The Art of
Waging Peace

The Art of
Waging Peace

A Strategic Approach
to Improving Our Lives
and the World

by Paul K. Chappell

PROSPECTA PRESS

For information about permission
to reproduce selections from this book, write to:

PROSPECTA PRESS
P. O. Box 3131
Westport, CT 06880
www.prospectapress.com

Book and cover design by Barbara Aronica-Buck.
Cover image of Monumento a los Caídos, a memorial dedicated to those who died in the
Spanish Civil War, located in Santa Cruz de Tenerife, Spain. Credit: Profimedia.com, Corbis.

Hardcover ISBN: 978-1-935212-78-2
E-book ISBN: 978-1-935212-68-3

For Jo Ann Deck,

goddess of compassion and strategic mastermind

CONTENTS

PROPHETS OF PEACE: GENERAL DOUGLAS MACARTHUR SPEAKING ON THE NEED TO ABOLISH WAR

The leaders are the laggards. The disease of power seems to confuse and befuddle them . . . They debate and turmoil over a hundred issues—they bring us to the verge of despair or raise our hopes to utopian heights over the corollary misunderstandings that stem from the threat of war—but never in the chancelleries of the world or the halls of the United Nations is the real problem raised. Never do they dare to state the bald truth, that the next great advance in the evolution of civilization cannot take place until war is abolished . . .

I am sure that every pundit in the world, every cynic and hypocrite, every paid brain washer, every egotist, every troublemaker, and many others of entirely different mold, will tell you with mockery and ridicule that [the abolition of war] can be only a dream—that it is but the vague imaginings of a visionary. But, as David Lloyd George once said in Commons at the crisis of the First World War, "We must go on or we will go under." And the great criticism we can make of the world's leaders is their lack of a plan which will enable us "to go on." All they propose merely gravitates around but dares not face the real problem. They increase preparedness [for war] by alliances, by distributing resources throughout the world, by feverish activity in developing new and deadlier weapons . . . We are told that this increases the chances of peace—which is doubtful—and increases the chances of victory if war comes—which would be incontestable if the other side did not increase in like proportion. Actually, the truth is that the relative strengths of the two change little with the years. Action by one is promptly matched by reaction from the other . . .

I recall so vividly this problem when it faced the Japanese in their new Constitution. They are realists; and they are the only ones that know by dread experience the fearful effect of mass annihilation. They realize in their limited geographical area, caught up as a sort of no man's land between two great ideologies, that to engage in another war, whether on the winning or the losing side, would spell the probable doom of their race. And their wise old Prime Minister, Shidehara, came to me and urged that to save themselves they should abolish war as an international instrument. When I agreed, he turned to me and said, "The world will laugh and mock us as impractical visionaries, but a hundred years from now we will be called prophets."

Sooner or later the world, if it is to survive, must reach this decision. The only question is, When? Must we fight again before we learn? When will some great figure in power have sufficient imagination and moral courage to translate this universal wish—which is rapidly becoming a universal necessity—into actuality? We are in a new era. The old methods and solutions no longer suffice. We must have new thoughts, new ideas, new concepts, just as did our venerated forefathers when they faced a new world. We must break out of the straitjacket of the past. There must always be one to lead, and we should be that one. We should now proclaim our readiness to abolish war in concert with the great powers of the world. The result would be magical.*

---

* Excerpt from an untitled speech General MacArthur gave to the Los Angeles City Council of the American Legion, January 26, 1955. *General MacArthur: Speeches and Reports: 1908–1964*, Edward T. Imparato, ed. (Paducah, KY: Turner Publishing, 2000), 225–26. "Prophets of Peace" is a title I came up with for this excerpt.

West Point and the U.S. Army trained me how to be a peace activist. If you think working for world peace means pursuing a naive and impossible dream, what I learned in the military may change your mind, just as it transformed my understanding of humanity's potential for peace. To explain my transformation, this book will shatter commonly held stereotypes about soldiers and peace activists. These stereotypes not only deceive and divide us, but they also prevent us from understanding the art of waging peace and the power it gives us to solve our national and global problems. Before I can explain what waging peace is and how I learned the deepest secrets of this art while serving in the military, I must first tell you an unlikely story. It is the story of who I am, and how I got here.

Societal Change

Waging peace empowers us to create three forms of change. My life embodies these three forms; they are the reason I am able to write these words and work for peace today. The first form, which has affected my life and the lives of countless others, is *societal change*.

I am a descendant of African slaves, and I grew up in Alabama. Although I was born in 1980, my father taught me to think like someone living before the civil rights movement. During my childhood, my father always told me, "The army is the only place in America where black men are given a fair chance. You'll never be able to get a decent job unless you're in the army." *

Half black and half white, my father was born in 1925 and grew up in Virginia during segregation and the Great Depression. The U.S. Army was desegregated in the early 1950s, many years before segregation ended in the South. This made a strong impression on my father. During the 1940s and 1950s, his belief that he only had opportunity in the military was largely true. A hard worker who began picking fruit when he was six years old to earn extra income for his family, he fought in the Korean and Vietnam Wars and retired as a command sergeant major, the highest enlisted rank.

I graduated from West Point in 2002 and served in the army for seven years. My mother is Korean, and when I told her in 2009 that I was leaving active duty, she said: "Are you out of your mind? Nobody is going to hire you. It's bad enough you look Asian, but you're also part black. Nobody is going to give a job to a black man who looks Asian." My parents did not tell me lies. On the contrary, they told me *their* truth. They were describing life as they had experienced it and trying to protect me from the suffering they endured. Although I experienced racism as a child, as an adult I began to realize that my multi-ethnic background was no longer the hindrance my parents believed it to be, and that I owed my very existence to the power of waging peace and its ability to change our society for the better.

America's Founding Fathers rebelled against Great Britain because they felt unfairly treated. They believed it was unjust to be taxed or controlled without the opportunity to participate in the political process. They also believed that those who govern must gain the consent of the governed. The motto "No taxation without representation" echoed their outrage and became a call to arms, leading to the American Revolution (1775–1783). Yet decades after the war ended, less than 10 percent of the American population could vote in national elections. Women could not vote. African Americans could not vote. And most white people could not vote unless

---

* But prior to the civil rights movement, weren't a few black men successful outside of the military? In his book *Why We Can't Wait*, Martin Luther King Jr. described the limited success of black men in American society as "tokenism," a practice that allowed a small number of African Americans to attain middle-class professional occupations in order to create the illusion of progress and hide the brutal conditions of segregation, unemployment, and poverty experienced by millions of African Americans.

they owned land. During the early nineteenth century "No taxation without representation" only seemed to apply to the rich.[1]

How did so many Americans increase their liberties during the past two hundred years? Did nonlandowners fight a war to obtain the right to vote? Did women fight a war to get the right to vote? Did African Americans fight a war to attain their civil rights? Did American workers fight a war to gain their rights? Was a war fought for child labor laws? These victories for liberty and justice were achieved because people waged peace, but this is a part of our history many people do not remember.

This is not the only part of our history that has been largely forgotten. By exploring the truth of our *human history,* in addition to the history of our country, we can understand how far humanity has come, how much further we can go, and how we can get there.

Five hundred years ago ideals such as democracy, the right to vote, freedom of speech, freedom of religion, freedom of the press, and women's and civil rights virtually did not exist. And how many democratic countries were there two hundred years ago? Napoleon overthrew the democratic government in France, and the United States was not a democracy for African Americans, women, and even many white people, since owning land was a common requirement for voting. But because people in the past took action, democracies now exist in many parts of the world, and America has become a place where I can write these words today.*

The simple idea that all human beings have a right to liberty, which once sounded radical and dangerous to most people around the world, has now become so common that many of us take this idea for granted. Today if I said, "It's not in the nature of some races to be slaves. Human beings have an innate yearning for freedom, and to enslave a group of people harsh techniques must be used to break their will and suppress their human nature," most of us would agree it is a self-evident statement that makes common sense. But this was not common sense several hundred years ago.

By the eighteenth century, state-sanctioned slavery had existed since the beginning of recorded history and was an integral part of the global economy. Thomas Clarkson and other abolitionists believed all human beings

---

* Although we are technically a republic (which is a form of representative democracy), today the word "democracy" refers to direct democracies, representative democracies, and democratic ideals.

should have the gift of freedom, yet they were ridiculed and threatened for opposing slavery. The idea that slavery is wrong—which was once ridiculed—has now become so widely accepted that anyone advocating slavery today would be called insane.

For most of recorded history, women around the world had virtually no rights.[2] During the eighteenth century they were not only forbidden from voting or owning property; in most places they *were* property. Those who advocated women's rights were ridiculed and threatened for challenging the oppression of women, but today if an American politician said that women should not be allowed to vote or own property, many would call him insane.

Today it would be political suicide for any American politician to say, "We should bring back slavery and segregation, and women should not be allowed to vote or own property." But two hundred years ago nearly all American politicians openly supported slavery and the oppression of women. How did this progress happen, and how can we also change attitudes toward war, environmental destruction, and the other problems that threaten humanity? How can we become prophets of peace who not only possess the ability to predict a peaceful future, but the power to *create* a peaceful future? This book will help answer those questions.

Spiritual Change

When I left active duty in 2009, I began serving as the Peace Leadership Director for the Nuclear Age Peace Foundation. One responsibility I have in this new role is speaking to colleges, high schools, churches, and activist organizations around the country. During a lecture I gave at a law school in 2010, I mentioned that state-sanctioned slavery and the oppression of women had existed since the beginning of recorded history. But in the past two hundred years, humanity abolished state-sanctioned slavery on a global scale and dramatically improved women's rights in many parts of the world. This demonstrates that positive change is possible, and that we also have the power to make a difference for the better.

After my lecture, a female student said to me, "You naively think the world is getting better, but illegal slavery still exists, and women are still oppressed in some parts of the world."

I responded by saying, "Yes, illegal forms of slavery still exist, but if we have made progress, why can't we continue making progress? I am not saying that our global community is completely healthy. On the contrary, our global community is like an unhealthy person who used to weigh six hundred pounds, but through diet and exercise now weighs four hundred pounds. Just as a four-hundred-pound person still has a couple hundred pounds of fat to shed before being healthy, our global community also has a couple hundred pounds of injustice to shed before achieving its full potential. The fact that a woman such as yourself is even able to attend law school—which would have been unimaginable a couple hundred years ago—and the fact that I can speak in front of you despite being part African American, is proof that positive change is possible. As American citizens and citizens of the world, you and I now have a responsibility to help our country and global community take additional steps on the path of positive change." *

She replied, "But how do you know your life is any better than your ancestors who were slaves? Workers in America are still oppressed and exploited, so nothing has really changed for the better. Can you honestly say that workers in America today are any better off than African American slaves two hundred years ago?"

I smiled calmly and replied, "It might seem as if nothing ever changes for the better, but have you read the personal accounts of slaves such as Frederick Douglass and Sojourner Truth? If you read about their experiences, you will see that I am a lot better off as a free person than they were under slavery. I am simply asking people to hold two thoughts in their head at the same time. The first thought is that we have come a long way on the journey toward peace and justice. The second thought is that we still have a long way to go."

That conversation made me feel slightly uncomfortable, and later I reflected upon the experience to understand why. As a descendant of slaves, I always feel a little insulted when people sugarcoat the horrors of slavery by saying people are not better off today. It reminds me of the pro-slavery and pro-segregation propaganda in the South that argued slavery wasn't that bad.

* Illegal slavery is certainly a problem and I discuss it further in a later chapter.

Improving the living conditions of people in America and around the world is one of the most important endeavors we can be involved in, but let's not distort the reality of what slavery was. To understand what state-sanctioned slavery truly was in America, a more accurate name for it would be "state-sanctioned rape and murder upon a country's own people."

It was common for slave masters to rape slave women and murder rebellious slaves, and these crimes were tolerated by the legal system. Frederick Douglass, who was born in 1818 and rumored to be descended from his white master and a black slave, described his life under slavery:

> My mother and I were separated when I was but an infant—before I knew her as my mother. It is a common custom, in the part of Maryland from which I ran away, to part children from their mothers at a very early age. Frequently, before the child has reached its twelfth month, its mother is taken from it, and hired out on some farm a considerable distance off, and the child is placed under the care of an old woman, too old for field labor. For what [purpose] this separation is done, I do not know, unless it be to hinder the development of the child's affection toward its mother, and to blunt and destroy the natural affection of the mother for the child. This is the inevitable result. I never saw my mother, to know her as such, more than four or five times in my life; and each of these times was very short in duration, and at night . . .
>
> [My master] was a cruel man, hardened by a long life of slaveholding. He would at times seem to take great pleasure in whipping a slave. I have often been awakened at the dawn of day by the most heart-rending shrieks of an own aunt of mine, whom he used to tie up to a joist, and whip upon her naked back till she was literally covered with blood. No words, no tears, no prayers, from his gory victim, seemed to move his iron heart from its bloody purpose. The louder she screamed, the harder he whipped; and where the blood ran fastest, there he whipped longest.

He would whip her to make her scream, and whip her to make her hush; and not until overcome by fatigue, would he cease to swing the blood-clotted cowskin. I remember the first time I ever witnessed this horrible exhibition. I was quite a child, but I well remember it . . . It was the first of a long series of such outrages, of which I was doomed to be a witness and a participant. It struck me with awful force. It was the blood-stained gate, the entrance to the hell of slavery, through which I was about to pass.[3]

When I was growing up in Alabama, I heard people say that black slaves living two hundred years ago had better lives than the poor in America today, because slave owners kept all of their slaves well fed and properly clothed. But this is not true. In fact, many plantation slaves were kept on the verge of starvation in order to break their spirit. Frederick Douglass described how the slaves on his plantation were starved, barely clothed, and treated worse than farm animals:

It was the boast of slaveholders that their slaves enjoyed more of the physical comforts of life than the peasantry of any country in the world. My experience contradicts this . . . Children under ten years old had neither shoes, stockings, jackets, nor trousers. They had two coarse tow linen shirts per year, and when these were worn out they went naked till the next allowance day—and this was the condition of the little girls as well as of the boys . . .

[As a young child] the insufficiency of both food and clothing was a serious trial to me, especially the lack of clothing. In hottest summer and coldest winter I was kept almost in a state of nudity. My only clothing—a little coarse sackcloth or tow linen sort of shirt, scarcely reaching to my knees, was worn night and day and changed once a week. In the day time I could protect myself [from cold] by keeping on the sunny side of the house, or, in stormy weather, in the corner of the kitchen chimney. But the great difficulty was to keep warm during the night. The pigs in the pen had leaves, and the horses in the stable had straw, but the children had no beds. They lodged anywhere in the ample kitchen. I slept generally in a little closet, without even a blanket to cover me . . . My feet have been so cracked with the frost that the pen with which I am writing might be laid in the gashes.

Our cornmeal mush, which was our only regular if not all-sufficing diet, was, when sufficiently cooled from the cooking, placed in a large tray or trough. This was set down either on the floor of the kitchen, or out of doors on the ground, and the children were called like so many pigs, and like so many pigs would come, some with oyster-shells, some with pieces of shingles, but none with spoons, and literally devour the mush. He who could eat fastest got most, and he who was strongest got the best place, but few left the trough really satisfied . . . I have often been so pinched with hunger as to dispute with old "Nep," the dog, for the crumbs which fell from the kitchen table. Many times have I followed, with eager step, the waiting-girl when she shook the tablecloth, to get the crumbs and small bones flung out for the dogs and cats . . . [During my teenage years on Thomas Auld's plantation] so wretchedly starved were we that we were compelled to live at the expense of our neighbors, or to steal from the home larder.[4]

Commenting on the brutality that Frederick Douglass experienced before escaping from slavery, abolitionist William Lloyd Garrison said:

The experience of Frederick Douglass, as a slave, was not a peculiar one; his lot was not especially a hard one; his case may be regarded as a very fair specimen of the treatment of slaves in Maryland, in which State it is conceded that they are better fed and less cruelly treated than in Georgia, Alabama, or Louisiana. Many have suffered incomparably more, while very few on the plantations have suffered less, than himself. Yet how deplorable was his situation . . . how like a brute was he treated, even by those professing to have the same mind in them that was in Christ Jesus!

[Frederick Douglass] relates two instances of murderous cruelty—in one of which a planter deliberately shot a slave belonging to a neighboring plantation, who had unintentionally gotten within his lordly domain in quest of fish; and in the other, an overseer blew out the brains of a slave who had fled to a stream of water to escape a bloody scourging. Mr. Douglass states that in neither of these instances was any thing done by way of legal arrest or judicial investigation . . .

Let it never be forgotten, that no slaveholder or overseer can be convicted of any outrage perpetrated on the person of a slave, however diabolical it may be, on the testimony of colored witnesses, whether bond or free. By the slave code, they are adjudged to be as incompetent to testify against a white man . . . Hence, there is no legal protection in fact, whatever there may be in form, for the slave population; and any amount of cruelty may be inflicted on them with impunity. Is it possible for the human mind to conceive of a more horrible state of society?[5]

Although state-sanctioned slavery has been abolished, many people in the world are still living under terrible oppression. However, it would be difficult to find a population today that suffers from the many horrors of state-sanctioned slavery, where people were beaten, murdered, raped, worked relentlessly without pay, separated from their mothers as infants, bought and sold as property, and given no legal protection against these assaults. Illegal slavery still exists, but imagine if the role of American law enforcement officers was not to punish people caught with slaves, but to return their escaped slaves to them. According to the Fugitive Slave Act of 1850, any U.S marshal who refused to arrest a runaway slave should be heavily fined, and any person helping an escaped slave by providing food, shelter, or any form of assistance should be heavily fined and imprisoned.[6]

The fact that a descendant of slaves is able to write these words today is proof that progress does happen, yet I cannot forget about those still living under oppression. For many years, when I heard about the injustices still occurring in our world, I wanted to kill those who profit from oppression, injustice, and war. It might sound surprising to hear a peace activist admit to having violent tendencies, but violence is the reason why I began walking the road to peace.

My personality was forged in the fire of violence. I grew up in a violent household and had a traumatic upbringing, and I experienced racism as a child in Alabama. I owe my life to an ongoing spiritual transformation that is helping me heal the agony and hatred in my heart. When I use the word "spiritual," I am not referring to a supernatural spirituality, but an intellectual, emotional, and philosophical spirituality. Spiritual change allows us to heal our psychological wounds, and when we heal these inner wounds we become more effective at healing the outer wounds of our society. If we ignore our psychological wounds and allow them to fester, they can infect and destroy our human relationships, ability to savor life, and efforts to create a better world.

Martin Luther King Jr. taught us that peaceful ends require peaceful means, and if we want to be effective at creating peace in the world, we must first strive to create peace within ourselves. According to King, the love that arises from spiritual change gives us immense power in our efforts to wage peace: "Hatred and bitterness can never cure the disease of fear; only love can do that. Hatred paralyzes life; love releases it. Hatred confuses life; love harmonizes it. Hatred darkens life; love illumines it."[7]

The art of waging peace allows us to create not just societal change, but also spiritual change. When we understand the secrets of this art, we become empowered to not only reduce the suffering in our society, but to heal the suffering within us. To explain how we can all achieve spiritual change in our lives, this book will translate the language of trauma.

Trauma has its own language and logic. Behavior that seems destructive and illogical to others can make complete sense to someone trapped in the distorted logic of trauma. When a person does not speak or understand the language of trauma, it can be difficult to comprehend why human beings are capable of doing such terrible things.

By discussing the causes and consequences of my trauma, I hope to help those who have shared similar experiences, and help those who haven't experienced trauma to better understand its true nature. Many of the painful experiences I describe in this book are actually quite common in our society, and people suffer from these problems in varying degrees. By translating my rage and self-loathing into a language that can be understood, I will shed light on the many truths that lie hidden in the heart of darkness, where people seldom look.

Ideological Change

I grew up surrounded by conservatives in Alabama, and during high school I listened to conservative talk-radio religiously. For much of my life I believed war was the best way to solve conflicts between countries and violence was an effective way to solve problems between individuals. My views have changed dramatically since leaving high school, but this does not mean that I now call myself a liberal.

When people first hear about my personal transformation from war to peace, they usually assume that I converted from being a war-mongering conservative to a peace-loving liberal. But what really happened is far more complex, and far more useful for anyone who wants to understand peace, conflict, and how the human mind truly works.

As my views changed dramatically during my time in the military, something occurred that I did not expect. Instead of becoming alienated from my conservative upbringing, I began to feel more empathy for people who call themselves conservative. As I journeyed on the road to peace, I realized that we have been deceived into thinking that conservatives and liberals are so different from each other. I also saw how our shared humanity transcends our various political views. Most importantly, I learned how to communicate with people on a deeper human level, instead of demonizing those who disagree with me.

This book will not only shatter stereotypes about soldiers and peace activists, but also conservatives and liberals. The purpose of this book is to teach us not only how to create peace in our hearts and peace between countries, but peace within our own country. The division in America is so severe that many conservatives and liberals cannot even speak to each other in a respectful way, let alone have a productive conversation. As each side demonizes the other, I will show how much they really have in common. As each side seems less willing to listen to and dialogue with its opponents, I will show how we can not only dialogue with those who disagree with us, but transform how they think. To do this, I will teach you a new form of combat.

Where do our societal problems come from? What is the underlying cause of war, racism, sexism, injustice, oppression, environmental destruction, and poverty? All these problems come from the human mind, from how people think. To solve these problems, we must get to their root by understanding how the human mind works, why people think the way they do, and how to transform people's views about controversial issues.

To transform how people think about controversial issues, I have spent years developing a *mental martial art* that allows us to engage in combat not in the physical world, but in the realm of ideas. What is the realm of ideas? It is the battlefield where the idea of universal human freedom fought against the idea of state-sanctioned slavery, where the idea of women's equality fought against the idea of gender inequality, and where the idea of peace is now fighting against the idea of war.

Earlier I said that it would be political suicide for any American politician to say, "We should bring back slavery and segregation, and women should not be allowed to vote or own property." But two hundred years ago nearly all American politicians openly supported slavery and the oppression of women. This book will explain how the changes in our understanding of these issues did not happen by accident. Frederick Douglass, Martin Luther King Jr., and many others were powerful warriors in the realm of ideas. They knew how to do more than preach to the choir, and they were black belts in the mental martial art of transforming how people think.

The mental martial art *is* the art of waging peace. I call waging peace a martial art to break the stereotype that peace activists are passive and weak. True peace activism is more than meditating alone in a quiet room. It is a fight. But instead of attacking people, waging peace attacks the ignorance and misunderstandings that hold people hostage. Waging peace is not physical combat with bombs and bullets, but mental and spiritual combat against hatred, greed, deception, and apathy.

Is it possible to fight for peace? It depends on how we define the word "fight." If we define it not as violence but as struggle, then we must fight for peace. Waging peace is certainly a struggle. Bernard Lafayette, a civil rights activist who helped desegregate Nashville, Tennessee, explained: "Unfortunately, the concept of nonviolence for many people is that you get hit on one cheek, you turn the other cheek, and you don't do anything. But nonviolence means fighting back, but you are fighting back with another purpose, and other weapons. Number one, your fight is to win that person over, and that is a fight, that is a struggle. That is much more challenging than fisticuffs . . . We were warriors in that sense."[8]

Some peace activists might criticize my use of martial arts metaphors. A peace activist once commented on an article I wrote by saying, "No, what we need is to stop using militaristic language at all. Period . . . Could you imagine Gandhi, or Martin Luther King using militaristic metaphors to define themselves or their movement?"

Actually, Gandhi and Martin Luther King Jr. were the ones who taught me to use militaristic metaphors. Gandhi said, "I regard myself as a soldier, though a soldier of peace. I know the value of discipline and truth."[9] King described the civil rights movement by saying, "We did not hesitate to call our movement an army . . . It was an army that would move but not maul . . . It was an army to storm bastions of hatred, to lay siege to the fortresses of segregation, to surround symbols of discrimination . . . The battle hymn of our movement [was] 'We Shall Overcome.'"[10] King also said, "Nonviolence is a powerful and just weapon. It is a weapon unique in history, which cuts without wounding and ennobles the man who wields it. It is a sword that heals."[11]

At one time I was so bitter toward the army that I rejected all militaristic metaphors, but Gandhi and King taught me how useful and powerful these metaphors can be. As I will show throughout this book, not only are martial arts metaphors extremely effective at helping us understand how waging peace works, but martial arts philosophy and waging peace have far more in common than most people realize.

To understand why waging peace is more effective than bombs and bullets at solving our national and global problems, Henry David Thoreau tells us: "There are a thousand hacking at the branches of evil to one who is striking at the root."[12] Waging peace is a sword that strikes our problems at their root, because it gives us the power to transform how people think about important issues. I call this transformation *ideological change.*

Societal, spiritual, and ideological change are deeply interconnected, and when one form of change is blocked the others also suffer. Peace is like a beautiful human body, and societal change is the blood, spiritual change is the heart, and ideological change is the brain. If the heart of spiritual change ceases to beat with compassion, the blood of societal change cannot flow and our society's progress will end. If the brain of ideological change does not transform how people think about important issues, the health of our society and spirit in each person will fade, even perish. And if the blood of societal change is poisoned by political and media propaganda, this deception will also poison the heart and brain in the beautiful body of peace.

The three forms of change make other forms of change, such as scientific change, possible. During the seventeenth century, Galileo Galilei offered scientific evidence showing the earth revolved around the sun. Threatened by his new evidence, the Roman Catholic Church gave him the choice of recanting his ideas or facing execution. Even if he recanted, the church would ban Galileo's books and put him under house arrest for the rest of his life. At this time freedom of speech did not exist, and Galileo recanted his ideas in order to avoid being killed.[13]

But today if someone said, "People who say the earth revolves around the sun should be executed," that person would sound insane. All scientific change depends on the three forms of change, because societal change gives us the freedom of speech to express new ideas, spiritual change makes us more open to new ideas, and ideological change has transformed the once radical idea that the earth revolves around the sun into an accepted part of our modern ideology.

I am living proof the three forms of change are possible, and I have realized how we can all help create the positive change our world so desperately needs. By learning and practicing the art of waging peace, the heart of spiritual change will beat stronger in each of us, the brain of ideological change will empower us with the strategic thinking to do more than preach to the choir, and the blood of societal change will flow into those places where it is needed most.

A Disciplined Approach to Peacemaking

I experienced a surreal moment while attending a peace conference in Berkeley, California. It happened when one of the speakers had all the participants sing a song that went, "I ain't gonna study war no more. I ain't gonna study war no more. I ain't gonna study war no more."

I thought this was very odd. To me, it would be like doctors at a medical conference singing, "I ain't gonna study disease no more. I ain't gonna study disease no more. I ain't gonna study disease no more." If the purpose of doctors is to promote health, then shouldn't they be experts on disease and illness? And if the purpose of peace activists is to promote peace, then shouldn't we be experts on war and violence? The only way to cure any sickness is to first study and understand it. Only then can we learn its secrets. Only then can we defeat it. Isn't the same true for war and violence?

During my interactions with peace activists around America, I have met many who feel no need to study war. I have also met many who want to develop a deeper understanding of war but do not know where to begin. After speaking with a peace group in the Los Angeles area about the importance of studying and understanding war, I received an e-mail that said:

> I used to be a "we ain't gonna study war no more" type, thinking that if we elected to starve the knowledge of how to wage war from ourselves and our society, it would shrivel and die . . . that thinking for me extended to being uncomfortable with militaristic words and phrases being used in peace contexts, such as "fighting for peace" or "choosing your battles" or anything about weapons. In the space of your talk you transformed that for me, where I'm willing to explore that phrasing as a way of reclaiming and reframing it.

I began my reply by again comparing peace activists to doctors, but then I went further by explaining some of the practical reasons to study war as we strive to create peace:

> Doctors work to promote health,* and to do this they must be experts on disease and illness (the things that prevent health), and if our job is to promote peace, we must also be experts on war and violence (the things that prevent peace). Our opponents are war and violence, and we must know our opponents very well in order to defeat them. The key to ending war is not necessarily starving the knowledge about war, but understanding war so deeply that we are capable of seeing through the illusions and myths that keep the war system going and helping others also see through these illusions and myths. One reason the war system persists is because so few people truly understand it, which allows its many flaws to remain hidden, and most of what people know about war comes from Hollywood and television.

This e-mail exchange reveals a lot. The idea that peace activists must study and understand war sounds radical to some in the peace movement, but to many it sounds like common sense after I explain my reasoning. "I ain't gonna study war no more" is actually a quote from Martin Luther King Jr., but there is more to the quote. Referencing a passage from the Bible, he said, "Men will beat their swords into plowshares and their spears into pruning hooks. And nations will not rise up against nations, neither shall they study war anymore. And I don't know about you, I ain't gonna study war no more."[14] What I think King meant is that we should no longer study war for the purpose of waging it. But what I am proposing is that we must study war, just as doctors study disease and illness, if our purpose is to end it.

During a lecture I gave at a university, someone asked me, "But how do you expect us to study war? We didn't graduate from West Point and serve

---

* I am referring to the ideal that doctors are supposed to aspire toward – the ideal of being knowledgeable, compassionate, and conscientious. Not all doctors achieve this ideal.

in the military like you did." I reminded the audience that "I have spent most of my life studying war, aggression, and violence, and I hope you can benefit from what I have learned. As a result of this intensive study, which consisted of rigorous research and life-changing personal experiences, I have written several books that dispel the many myths of war."

To truly understand peace, I realized that I first had to understand war. But before I could understand war, I realized that I first had to understand human nature. As I say in my first book, *Will War Ever End?,* "Trying to end war without understanding human nature is like trying to go to the moon without understanding the laws of physics." By uncovering vital truths about war, aggression, and violence, my first three books shed new light on human nature and the road to peace. *The Art of Waging Peace*, the fourth book in this series, will give us the training we need to make peace a reality.

In the military I learned that training is necessary to accomplish any challenging goal, and I was surprised to learn that so many peace activists have little to no training in how to effectively wage peace. If we compare how much the average twenty-five-year-old army officer knows about waging war and how much the average twenty-five-year-old activist knows about waging peace, there is a big difference. Although I admire their deep commitment to waging peace, many activists have not had enough training in the nonviolent methods that lead to positive change. Many activists have not thoroughly studied the brilliant techniques of Mahatma Gandhi, Martin Luther King Jr., and others who have so much to teach us.

Good intentions are simply not enough. If they were enough, then war, injustice, and oppression would have ended many years ago. To solve our national and global problems, we need more than just good intentions. We must also be disciplined, strategic, and well trained. Civil rights leader James Lawson, whom Martin Luther King Jr. called "the leading theorist and strategist of nonviolence in the world," said, "The difficulty with nonviolent people and efforts is that they don't recognize the necessity of fierce discipline, and training, and strategizing, and planning, and recruiting."[15]

Just as studying painting, writing, or any art unlocks our creativity by giving us the skills to effectively express ourselves, the same is true when we study the art of waging peace. And just as a great artist like Leonardo da Vinci had the discipline to hone his skills through hard work, we must also have a disciplined approach to peacemaking. In the twenty-first century, issues such as war, nuclear weapons, and environmental destruction threaten human survival. The stakes are much too high, and the opponents of peace far too strong, for us to not take our passion for peace seriously.

Sun Tzu wrote *The Art of War* nearly twenty-five hundred years ago, and humanity has spent thousands of years exploring and improving the methods of waging war. In many ways, humanity's exploration of waging peace has just begun. Gandhi said that his understanding of nonviolence was equivalent to the limited understanding of electricity during Thomas Edison's time.[16] In our era, the paradigm of war still controls most nations and the minds of countless people. To replace the old paradigm of war with a new paradigm of waging peace, we must be pioneers who can push the boundaries of human understanding. We must be doctors who can cure the virus of violence. We must be soldiers of peace who can do more than preach to the choir. And we must be artists who will make the world our masterpiece.

PART I

The
Infinite Shield

CHAPTER 1

The Labyrinth of Trauma

The Wars That Followed My Father Home

The unconscious mind has no past. Like a bizarre alternate universe where time does not exist, the unconscious mind relives traumatic experiences from long ago as if they were happening in the present. This explains why so many soldiers return from war, but their minds never truly come home. I began to realize this as a child, because my father fought in the Korean and Vietnam Wars. Like many soldiers, his body came home alive, but his mind never fully returned from the battle overseas.

In his book *Achilles in Vietnam*, psychiatrist Jonathan Shay shares the story of a Vietnam veteran whose unconscious mind relives traumatic events from the war, such as the fear of a night ambush. When a person's mind is stuck in the alternate universe of trauma, the line between past and present ceases to exist.

> I haven't really slept for twenty years. I lie down, but I don't sleep. I'm always watching the door, the window, then back to the door. I get up at least five times to walk my perimeter, sometimes it's ten or fifteen times. There's always something within reach, maybe a baseball bat or a knife, at every door. I used to sleep with a gun under my pillow, another under my mattress, and another in the drawer next to the bed . . . So it's like that until the sun begins to come up, then I can sleep for an hour or two . . .

I was real lucky [my employers] kept me so long. They understood that sometimes I just had to leave work. And they never laughed at me when I hit the floor if there was a loud bang or something. I know guys here [in the treatment program] who work other places who had fire-crackers lit off just to see them dive over a conveyer belt or something like that. Or their supervisors pushing them, mind-fucking them, pushing them till they lost it, so they could get rid of them. That never happened to me. Once a lamp in the ceiling exploded with a loud bang, and I dove into a tank of lubricant for the cutting machines. Oof! It was awful. But nobody laughed at me . . .

I don't deserve my wife. What kind of life is it for her married to me? She says, "Let's take the kids out for din-ner." And I say, "Sure, let's go." So we get to the restaurant and we walk in the door and I say, "Whoa!" when I look around and see all those people. So the hostess shows us to a table right in the middle, and I say, "How about there in the corner?" and she says, "There's people there," and I say, "We'll wait." Meantime my wife is looking at me and there's sweat running down my face. I can't sit with my back uncovered . . . So after we wait thirty minutes for the table in the corner we start walking through the restaurant to it and my heart's pounding, pounding and the sweat's rolling off me and I say, "I gotta go." So they sit down and eat and I stand up in the parking garage, the second floor overlooking the entrance to the restaurant where I have a real good line on everything going on.[1]

Like mud that sticks to the soles of our shoes, war has a way of sticking to the human mind and following people home. As a child my life was turned upside down when the wars from my father's past reemerged in the present, away from the battlefield and behind closed doors. I have fond memories of being three years old and watching my father tend to his garden, feed the birds in our backyard, and chase away a spider that almost frightened me to death. But when I was four years old, everything changed.

I was sleeping peacefully late one night when I felt someone grab my leg and drag me from my bed onto the floor. My leg was pulled so hard I heard my pajama pants rip down the middle. Looking up and seeing my father, I began to panic as he pulled my hair and told me he was going to kill me. His cursing and my screaming woke my mother, who ran into the room and bear-hugged him until he finally calmed down.

When I was four something else occurred that I could not understand at the time, but that I later attributed to my father's war experiences. One evening I heard him screaming at my mother and threatening to shoot himself with his pistol. This was the first time I heard him threaten to commit suicide, but it would not be the last. Throughout my childhood, I watched my father lose his grip on reality, and this frightening behavior caused me to struggle with my own sanity. As I grew older, the trauma I inherited from my father caused me to embark on a relentless search for understanding, peace, and trust.

The Search for Trust

To me the army was more than just a profession. It was also a family. I grew up as an only child in Alabama, and by sixth grade my father's paranoia had become so severe that he stopped letting me visit with friends. In my parents' house I ate all my meals alone. I spent most of my time alone. I felt alone in society, drifting in a sea of strangers. Other children bullied me because of my racial background, and I received countless beatings from my father. But in the army I found a group of people who would not only die for me, but they would kill in order to protect me. This is a powerful experience for anyone who has ever been beaten, bullied, or abused. It is one among many reasons why troubled young people join gangs.

The army is not a perfect organization, nor is it filled with perfect people. Soldiers are vulnerable to the same problems that affected my father, so what reason did I have to trust them? If my own father could beat me to a point where I feared for my life, what reason did I have to trust anyone? When I went to West Point in 1998 I had difficulty trusting my classmates, but I quickly realized that the military allowed me to test people's trustworthiness.

An army unit functions as a team, and soldiers must trust each other with their lives. The army relies heavily on cooperation to accomplish its objectives, and even to complete mundane tasks. This gave me numerous opportunities to test people's trustworthiness. Would my comrades come through for me when I was relying on them? Would they fulfill their responsibilities to help the group succeed? Did they have my back, or would they instead stab me in the back?

My father severely damaged my ability to trust, and in the army I learned to trust people for the first time since my early childhood. But when I left the army in 2009 I again lost my ability to trust. Embarking on a new life as a civilian, I moved from El Paso, Texas, (where I was stationed at Fort Bliss) to Santa Barbara, California. I had never been to this city before. As I drove along the radiant California coast to my new home, the ocean looked magical and otherworldly. The sunlight danced across deep shades of blue in ways that were primordial and hypnotic.

California seemed like a different planet compared to Alabama, but that soon changed. After a few days something happened that I never expected. Santa Barbara began to remind me of my childhood for various reasons, causing my old psychological wounds to reopen. Painful memories began to replay in my mind, like a bad song stuck in my head. Although I was surrounded by beautiful California beaches, my mind was far away. Physically I lived in Santa Barbara, but mentally I was lost in the *labyrinth of trauma*.

By exploring the story of the labyrinth from Greek mythology, we can better understand the nature of trauma, and why it can be so difficult to escape its wrath. According to Greek legend, the labyrinth was created because of a traumatic event. The Greek god Poseidon gave King Minos a white bull, on the condition that Minos would sacrifice the bull to Poseidon. However, the animal was so beautiful that Minos refused to sacrifice it. To punish the king for not sacrificing the bull, Poseidon put a curse on Minos's wife, Pasiphae, by making her feel lust for the animal. After she mated with the bull, she produced an offspring known as the Minotaur, a creature with the head of a bull and body of a man.

Horrified by what happened, Minos consulted an oracle for advice. She advised him to build a maze where the monstrous Minotaur could be hidden. Anxious to protect his wife from disgrace, Minos had the master craftsman Daedalus build a maze, known as the labyrinth, to contain the Minotaur. Every year Minos ordered the Athenians to offer him seven boys and seven girls, whom he sent into the labyrinth as food for the monster. Anyone entering the labyrinth found it impossible to escape because of its many winding passages.[2]

Around every psychological wound, a labyrinth is built deep in our unconscious mind. The more traumatic the wound, the more complex the labyrinth. The Minotaur symbolizes our psychological wounds, agonizing humiliations, and dark secrets. Like sacrificial children trapped in the labyrinth of the Minotaur, soldiers who return from war can wander lost and alone in the winding tunnels of trauma for the remainder of their lives. Just as the Minotaur kills people in its labyrinth, our psychological wounds can destroy us when we become lost in the labyrinth of trauma. The Minotaur kills with horns, fists, and rage, while trauma kills by driving people to madness, drug addiction, and suicide.

Like the Minotaur, trauma is a beast that has ended many lives. Trauma is also a monster that can assume countless shapes and sizes, and war trauma is only one among many forms of trauma. In his book *The Boy Who Was Raised As a Dog*, psychiatrist Bruce Perry describes the common misconceptions about childhood trauma that he noticed during his work in the 1980s:

> Unfortunately, the prevailing view of children and trauma at the time—one that persists to a large degree to this day—is that "children are resilient." . . . If anything, children are more vulnerable to trauma than adults; I knew this from Seymour Levine's work and the work of dozens of others by then . . . The developing brain is most malleable and most sensitive to experience—both good and bad—early in life. (This is why we so easily and rapidly learn language, social nuance, motor skills and dozens of other things in childhood, and why we speak of "formative" experiences.) . . . Consequently, we are also rapidly and

easily transformed by trauma when we are young. Though
its effects may not always be visible to the untrained eye,
when you know what trauma can do to children, sadly, you
begin to see its aftermath everywhere . . .

In sensitization a pattern of stimulus leads to
increased sensitivity to future similar stimulus. This is
what is seen in the Vietnam veterans and the rats that were
genetically oversensitive to stress or became that way
because of early exposure to it. When the brain becomes
sensitized, even small stressors can provoke large
responses.[3]

During my childhood my brain became sensitized to violence. "Sensitization" means that our mind has been wounded by a traumatic event. Just
as an open flesh wound is so sensitive that gently touching it can cause
immense pain, a situation that remotely reminds us of past trauma can
inflame sensitive psychological wounds. To protect these wounds our mind
often develops defense mechanisms. For example, when I was four years old
I was beaten by my father to the point where I feared for my life, and these
beatings continued throughout most of my childhood. One defense mech-
anism I developed was an inability to trust people. My inability to trust is
actually a survival technique. As I mentioned earlier, trauma has its own language and logic. When the people closest to us have made us fear for our
lives, being distrustful and not letting others get too close to us makes complete sense within the distorted logic of trauma.

Before moving to Santa Barbara, I had spent my entire adult life in the
military. I went to West Point in 1998 when I was eighteen years old, graduated in 2002, and stayed on active duty until 2009. The army allowed me
to test people's trustworthiness, but when I left the army and moved to Santa
Barbara as a civilian, I could no longer test whether I could trust people. To
keep me safe, the old defense mechanisms from my childhood reemerged. I
kept people at a distance, becoming a recluse. I again found myself drifting
alone in a sea of strangers, and I perceived everyone around me as a potential
threat. I was lost in the labyrinth of trauma, unable to find my way home. I
was searching for trust, not realizing how difficult it would be to find again.

To better understand why it can be so difficult to escape the labyrinth of trauma, consider the following scenario. Imagine how difficult it would be for someone with a phobia of cockroaches, nonpoisonous spiders, or harmless snakes to lie next to these creatures. Most people with such a phobia would find it unbearable. Now imagine if the creatures that frightened these people were not harmless, but had repeatedly hurt them over a long period of time and even come close to killing them. This is how traumatized war veterans and abused children can feel around other human beings.*

As I explained earlier, the three forms of change are societal, spiritual, and ideological. Understanding the nature of trauma can help us achieve spiritual change. Those who have not experienced severe trauma can still benefit from learning about it, because human beings share many common experiences. Although my trauma is based on betrayal, mistrust, anger, and loneliness, doesn't every person experience these forms of suffering to at least some extent? By experiencing them in extreme amounts, I have been able to thoroughly study these aspects of our existence and shed new light on these problems.

To achieve spiritual change, we must also understand how trauma from our past can inhibit our ability to wage peace. A violent upbringing led to my obsession with peace, and during my interactions with the peace movement I was surprised to learn that I am not an anomaly. I have met many peace activists who are drawn to activism because of painful life experiences. However, if we do not learn to navigate the labyrinth of trauma and heal our agony, the anger we bring into the peace movement can destroy the very cause we are trying to promote.

How can we navigate the labyrinth of trauma and achieve spiritual change? I know firsthand how difficult this can be, and I do not underestimate the challenge of overcoming trauma. I have seen many self-help gurus

---

* I once heard someone say, "Every time we drive we demonstrate trust, because we are trusting the other drivers not to hit us." But when I talk about trust and mistrust, I am referring to something much deeper. First of all, if another driver hits my vehicle while I am driving, he or she could be injured or even killed, and also face financial and legal consequences for reckless driving. The kind of trust I am referring to goes much deeper than this, because it deals with the bonds that make family, friendship, and close community possible. Real trust exists when people have the ability to harm us with little or no risk to themselves. Jonathan Shay refers to the mistrust caused by trauma as the "persistent expectation of betrayal and exploitation" (I would also add "humiliation"). The people who have the greatest ability to betray, exploit, and humiliate us are not strangers driving in cars, but the people we rely on and those closest to us.

offer shallow and oversimplistic solutions, which can be harmful to those with severe trauma. A psychological wound by itself can be dangerous, and several wounds have a way of getting tangled together. I spent most of my childhood living in fear, believing that at any moment my father could lose his temper and beat me to death. When I deployed to Iraq in 2006, I again felt that people were trying to kill me. This exacerbated my earlier trauma and led to other psychological problems. Since trauma is a complex maze that leads countless people to madness, drug addiction, and suicide, is there any hope for me and so many others?

In Greek mythology the hero Theseus volunteered to enter the labyrinth, taking the place of a child about to be sacrificed. With sword in hand, he found his way to the Minotaur and killed the beast. I wish overcoming trauma were that simple. I wish I could metaphorically kill the parts of my mind that were in agony. According to the two psychiatrists I quoted earlier, Jonathan Shay and Bruce Perry, a person never completely gets rid of their trauma. It leaves a mark in the brain, like metaphorical scar tissue. But as I will explain in this book, I am hopeful because I have seen that it is possible to live with trauma and still find meaning and fulfillment. Even if we have been lost in the labyrinth of trauma for many years, we can learn to trust and love humanity. Even if we have suffered deeply, we can make peace with the wounded parts of ourselves.

CHAPTER 2

The Siren Song of Rage

The Trauma of Racism

The paramedic gently removed the small fragments of glass from my bleeding hand. "You won't need stitches," he said. A police officer stood nearby, keeping a close eye on me.

"You are lucky the glass shattered the way it did," said another paramedic as he filled out a report. "Otherwise you could have hurt yourself a lot worse, or injured someone else."

It was March 2011, and I had been living in Santa Barbara for over a year. The paramedics and police were called to my apartment because I lost my temper and punched out a large window in my living room. I lived in a second-floor apartment, and breaking the window caused big shards of glass to spill onto the sidewalk below. Now that I had come to my senses, I breathed a sigh of relief, grateful that no one got hurt. But half an hour earlier, I had been in a completely different state of mind. I had wandered into one of the deepest and most dangerous parts of the labyrinth of trauma. I had become lost in the dark tunnels where rage is born.

These tunnels were constructed during my violent upbringing, but also as a result of events that happened hundreds of years ago. My father was born in 1925, and I was born when he was fifty-four years old. Growing up in Virginia under segregation during the Great Depression, his upbringing was shaped by the aftermath of slavery and trauma of racism. To protect me from the pain he experienced, he taught me to think like someone living before the civil rights movement.

"White people can't stand to see a black person succeed in this country," he told me. "They want you to fail, and if they see you doing well they will try to ruin your life. You'll be a lot safer if you don't trust them or anyone else." It might sound like my father was filling my head with paranoia and nonsense, but he was actually passing down a survival technique that had saved the lives of my ancestors. Frederick Douglass explains the conditions that caused mistrust to become a survival technique for African Americans:

> To describe the wealth of Colonel Lloyd would be almost equal to describing the riches of Job . . . He was said to own a thousand slaves . . . Colonel Lloyd owned so many that he did not know them when he saw them; nor did all the slaves of the out-farms know him. It is reported of him, that, while riding along the road one day, he met a colored man, and addressed him in the usual manner of speaking to colored people on the public high-ways of the south: "Well, boy, whom do you belong to?" "To Colonel Lloyd," replied the slave. "Well, does the colonel treat you well?" "No, sir," was the ready reply. "What, does he work you too hard?" "Yes, sir." "Well, don't he give you enough to eat?" "Yes, sir, he gives me enough, such as it is."
>
> The colonel, after ascertaining where the slave belonged, rode on; the man also went on about his business, not dreaming that he had been conversing with his master. He thought, said, and heard nothing more of the matter, until two or three weeks afterwards. The poor man was then informed by his overseer that, for having found fault with his master, he was now to be sold to a Georgia trader. He was immediately chained and handcuffed; and thus, without a moment's warning, he was snatched away, and forever sundered, from his family and friends, by a hand more unrelenting than death. This is the penalty of telling the truth, of telling the simple truth, in answer to a series of plain questions.

It is partly in consequence of such facts, that slaves, when inquired of as to their condition and the character of their masters, almost universally say they are contented, and that their masters are kind. The slaveholders have been known to send in spies among their slaves, to ascertain their views and feelings in regard to their condition. The frequency of this has had the effect to establish among the slaves the maxim, that a still tongue makes a wise head. They suppress the truth rather than take the consequences of telling it.[1]

Most African Americans born in 1980 are five generations removed from slavery, but I am only three generations removed. My father, who had me at fifty-four, was old enough to be my grandfather when I was born, thus a generation was skipped between me and him. Furthermore, my grandfather was raised not by his parents, but by his grandparents, two former slaves named Wyatt and Frances Chappell; thus another generation was skipped. Wyatt Chappell was born a slave in Alabama in 1835 and Francis Chappell was born a slave in Virginia in 1842.[2]

Although I look Asian, I was raised to see the world like a black person living in the nineteenth century. If two of the generations separating me from slavery had not been skipped, perhaps I would have grown up with a more trusting attitude toward white people. My mistrust was not based solely on what my father told me. It was also reinforced by the racism I experienced as a child in Alabama.

As a child I tried to hide the fact that I was part African American, because to me it was bad enough being half Korean, since I was often bullied because of my Asian eyes. No matter how hard I tried to hide my African American blood, however, my parents reminded me that people would eventually find out. The army classified me as black in my military records, but when I was growing up my father always told me, "The army is the only place in America where black men are given a fair chance." In 1990, when General Colin Powell was chairman of the Joint Chiefs of Staff, the highest-ranking position in the military, my father added, "Just look at Colin Powell. He is the highest-ranking soldier, and he is black! Where else in America is such a thing possible? Have you ever seen a black president?" My father died in 2004, before the first African American president was elected.

Mistrust was a survival technique that kept my ancestors alive for many generations, but in the army I no longer needed mistrust to survive. I saw my white comrades as family, and race did not matter anymore. I would die for them, and they would die for me. When I moved to Santa Barbara as a civilian, my military comrades were replaced by complete strangers. In order to protect myself, I resurrected the old survival techniques I had learned from my father. I relied on mistrust for my safety, regressing back into the fearful mindset of my childhood.

Spiritual change requires us to strengthen our ability to trust, because to truly love people we must first be able to trust them, and trust also creates the conditions that make strong communities possible. But when mistrust becomes a survival technique, people often have great difficulty letting it go. Many hold on to it just in case, even when it is not needed, because they would rather be safe than sorry. The difficult task of releasing mistrust is actually a common human experience that transcends race, because betrayal is not limited to the trauma of racism. Countless people have been stabbed with the dagger of betrayal in relationships, friendships, and in the workplace. Is there any hope for all those who have been betrayed, and who now hold on to mistrust as a way of protecting themselves? Is it possible to trust again?

When we look at the life of Frederick Douglass, we see that human beings have an incredible capacity to overcome their feelings of mistrust. Douglass shows that we all have the power to trust again, no matter how much we have been hurt. During the nineteenth century, Douglass worked with many white people toward the creation of women's rights and abolition of slavery, after spending much of his life unable to trust white people. As he explains, he could not even trust their kindness:

> I went one day down on the wharf . . . and seeing two Irishmen unloading a scow of stone, I went, unasked, and helped them. When we had finished, one of them came to me and asked me if I were a slave. I told him I was. He asked, "Are ye a slave for life?" I told him that I was. The good Irishman seemed to be deeply affected by

the statement. He said to the other that it was a pity so fine a little fellow as myself should be a slave for life. He said it was a shame to hold me. They both advised me to run away to the north; that I should find friends there, and that I should be free. I pretended not to be interested in what they said, and treated them as if I did not understand them; for I feared they might be treacherous. White men have been known to encourage slaves to escape, and then, to get the reward, catch them and return them to their masters. I was afraid that these seemingly good men might use me so; but I nevertheless remembered their advice, and from that time I resolved to run away."[3]

Martin Luther King Jr. said the mistrust African Americans feel toward white people remained well into the 1950s, especially in the segregated South. Remnants of this mistrust still exist today. I often hear people say, "Slavery ended a long time ago, and race shouldn't be an issue anymore. Why can't we all just be colorblind toward the issue of race? Why can't African Americans simply let go of the past?" But the problem with race relations in America is far more complex. A United Nations fact sheet on slavery states: "Even when abolished, slavery leaves traces. It can persist as a state of mind—among its victims and their descendants and among the inheritors of those who practiced it—long after it has formally disappeared."[4]

To improve the health of America and heal the racial trauma from our past, we must all do our part to rebuild trust with each other. This is a challenging path, and the first step involves recognizing that it is possible to trust again. Frederick Douglass and Martin Luther King Jr. demonstrated this by developing strong bonds of trust with white people. Even Malcolm X, a controversial civil rights activist, demonstrated our remarkable human ability to gradually overcome mistrust.

Malcolm Little was born in 1925, the same year as my father. He later changed his last name to "X," symbolizing the Africans who lost their names when taken to America as slaves. Malcolm X said he inherited his light skin when a white man raped his black grandmother. Describing how his childhood was affected by racism, he explained, "The Ku Klux Klan burned down [my family's home] in Omaha . . . When we moved to Lansing, Michigan, our home was burned down again. In fact, my father was killed by the Ku Klux Klan."[5]

Turning to a life of crime, Malcolm X spent seventy-seven months in prison.[6] He often called white people "devils" and said, "I don't care how nice [a white person] is to you; the thing you must always remember is that almost never does he really see you as he sees himself, as he sees his own kind. He may stand with you through thin, but not thick; when the chips are down, you'll find that as fixed in him as his bone structure is his sometimes subconscious conviction that he's better than anybody black."[7]

Later in his life Malcolm X had a change of heart due to honest self-reflection and life-changing personal experiences. He said, "I tried in every speech I made to clarify my new position regarding white people—'I don't speak against the sincere, well-meaning, good white people. I have learned that there *are* some. I have learned that not all white people are racists.'"[8]

Toward the end of his life Malcolm X realized that our shared humanity transcends our racial differences. His understanding that he belonged to a global human family continued to grow until he was assassinated on February 21, 1965, at the age of thirty-nine. One month before his death, he said: "I believe in recognizing every human being as a human being, neither white, black, brown nor red. When you are dealing with humanity as one family, there's no question of integration or intermarriage. It's just one human being marrying another human being, or one human being living around and with another human being."[9]

Two days before his assassination, Malcolm X said the following during an interview with Gordon Parks:

> I realized racism isn't just a black and white problem. It's brought bloodbaths to about every nation on earth at one time or another. Brother, remember the time that white college girl came into the restaurant—the one who wanted to help the [Black] Muslims and the whites get together—and I told her there wasn't a ghost of a chance and she went away crying? . . . Well, I've lived to regret that incident. In many parts of the African continent I saw

white students helping black people. Something like this kills a lot of argument [that all white people are racist]. I did many things as a [Black] Muslim that I'm sorry for now. I was a zombie then—like all [Black] Muslims—I was hypnotized, pointed in a certain direction and told to march. Well, I guess a man's entitled to make a fool of himself if he's ready to pay the cost. It cost me twelve years. That was a bad scene, brother. The sickness and madness of those days—I'm glad to be free of them. It's a time for martyrs now. And if I'm to be one, it will be in the cause of brotherhood. That's the only thing that can save this country. I've learned it the hard way— but I've learned it.[10]

If Malcolm X could overcome so much adversity and learn to trust and forgive many of the people he had once hated, it reveals a lot about our own human capacity to develop trust and forgiveness, despite the obstacles that life throws at us. I have worked to overcome my own feelings of mistrust, and although I have made progress, it hasn't been easy. I have struggled to abandon mistrust as a survival technique, realizing that when my parents warned me about the dangers of not being white in America they did not tell me lies. On the contrary, they told me *their* truth. They were describing life as they had experienced it and trying to protect me from the suffering they endured.

My parents raised me the best they could in difficult circumstances. Interracial marriage did not become legal in all U.S. states until 1967, when the Supreme Court ruled in *Loving v. Virginia* that laws banning interracial marriage were unconstitutional. Although interracial marriage was illegal in nearly all the southern states prior to 1967, white people were not the only ones opposed to it. Marrying in 1975 when interracial marriage was still controversial in many parts of the country, my parents did not feel welcome in African American or Korean communities. Many Koreans did not like that my mother had married a black man, and many African Americans did not like that my father had married an Asian woman. This rejection made my life journey much more challenging. A strong community can protect children from some of the worst aspects of racism, such as self-loathing and low self-respect. Martin Luther King Jr. grew up in a strong black community where his father and other African Americans helped him recognize his full dignity and worth as a human being.

I did not grow up around any African Americans or Koreans other than my parents. Because I was racially isolated when dealing with racism, I developed intense feelings of self-loathing and I began to hate the African American and Asian blood that flowed through my veins. When combined with my violent upbringing, this led me deeper into the dark tunnels where the siren song of rage became louder, louder, louder.

The Berserker

In Greek mythology, the Sirens were monsters who killed sailors passing by their island. Possessing a woman's head and bird's body, they lured people to their deaths by hypnotizing them with their magical singing voices. When Odysseus, the hero of Homer's epic the *Odyssey*, sailed by the island where the Sirens lived, he ordered his sailors to plug their ears with beeswax. Because he wanted to hear the Sirens' beautiful music, however, he did not plug his ears and instead had his crew tie him to the ship's mast.

The Sirens quickly hypnotized Odysseus with their magical song, calling him to them. He tried desperately to break free from the ropes, but he was tied too tightly. So he begged his crew to untie him, but the sailors knew he would be killed if allowed to visit the Sirens. Eventually his ship passed beyond the reach of the Sirens' mesmerizing voices, and Odysseus survived.

Today the term *siren song* refers to a temptation that is difficult to resist, but if pursued will lead to our destruction.[11] The more a person has been beaten, abused, and humiliated, the louder the siren song of rage becomes. The seductive voice of rage tells us to kill, maim, and destroy. If we obey its sinister commands, it promises to protect us. It promises to never let anyone hurt us again.

When people are physically threatened they often experience the fight-or-flight response, which gives them the options of becoming aggressive toward the threat or fleeing to safety. But what happens when fleeing is not an option? What happens when someone is trapped, unable to run away, and terrified? What happens when someone has been abused for so long that he or she would rather die in a violent confrontation than continue to live in fear? When nothing else in the world is able to protect us, rage can come to our rescue.

When a person is drunk with rage, it is known as *going berserk.* Just as doctors must understand illness in order to promote health, understanding the berserker mindset is essential for healing the worst forms of violent behavior and creating a more peaceful society. The factors that cause people to go berserk are rarely discussed today, but Sun Tzu understood them over two thousand years ago. In *The Art of War* he said, "When you surround an army, leave an outlet free. Do not press a desperate foe too hard."[12]

Sun Tzu realized that a combination of two factors, like an explosive chemical reaction, causes people to go berserk. The first is feeling that one's life is in imminent danger, and the second is feeling trapped and unable to escape. Accordingly, Sun Tzu advised military commanders to always give an opposing army an escape route, because when soldiers are trapped and about to be killed they are more likely to go berserk. In his book *Achilles in Vietnam*, Jonathan Shay explains: "When a soldier is trapped, surrounded, or overrun and facing certain death, the berserk state has apparent survival value, because he apparently has nothing to lose and everything to gain from reckless frenzy."[13]

In ancient battles, most casualties were inflicted by forcing an opposing army to retreat and killing the fleeing soldiers as they ran away. When an opposing army was trapped and unable to escape, the berserk state became a desperate "Hail Mary pass" in the struggle for survival, a last-ditch effort to stay alive. Similar to humans, wild animals are also most dangerous when cornered and unable to flee. If death seems imminent, going into a reckless violent frenzy can seem like the best option. What do you have to lose?

The berserk state helped our earliest ancestors survive in the wild. To understand how, consider the following scenario. If you lived on the African savannah thousands of years ago and saw a large male leopard sneaking toward you, how would you protect yourself? You could flee, or you could try to frighten the animal away by yelling, waving your arms to appear larger than you really were, and throwing rocks. These attempts to frighten the animal away in order to avoid a violent confrontation are known as *posturing.*

But what happens if a large male leopard sneaks up on you and jumps on your back? At that point you can no longer flee or posture. Your only options are dying or going berserk.

Now here is a question for you. If a large male leopard jumped on you right now and you had only six seconds before he inflicted a lethal wound, how would you convince him to leave you alone? Would you play dead? Would you punch him? Would you scream? Take a moment to ponder this. If it takes you more than six seconds to think of an answer, it's too late.

To stay alive in this extreme life-or-death situation where there is no time to think, we must go into a beastlike state of mind where thinking is not necessary and instinct takes over. The berserker mindset knows exactly what to do when a large male leopard has knocked you to the ground and is six seconds away from inflicting a lethal wound. Gouge out his eyes with your fingers. Use your hands to tear off his genitals, or if necessary bite them off. Rip off his ears or a chunk of his nose. With insane frenzy, use your hands and teeth to pull off any piece of flesh within your reach. This will not guarantee your survival. It might not even give you a good chance at staying alive. But in a situation where you are about to die and have nothing to lose, it will give you the best chance of causing the leopard so much pain that he lets you go. As I mentioned earlier, the berserk state is a desperate Hail Mary pass in the struggle for survival, a last-ditch effort to stay alive.

The sensory and reproductive organs of animals are very sensitive, and to inflict as much pain as possible the berserker can fixate on damaging those parts of the body. The berserker is not just intent on killing, but mutilating flesh and causing immense pain. Most people would cringe at the thought of gouging out a leopard's eyes or ripping off his genitals, even if they were about to be killed. To commit these horrifying and revolting acts, a person in the berserk state becomes practically insane. A chemical change occurs in the brain that makes the thought of gouging out a living creature's eyes no longer seem disgusting, but irresistible—like a dark and seductive siren song. The siren song of rage tells us: "If you have no mercy, you will find safety."

This is one reason a soldier who goes berserk in war can gouge out people's eyes, cut off their ears, and mutilate their bodies in other grotesque ways. These forms of mutilation are directed not only at the living, but also at corpses. Like smoldering embers that remain long after a fire has died, berserker rage can linger long after a threat has disappeared, especially in the hostile environment of war where a person never truly feels safe. When the inferno of berserker rage has been ignited but not fully satisfied, innocent people can also become targets. A berserker can perceive women and children as if they were leopards—as lethal threats that must be destroyed.

Jonathan Shay tells us, "The berserker is figuratively—sometimes literally—blind to everything but his destructive aim. He cannot see the distinction between civilian and combatant or even the distinction between comrade and enemy. One of our veterans was tied up by his own men and taken to the rear while berserk. He has no clear memory but suspects that he had become a serious threat to them."[14] The army views berserkers as potentially dangerous, because they can endanger their own comrades. There are many examples of berserkers engaging in extremely reckless behavior that puts their fellow soldiers at risk.

Evidence of berserker rage can be seen throughout military history, from the ancient Greeks to modern soldiers. The word "berserker" originally referred to Nordic warriors who fought with uncontrollable rage. During the Vietnam War, both sides demonstrated berserker rage by mutilating living people and corpses in horrific ways. To understand why people are never the same after they go berserk, I am reminded of something I learned in the army. The army taught me that when people suffer from heat stroke for the first time, it creates a physiological change in the body that makes them more vulnerable to heat stroke in the future. In a similar way, Jonathan Shay theorizes that when people fully go berserk for the first time, it permanently changes the brain, making them more vulnerable to future incidents of berserker rage. He shares an account of a Vietnam veteran that illustrates how a person can descend into the dark tunnels of berserker madness:

> I was walking point. I had seen this NVA [North Vietnamese Army] soldier at a distance. We were approaching him and he spotted us. We spread out to look for him. I was coming around a stand of grass and heard noise. I couldn't tell who it was, us or him. I stuck my head in the bush and saw this NVA hiding there and told him to come out . . . He fired and I felt this burning on my

cheek . . . I emptied everything I had into him. Then I saw blood dripping on the back of my hand and I just went crazy. I pulled him out into the paddy and carved him up with my knife. When I was done with him, he looked like a rag doll that a dog had been playing with. Even then I wasn't satisfied. I was fighting with the [medical] corpsmen trying to take care of me. I was trying to get at him for more . . .

I felt betrayed by trying to give the guy a chance and I got blasted. I lost all my mercy. I felt a drastic change after that. I just couldn't get enough. I built up such hate, I couldn't do enough damage . . . especially seeing what they did to guys in the outfit they got hold of—cut off their dicks, cut off their ears . . . Got worse as time went by. I really loved fucking killing, couldn't get enough. For every one that I killed I felt better. Made some of the hurt went away. Every time you lost a friend it seemed like a part of you was gone. Get one of them to compensate what they had done to me. I got very hard, cold, merciless. I lost all my mercy.[15]

Many soldiers in combat don't go berserk, and many people attacked by wild animals don't descend into a berserker rage. It is unclear why some people go berserk and others do not, but the situations that make people most likely to go berserk are well known. The feeling of being terrified and trapped is the most common cause of berserker rage. In addition, the brutal death of a loved one and extreme forms of humiliation and betrayal can also cause people to snap and go berserk. It seems that the berserk state can be ignited not only when our physical body is threatened and trapped, but also when an important part of our identity is severely threatened or destroyed.

The numerous examples of soldiers going berserk show that people can experience berserker rage in different amounts. Some people go berserk to greater extremes than others, yet anyone who goes berserk shares similar characteristics. Jonathan Shay uses the following words to describe the berserker mindset: beastlike, insane, enraged, cruel, without restraint or discrimination, insatiable, intoxicated, frenzy.

In *Achilles in Vietnam*, Jonathan Shay says:

> The *Iliad* climaxes with Achilles' beastlike and godlike rampage. The berserk state is the most important and distinctive element of combat trauma . . . Achilles defines himself here as a lion or a wolf, not a human . . . Homer compares attacking warriors to wild animals dozens of times. This was clearly a conventional metaphor used to praise warrior ferocity . . . However, when veterans and Achilles refer to themselves as animals they are not using conventional metaphors of strength and ferocity . . . When soldiers speak of themselves this way they are speaking of a loss of human restraint, powerfully symbolized by Achilles' longing to eat Hector's raw flesh.[16]

War is not the only experience that fills people with berserker rage. Mike Tyson, the youngest heavyweight champion in boxing history, suffered from berserker rage throughout his life. After Evander Holyfield headbutted Tyson multiple times during their 1997 rematch, he bit off part of Holyfield's ear. In the excellent 2009 documentary *Tyson*, he explained what went through his mind:

> He butts me again. He's taller than me. What is his head doing underneath my head? I received a cut eye. He started looking at the eye. He butts me again. I complain to the referee. The referee doesn't do anything. I become ferocious . . . I'm mad. I get so mad I want to kill him . . . At the moment I'm enraged and I lose all composure and discipline. I fight and fight and fight and I want to choke him. I bit him . . . I wanted to just kick him right in his groin . . . I wanted to kill this guy . . . And I'm insane at the moment. I'm a good person, but at that moment I went insane. I was enraged . . . he butted me with his head intentionally to hurt me and my eye, so I wanted to

intentionally hurt him, and so when I bit him again and [referee] Mills Lane came and disqualified me, I didn't really care. I wanted to inflict as much pain as possible on that man, because I was totally insane at that moment."[17]

My other books show that human beings are not naturally violent, by citing abundant evidence from military history. But if people become extremely violent when they go berserk, does this contradict my view? Exploring the berserker mindset actually supports the view that human beings are not naturally violent by offering four pieces of evidence. First, people are not born as berserkers, and going berserk requires certain kinds of trauma, conditioning, or feelings of desperation. Second, going berserk is a last resort that results when other options, such as fleeing from danger and posturing, seem unlikely to work. Third, going berserk isn't a part of our normal human experience. Like a rubber band that is pulled so hard it breaks, people go berserk in extreme situations: when they are threatened and trapped, their loved one is brutally killed, or they are severely humiliated or betrayed. Fourth, even in extreme situations many people do not go berserk, and many go berserk only after repeated instances of abuse. When Tyson was a child, he was afraid of fighting, and it took years of abuse for him to slip into his first berserker rage. He describes how he was bullied as a child for being short, obese, and wearing glasses, yet he chose to run rather than fight:

> I can remember going to school and being bullied and people taking my glasses and putting them in the trunk of a milk cart. I've never had any kind of physical altercation with anybody at that particular time in my life, so I couldn't believe a human being would do that. I never dreamed somebody, an absolute stranger would do that to me. I didn't know why . . . I just ran. And I think that's why people like myself become more assertive in life and become more aggressive . . . because they fear that they don't want that to happen to them no more and they don't want to be humiliated in that particular fashion any more.

And that's why I believe I'm the person that I am. And
people have a misconception that I'm something else, but
I'm just afraid of being that way again, of being treated
that way again, of being physically humiliated in the
streets again . . . And I just wish I knew how to fight back
then . . . I was afraid to fight . . . I was so afraid.[18]

Although Tyson was afraid of fighting, a traumatizing incident led to
his first street fight. Growing up in one of the most violent sections of Brook-
lyn, he loved raising pigeons. They gave him the sense of security and comfort all children need and provided a sanctuary from his abusive
surroundings. Unlike people, his birds were loyal and did not hurt him.

One day a group of bullies found his pigeons and took one. He shouted,
"Give me my bird back!" The bully holding the bird responded by ripping
off its head and throwing the dead bird at Tyson, saying, "There, you can
have it." Enraged, Tyson beat up the larger boy. It was his first fight but
would not be his last.

By the time Tyson was thirteen he had been arrested thirty-eight times.
Like many people who become violent, he was the product of the kind of
abuse, fear, and humiliation that breeds violence. In the documentary *Tyson*,
he described how he felt after learning to box. Barely able to hold back his
tears, he said, "I just never had to worry about anyone bullying me again. I
knew that would never happen again. Because I knew I would fucking kill
them if they fucked with me."[19]

As a teenager I was fed up with being bullied by other children and
beaten by my father. When I started lifting weights during high school, my
father sensed a dark change in my behavior. He stopped hitting me, because
I think he feared I would retaliate and possibly kill him. The siren song of
rage told me, "If anyone tries to hurt you again as your father did, I will protect you. Your parents taught you about the dangers of not being white in
America, but I am here for you. Your enslaved ancestors suffered so much,
and if anyone tries to harm you in that way I will keep you safe. I will make
you invincible and give you the power to kill them."

Jonathan Shay says going berserk also makes people feel invincible,
immune to physical pain, and godlike. If a leopard were on top of you,

sinking his claws and teeth into your flesh, not being distracted by physical pain or even your own safety would allow you to focus all your energy on the act of maiming and destroying. The sensation of feeling invincible can be very addictive, especially for people who have been abused. If you had to choose between feeling constant fear, physical pain, and helplessness as a result of being beaten up all your life, or you could instead feel invincible, immune to pain, and godlike, what would you choose? The siren song of rage is so seductive because it promises to protect us. The more abuse and trauma a person has experienced, the more seductive the siren song of rage becomes.

Because berserker rage makes people feel invincible, it can cause them to behave in ways that *appear* suicidal. Berserking soldiers often expose themselves to extreme and unnecessary danger during combat. For example, when soldiers feel trapped and go berserk they may run wildly toward the enemy or stand up in the middle of a firefight, shooting their rifle or machine gun with reckless frenzy. This is not because they are suicidal, but because they feel godlike and invincible. As I mentioned earlier, this is why Sun Tzu advised military commanders to never trap their opponents into a corner but to always give them an escape route. Sun Tzu knew that berserking soldiers are extremely dangerous. Adachi Masahiro, a Japanese martial artist and military scientist who wrote during the eighteenth century, described how dangerous a berserker can be:

> Once when a servant of a certain master of the One Sword school was summoned by another distinguished personage, toward whom he'd committed a discourtesy, the sword master called his servant to him and said, "You were discourteous to so-and-so, and now he's asked me to turn you over to him. I'm sorry, but I have no choice but to send you to him. No doubt he's going to kill you. Your life is over anyway, so I'll give you my sword and you can go away if you kill me. Otherwise he'll kill you."
>
> The servant said, "What can someone like me, with no skill at all, do to a famous person like you, master? Please excuse me."

The master said, "I've never faced someone who's gone berserk before. It'll serve as a test. So since you're a dead man anyway, I'm taking you on as an opponent for a test. Fight with all your might!"

The servant said, "Well, then, I'll have to take you on." Then when they dueled, [the servant went berserk and] the master unexpectedly retreated and was ultimately driven back to a wall. When he saw he was in danger, he shouted and cut his servant down in one fell swoop.

Turning to his disciples, who were watching, he said, "Well, now—going berserk is scary stuff! . . . If even a menial without skills is like this, how much the more so someone with first-class training—if he were to fight berserk, no one could stand up to him."[20]

At first glance the berserk state might appear to give people an advantage in combat, but looking deeper allows us to see a much different story. Feeling invincible in combat is not necessarily a good thing. Jonathan Shay tells us, "Berserking American soldiers invariably shed their helmets and flak jackets. They had no other armor. As one veteran said, 'Got rid of my helmet, got rid of my flak jacket. I just wanted to kill.' All the berserker feels he needs is a *weapon*; everything else is in the way. Achilles [when he goes berserk] wants to go after Hector just moments after he hears the grievous news of Pátroklos's death, despite the loss of his own armor."[21]

But don't many children also take dangerous and unnecessary risks? Don't many children also think they are invincible? When teenagers perform dangerous stunts on a skateboard while not wearing a helmet, does it mean they have gone berserk? The invincibility most children feel is different from berserker rage. As I explain in *Peaceful Revolution* when discussing the "universal human phobia," the vast majority of us are terrified of violence when it is up close and personal, and around 98 percent of people will have a phobic-level reaction to human aggression when it is directed at them. Most teenagers who perform dangerous stunts on a skateboard while not wearing a helmet would flee in terror if a man with a machete started chasing them. When the school shootings occurred at Columbine High School in 1999, most of the teenagers panicked and went into shock; some of the high school students were so terrified they clung to the SWAT team members, sobbing in horror and refusing to let go.[22] What makes berserkers unique is not only that they feel invincible, but also that they lose one of the most deeply ingrained instincts in human beings—the fear of lethal violence.

As I mentioned earlier, going berserk is a desperate Hail Mary pass in the struggle for survival, a last-ditch effort to stay alive. A berserker who feels invincible may *appear* to have an advantage in combat, but appearances are often deceptive. Feeling invincible can be useful in certain rare circumstances—such as when a person is trapped and has little chance of surviving—but it also leads to extremely reckless behavior that can easily get a berserker killed. Another problem is that berserking soldiers are nearly impossible to control, and the last thing most generals want is to lose control of their soldiers. Generals win battles and wars by utilizing strategies and tactics, but berserking soldiers have trouble obeying strategies and tactics because they are difficult to control and unable to listen. When Achilles goes berserk he shouts at his mother, "Do not attempt to keep me from the fight, though you love me; *you cannot make me listen* [emphasis added]."[23]

Not only is feeling invincible not necessarily a good thing, but berserking soldiers can endanger their comrades, friends, and family. Jonathan Shay explains:

> One [Vietnam] veteran went berserk after the death of his closest friend-in-arms and remained in that state for two years, until his behavior became so extreme that his own men tied him up and took him to the rear . . . [The veteran said] 'I carried this home with me. I lost all my friends, beat up my sister, went after my father. I mean, I just went after anybody and everything. Every three days I would totally explode, lose it for no reason at all. I'd be sitting there calm as could be, and this monster would come out of me.[24]

Frederick Douglass was abused to a point where he began to exhibit some characteristics of berserker rage such as complete disregard for personal safety in the midst of lethal violence.* After being beaten throughout his life, he started to court death as only a berserker does, by displaying the kind of rage that cares more about hurting others than personal safety. The penalty for a slave hitting a white man was death, but Douglass was determined to attack and potentially kill any white man who ever tried to beat him again. He realized that any white person who hit him would have to kill him, because he was prepared to fight to the death.

People go berserk to different degrees, and although Douglass never demonstrated full-blown berserker rage, he described an incident where he exhibited some characteristics of the berserk state. When he was a teenager a group of white men at a shipyard started insulting and hitting him. He became so enraged that he attacked the white men, even though they had weapons and greatly outnumbered him. And when they stopped attacking him and left him alone he ran after them, trying to assault them with a hand-spike, before some carpenters intervened and he was able to calm down. Doesn't Douglass's behavior seem suicidal? It was likely the armed group of white men would kill him, and if they did not he would have been lynched for hitting a white man, even if it was in self-defense. But like a berserker, he lost his fear of consequences and even death during the fight. Douglass described what happened:

> They began to put on airs, and talk about the "niggers" taking the country, saying we all ought to be killed . . . they commenced making my condition as hard as they could, by hectoring me around, and sometimes striking me. I, of course, kept the vow I made after the fight with Mr. Covey, and struck back again, regardless of consequences;

* I would not call boxing or mixed martial arts "lethal violence." Although a person can die during a match, this is rare, and there are strict rules along with a referee to protect the fighters. Unlike boxing and mixed martial arts, lethal violence has no rules or referee, and the likelihood of being maimed or killed is much higher due to the presence of weapons. There is a big difference between a boxing match with gloves, and fighting several hostile men wielding knives, baseball bats, or guns in a dark alley. Considering that a slave striking a white person could result in the death penalty, all of Frederick Douglass's fights with white men greatly endangered his life, and it is amazing he survived his years in slavery.

and while I kept them from combining, I succeeded very well; for I could whip the whole of them, taking them separately. They, however, at length combined, and came upon me, armed with sticks, stones, and heavy handspikes. One came in front with a half brick. There was one at each side of me, and one behind me. While I was attending to those in front, and on either side, the one behind ran up with the handspike, and struck me a heavy blow upon the head. It stunned me. I fell, and with this they all ran upon me, and fell to beating me with their fists. I let them lay on for a while, gathering strength. In an instant, I gave a sudden surge, and rose to my hands and knees. Just as I did that, one of their number gave me, with his heavy boot, a powerful kick in the left eye. My eyeball seemed to have burst. When they saw my eye closed, and badly swollen, they left me. With this I seized the handspike, *and for a time pursued them* [emphasis added]. But here the carpenters interfered.[25]

After the carpenters blocked Douglass's pursuit, he seemed to calm down and think about consequences and his personal safety. At this point he no longer resembled a berserker who felt invincible, and he decided to retreat: "I thought I might as well give it up. It was impossible to stand my hand against so many. All this took place in sight of not less than fifty white ship-carpenters, and not one interposed a friendly word; but some cried, 'Kill the damned nigger! Kill him! Kill him! He struck a white person.' I found my only chance for life was in flight. I succeeded in getting away without an additional blow, and barely so; for to strike a white man is death by Lynch law."[26]

Douglass first exhibited characteristics of berserker rage earlier in his life, when he was trying to escape a beating from the "slavebreaker" Mr. Covey. Unable to avoid the beating and *feeling trapped*, he noticed a dramatic change in his behavior. Comparing the way he felt to insanity, he called it "fighting madness." Douglass explained, "Whence came the daring spirit necessary to grapple with a man who, eight-and-forty hours before, could, with his slightest word, have made me tremble like a leaf in a storm, I do not know; at any rate, I was resolved to fight . . . The *fighting madness* [emphasis added] had come upon me, and I found my strong fingers firmly attached to the throat of the tyrant, as heedless of consequences, at the moment, as if we stood as equals before the law . . . I held him so firmly by the throat that his blood followed my nails."[27]

Douglass would have been put to death for fighting back against a white man, but Covey did not report this fight because he did not want people to know that a sixteen-year-old slave like Douglass had overpowered him. This would have ruined Covey's reputation within the white community, where he was valued as a man who could break even the most difficult slaves into submission. During the fight Douglass was focused on defending himself rather than causing harm, but after this incident he started having strong urges to seriously injure Covey. Exhibiting characteristics of berserker rage, he seemed to lose his fear of lethal violence, and maiming another human being became more important to him than staying alive.

Douglass explained: "[During my first fight with Mr. Covey] my aim had not been to injure him, but to prevent his injuring me . . . After this conflict with Mr. Covey I did, at times, purposely aim to provoke him to an attack, by refusing to keep with the other hands in the field, but I could never bully him to another battle. *I was determined on doing him serious damage* [emphasis added] if he ever again attempted to lay violent hands on me."[28] Covey seemed to know better than to get in another fight with Douglass. But just as berserker rage can sometimes protect us, it can more likely backfire and get us killed. Berserker rage is not a reliable form of self-defense, because it is based largely on illusions.

The comic book *Incredible Hulk* is a metaphor for the berserker mindset and its illusions. The main character, Bruce Banner, is a kind and mild-mannered person, but when he loses his temper he becomes the Hulk. Like the berserker, the Hulk is beastlike and drunk with rage. Immune to most physical pain and practically invincible, his power is godlike. Bruce Banner is afraid of transforming into the enraged Hulk because of the violent rampages that usually follow. Because of the Hulk's superhuman powers, he is nearly impossible to kill.

Unlike the fictional Hulk in the comic book, however, real-life berserker rage only creates the *illusion* of being invincible and godlike. When I broke the window in my apartment with my fist, the pain gave me so much pleasure that it is difficult to describe. It reminded me of the times I used to cut my arms in high school. Imagine feeling suffocating agony and not being able to cry or even scream. As the misery gets bottled up inside you, like a clogged pipe ready to explode, cutting yourself temporarily releases the tension that is strangling you on the inside. As the blood flowed from my wounds, it felt like the pain was dripping out of my body.

I broke the window because I missed a small typo when proofreading. I had read the words numerous times without seeing the mistake, and when I finally noticed it my temper erupted. When we are lost in the mazelike tunnels of our psychological wounds, it is like seeing the world through the distorted reflection of a fun-house mirror. Just as a fun-house mirror can exaggerate the size of our heads in relation to the rest of our bodies, trauma can blow something small out of proportion, causing us to see something harmless as a lethal threat. As a child I was often beaten for making small mistakes. Enraged at myself for missing the typo, my self-loathing caused me to explode. When I punched the window I wanted to hurt myself as much as I wanted to damage the glass. After the effects of berserker rage wore off and I calmed down, I was brought back to reality. My hand started to hurt, and because injuring myself did not deal with the source of my suffering, I knew that self-destruction cannot lead to peace.

So far in my adult life I have not assaulted anyone, and in *Peaceful Revolution* I explain how discipline has helped me control my rage. I am writing about berserker rage not to excuse the violent actions of those who go berserk, but to help us understand the causes and consequences of the berserker mindset. Only by exploring the nature of rage can we develop techniques to heal it. This chapter may help you have more compassion for those who go berserk, but we must remember that people are always responsible for their actions, even when drunk with rage. Mike Tyson took responsibility for biting off a part of Evander Holyfield's ear, saying, "I lost my composure. The worst thing a warrior, a soldier could ever do is lose his discipline."[29]

In his book *Man's Search for Meaning*, psychiatrist Victor Frankl says we should not excuse people's crimes, but hold them accountable for their actions and help them change for the better through rehabilitation. Frankl says attributing violent crime entirely to someone's circumstances is "tantamount to explaining away his or her guilt and to seeing in him or her not a free and responsible human being but a machine to be repaired. Even criminals themselves abhor this treatment and prefer to be held responsible for their deeds . . . When I addressed the prisoners in San Quentin, I told them that 'you are human beings like me, and as such you were free to commit a crime, to become guilty. Now, however, you are responsible for overcoming guilt by rising above it, by growing beyond yourselves, by changing for the better.'"[30]

I am sharing deeply personal information about myself not only to illustrate the ideas in this book, but to also help remove the taboos around trauma that prevent us from healing the violent behavior in our society. We must not be ashamed or afraid to discuss the underlying causes of violence, because that is where the truth can be found. Just as doctors understand illness, we must also understand violence. We must have terms and metaphors that give us the means to truly talk about violence and its causes, and we must be empowered with the tools to help each other. Like all people dealing with trauma I have good days and bad. Pursuing spiritual change allows us to have more good days than bad.

Many years ago the siren song of rage promised to protect me. For a long time I believed it, but then something odd happened. As the years passed I became more afraid of my own rage than I was of other people. I had been relying on a desperate Hail Mary pass, which should only be used as a last resort in the most extreme situations, as a way of keeping myself safe. But this was a dangerous way to live. How could I convince my rage that I no longer needed its protection? How could I transform the siren song of rage into a melody of peace? If I wanted to survive I would have to find a way, and that is why I developed a system of waging peace I call the *infinite shield*. I developed it not just to protect me from other people, but to also protect them from me.

CHAPTER 3

The First Line of Defense

The Best Martial Arts Self-Defense Technique

During the summer of 2010 I visited my friend Brett in Alabama. We met in high school, but became better friends after I graduated from West Point. On the first day of my visit, he and his friends wanted to go out drinking that evening. Although I don't drink alcohol, I decided to be social and join them. It was a relaxing and uneventful evening, until they decided to go to a Waffle House at 2:00 a.m.

We were sitting at a table, waiting to order our food. I was probably the only customer in the restaurant who had not consumed alcohol that evening. In the corner, a man who had just received his food was yelling at a waitress because his fork was dirty. He was drunk, and when she did not have a clean fork ready for him immediately, he stood up and walked toward my table. Seeing that I was still holding the menu and had not yet ordered, he took my fork. Another waitress saw what happened and quickly replaced the fork he took from me.

Brett's friend John was sitting next to me. Angered by the disrespectful behavior of the person who took my fork, he said, "That guy took your fork! Are you going to put up with that?"

I replied, "No harm was done. Now he has a fork. I have a fork. Everybody has forks."

The more John thought about it, the angrier he got. "You can't let him get away with taking your fork. I don't care if he sat down at a table with a dirty fork. It still doesn't give him a right to take something from you."

I said, "You have a point, and if he wasn't drunk I would consider confronting him about taking my fork. But it's difficult to reason with people when they're that drunk. People also make bad decisions when they're drunk, so let's give him the benefit of the doubt. Maybe he's nicer when he's sober. Also, it's not like he took my wallet. Now everybody has forks and everything is fine."

The more John thought about the way I had been disrespected, the angrier he got. As I looked at his body language, I could tell his temper was boiling. "I appreciate you wanting to defend my honor," I said jokingly, "But it's not worth getting in a fight over. Let's not worry about it."

But after seething with anger for several minutes, he finally said, "I'm not going to take this." Enraged, he walked over to the guy who took my fork and yelled, "He's a veteran! You can't take his fork!"

John pointed a hostile finger in the guy's face, who looked up from his food and began yelling back. The situation was quickly escalating toward a fight, and because I wasn't drunk I was able to look at the growing chaos with a clear head. First of all, the guy who took my fork was physically massive. He had a friend sitting next to him with a big chain around his neck. They had two other friends with them who were about six foot four, muscular, and wearing cowboy boots, cut-off "daisy-duke" jeans, tank tops, and women's wigs.

Martial arts training taught me that size does not accurately reflect how tough people are or how well they can fight. Nevertheless, this was not the kind of group I wanted to get in a fight with. Along with the legal risk of being arrested, sued, or imprisoned if someone got seriously injured, was it worth getting hurt or killed over a fork?

I also did not want John to get hurt, and if he were attacked I would have to jump in to help him. So I quickly stood up and tried to deescalate the situation. John yelled louder and louder. The guy who took my fork shouted back and became very aggressive. One of his friends yelled at John, "Shut up and get the fuck out of here!"

John would not back down, so I spoke directly to the guy who took my fork. I said, "We're not trying to be disrespectful. He's upset you took my fork, but I just want us to drop it." By that time a whole bunch of people were shouting and I could barely hear myself talk. I started to feel a little nervous and afraid. That was a good sign, I thought, because it meant I was not feeling fearless and invincible. It meant I had not gone berserk.

My memories of what happened next are vague, perhaps due to the chaos and commotion, but I remember trying to cut through the noise to communicate that no disrespect was intended and this wasn't worth fighting over. Then I grabbed John by the shoulders and pulled him back as he continued to yell.

Later on the guy with the chain around his neck came up to me and apologized. He said, "My friend is normally a nice guy, and he took your fork because he was drunk and pissed off. I apologize for his behavior, and let me pay for your meal to make up for it."

The reason I tell this story is because a mini-war was almost started just because people felt disrespected. There was no other reason to fight, because everyone had forks. There was also plenty of food for everyone, and nobody's personal property was taken. Someone could have gotten seriously injured or killed, simply because people felt disrespected.

Why do martial arts teach us to always respect everyone, including our opponents? The reason is because the majority of human conflict comes from people just feeling disrespected. Being respected is something human beings tend to like a lot. In all of human history, I don't think anyone has ever seriously said, "I hate it when people respect me! I can't stand it when people respect me!"

The times in my life when I most wanted to punch someone in the face occurred when I felt disrespected. Take a moment to ponder the times when someone most angered you, and the feeling of being disrespected probably had a lot to do with it. Martial arts philosophy focuses on self-defense, and martial arts taught me if we truly want to protect ourselves and others, the first line of defense is not being skilled at punching and kicking, but being skilled at giving respect.

Jesus, Gandhi, and Martin Luther King Jr. taught us to love everyone, but to many this seems impossible. This ideal is so high that most people do not even bother trying to attain this lofty goal. It is certainly difficult to love everyone, but a much more attainable goal is learning to respect everyone as human beings. That is a first step we can all strive toward. Not only will respecting everyone as human beings help us wage peace, but respect is the foundation for every genuine act of love, compassion, and kindness. In a television interview I saw many years ago, Jet Li, a famous martial artist, said, "I have the best martial arts self-defense technique. The best martial arts self-defense technique is to smile at people, because if you smile and treat people with respect and kindness, they usually don't want to fight you. Anyone who gets in a lot of fights has very poor martial arts self-defense" (paraphrased).

The Three Elements of Universal Respect

Every culture has different standards of respect. For example, in the military and many Asian cultures, being late is extremely rude, and showing up early is a sign of respect. In the army I heard a saying, "If you're early you're on time. If you're on time you're late." Since living in California, I have noticed that many people here do not consider it rude to show up a few minutes late. If someone is used to being late, their tardiness might greatly offend someone who served in the military or grew up in an Asian culture. Since respect varies from culture to culture, how can we prevent unintended incidents of disrespect?

Realizing how dangerous disrespect can be, becoming skilled at giving respect is one of the most effective and essential methods of waging peace. There are two important steps for maximizing the respect we give to others. The first is to not be ignorant of their culture and make an effort to educate ourselves about their social customs. To quote the old adage, "When in Rome, do as the Romans do." This means that when you are visiting another culture, it is important to be aware of their social customs and abide by their traditions when it is appropriate.

For example, in the army I was given cultural awareness classes about how to interact with people in the Middle East. I was taught to never show them the bottom of my shoes, never shake with my left hand, and always take off my sunglasses when speaking with people. The army taught me that in the Middle East it is rude to talk to someone while our eyes are covered, because so much of our humanity and trustworthiness is expressed through our eyes. In fact, we actually smile with our eyes, not just our mouth. A genuine smile occurs when the muscles around our eyes flex; if a person's mouth smiles while the muscles around their eyes remain still it is a clear sign of a fake smile.

The second step is to practice the *three elements of universal respect*. The three elements transcend cultures and convey respect in any society. Furthermore, they do not honor people because of their status, but instead give everyone basic human respect, from the richest king to the poorest peasant.

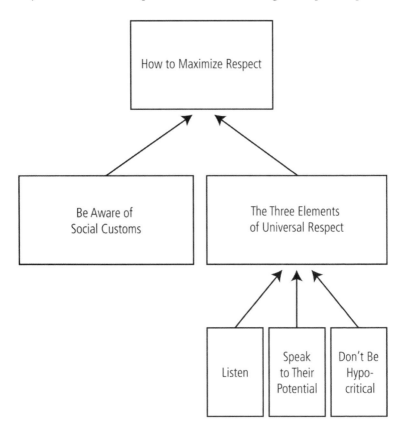

Figure 3.1 How to Maximize Respect

1. Listen: The First Element of Universal Respect

In all of human history, I don't think anyone has ever seriously said, "I hate it when people listen to me! I can't stand it when people listen to me!" Everyone likes to be listened to, and in the army I learned that listening is one of the greatest gifts we can give to people.

When I was promoted to captain I was transferred to a new unit, and things started to go badly during the first week. Because I had just joined the unit, they had not added me to their phone roster. As a result, when they called everyone in the unit at 4:00 a.m., ordering us to come in immediately for a surprise drug test, I never received the call. I did not find out about the drug test until I showed up to work later that morning.

When I came to work and started walking down the hall, I heard a colonel screaming and cursing as he told my supervisor what I had done. "I know Captain Chappell just showed up to the unit, but I can already tell he's a bad officer! He doesn't think he needs to show up to a drug test, and he just wants to do whatever he wants to do!" I tried to walk into the office to explain that I did not receive a phone call notifying me about the drug test, but the colonel yelled at me, ordering me to get out and wait in the hallway. The screaming and cursing seemed to go on for a long time as I waited. I felt helpless because I was unable to defend myself by explaining what had really happened.

I had just met my supervisor, only working with him for a couple of days. He knew almost nothing about me, and now a colonel was telling him all these bad things about me that were untrue. Soon after the colonel left, my supervisor asked to speak with me. I was nervous, because the colonel not only outranked me, but my supervisor had known him a lot longer than he had known me. Realizing that my supervisor probably had a bad impression of me based on what he had just heard, I tried to defend myself by saying that the colonel's anger had resulted from a misunderstanding.

But my supervisor interrupted me, saying, "I don't care what he said. He can yell all he wants, and I will just sit quietly and listen until he is done. I let him yell for so long because I know that if you let people vent and listen to them, they will eventually run out of steam and usually feel better. As for you, I won't make any judgments about you until I have heard your side of the story. As your supervisor I have a responsibility to at least hear your side of the story and give you the benefit of the doubt before condemning you."

I explained what happened and he completely understood, and I cannot express in words how wonderful it felt to be listened to and given the benefit of the doubt. Since then I have thought about the many conflicts that could be prevented and resolved if people simply learned how to listen. This is not easy, because listening is a challenging art form. Just as people work hard to become masters in the art of painting, music, or sculpting, it takes effort and commitment to become masters in the art of listening.

How can we listen deeply? How can we absorb what people say as soil absorbs the rain? To truly listen we must develop empathy. If we do not empathize with people we cannot really hear what they are saying. When we do not listen with empathy we hear only their words. But when we listen with empathy we also hear their emotions, hopes, and fears. We hear their humanity.

When we do not listen with empathy our conversations often become barriers that alienate us from the humanity of others. But when we listen with empathy our conversations become bridges that connect their humanity to ours. The art of listening is an essential life skill that can improve our friendships, relationships, and daily interactions with all kinds of people. Listening is also vital for effectively waging peace. Take a moment to think about a controversial issue that matters a lot to you. Now imagine discussing that issue with someone who passionately disagrees with you. Would you feel comfortable having a conversation with that person? Most people would feel uncomfortable and worry about the conversation devolving into a shouting match, but the art of listening transforms the blank canvas of a potentially hostile conversation into a masterpiece of possibilities.

Leslee Goodman, who interviewed me in the *Sun* magazine, explains how I was able to change the attitude of an adamant pro-war supporter:

> Chappell teaches through example. I met him at a weekly peace vigil on a downtown Santa Barbara, California, street corner, where he demonstrated how to engage even strident opponents with empathy and respect. I had lost patience with one such person after ten minutes of

unproductive dialogue. Then Chappell showed up. He respectfully engaged my critic for a full forty-five minutes. Their conversation ended with the man thanking Chappell for listening to him and accepting a copy of [his book] *The End of War.* A few weeks later Chappell ran into the man and learned that he had read the book and had changed his mind about war as a means of ending terrorism.

Martial arts taught me that even the best techniques are never 100 percent effective. In ideal circumstances the best techniques would succeed every time, but the circumstances we must work in are usually less than ideal. In a similar way, listening is an important technique that makes genuine dialogue possible, but sometimes a person is so stubborn and has so many biases that our best efforts do not succeed.

Singer Harry Belafonte, a friend of Martin Luther King Jr., describes how King was unable to convince a group of young African Americans to embrace the nonviolent methods of the civil rights movement. Noticing King's sadness, Belafonte asked him, "What troubles you, Martin?" King replied, "Well, I just came from that meeting with the young people in Newark and they said much that challenged me. They made great justification for why they saw violence as an important tool to their liberation. My task was to take the truths that they were experiencing, the pain they were experiencing, and say there is another way. When I left, I felt that I had not convinced them, that I had not gotten to them in the way which I would have loved to have gotten to them."[1]

Not even Martin Luther King Jr.—a black belt in waging peace—succeeded in persuading people 100 percent of the time. Although martial arts taught me that even the best techniques do not work every single time, I also learned that we can dramatically improve the success rate of our techniques. When I first tried to speak about peace in my early twenties, all I knew was how to preach to the choir. When I spoke to ten people who opposed my views on peace, I communicated in such a counterproductive way that I only persuaded one out of ten if I was lucky, and I probably alienated and offended the other nine due to the careless way I interacted with them.

As I learned the art of listening and grew more skilled at the other techniques of waging peace, I became empowered to do more than preach to the choir. This allowed me to persuade perhaps three out of ten who opposed my views on peace, and although the other seven might not agree with me, I was doing less to alienate and offend them. Today I think I can persuade perhaps six or seven out of ten, and I now speak in such a way that I alienate and offend far fewer people than I did before.

It is impossible to persuade or please everyone. At West Point I had a roommate who did not like chocolate. If chocolate cannot please everyone, how can any of us? Even Martin Luther King Jr. was hated by many despite his best efforts. But unlike some activists I have met, King did not want to just preach to the choir or alienate those who disagreed with him. He wanted to go beyond the choir by persuading as many as possible and alienating as few as possible. All social problems come from how people think, and all progress comes from transforming how people think. In a later chapter I will explain why we don't have to convince every single person for progress to happen. We just have to convince *enough* people, and the techniques of waging peace can help us persuade more and alienate less.

The first step is listening. If all you do is listen deeply when people passionately disagree with you about a controversial issue, that can be an important victory. Listening allows you to connect with their humanity, better understand where they are coming from and why they think the way they do, and gain insights into how you can more effectively reach them.

Listening also has the potential to make a strong impression on the people you are listening to. We live in a society where people seldom listen to each other, and when I watch television I see countless pundits and politicians who are disrespectful to each other and unwilling to listen. When you possess the rare ability to listen deeply, someone might walk away from a conversation with you, thinking, "I don't see eye to eye with those peace activists, but they sure are kind and really good listeners. I can't remember the last time someone really listened to me. My boss doesn't listen to me. My coworkers don't listen to me. I often feel like my wife (or husband) isn't even listening to me."

By listening deeply we plant a seed of change. Perhaps the seed will sprout long after the conversation has ended, causing the person to think about what you said and allowing your ideas to sink in. This might help the person develop a more positive attitude toward peace activists and become more open to future discussions about peace. Or maybe the seed will lie dormant and never significantly impact the person's way of thinking. People must choose to let peace bloom within them. But the more seeds of change we plant in people from all walks of life, the larger the potential harvest.

2. Speak to Their Potential: The Second Element of Universal Respect

For many years I viewed respect as a delicious meal, but its ingredients remained a secret. Just as a person can taste a flavorful soup and not know all of its ingredients, I had tasted respect but could not pinpoint exactly what was in it. If you had to summarize in words what makes someone respectful and another person disrespectful, how would you describe it? Is it their tone of voice, choice of words, or body language? It can be very difficult to capture the subtle differences between respect and disrespect in a few words, but then I had a deeper realization.

As I thought about all the times throughout my life when people spoke to me respectfully, they always talked to me as if deep down I was a good person, even if I was behaving badly. Martin Luther King Jr. referred to those who wanted to kill him as "our sick white brothers," recognizing that the white racists who wanted him dead were ill with hatred, but still his brothers. When people are disrespectful they talk to us as if we lack goodness, dignity, or worth as human beings. Disrespect makes us feel worthless, while respect recognizes our enormous human potential.

Human beings have the potential to live with integrity, reason, compassion, and conscience. However, not everyone lives up to their human potential. When we talk to people in a respectful way we must "speak to their potential" by speaking to their integrity, reason, compassion, and conscience. We must strive to communicate with and stimulate those parts of their humanity. Being respectful does not mean naively pretending that every person lives with these virtues. Instead, being respectful is a way to remind people of what it means to be fully human.

When soldiers make small, careless mistakes in the army, an example of *not* speaking to their potential would be, "Why are you so stupid? You are such an idiot!" On the other hand, an example of speaking to their potential would be, "Why did you do that? You know better, and because I have seen how well you can perform, I expect a lot out of you. Now what are you going to do to ensure that this doesn't happen again?" A quote attributed to the German poet Wolfgang von Goethe says, "If we treat people as they ought to be, we help them become what they are capable of becoming."

Some people view respect as naive and impractical in the real world, but this could not be further from the truth. Martial arts philosophy teaches that respect is vital for self-defense, and Gandhi, King, and Mandela harnessed the power of respect to advance their causes in extremely difficult circumstances. Christo Brand started working at Robben Island, where Nelson Mandela was imprisoned, in 1978. Brand was an unquestioningly pro-apartheid eighteen-year-old white prison guard. Despite their differences in race, age, and political views, Mandela respected the young prison guard. Brand explained how this affected him: "When I came to the prison, Nelson Mandela was already 60. He was down-to-earth and courteous. He treated me with respect and my respect for him grew. After a while, even though he was a prisoner, a friendship grew."[2]

Brand started doing favors for Mandela, smuggling in bread and bringing him messages. He also broke the rules in order to let Mandela hold his infant grandson.[3] But as Brand explains, Mandela seemed more concerned about the well-being of the young prison guard than the favors he was receiving: "Mandela was worried that I would get caught and be punished. He wrote to my wife telling her that I must continue my studies. Even as a prisoner he was encouraging a warder to study."[4] If Mandela could have such an influential impact on his white pro-apartheid prison guard, think of the many ways respect can bridge the divides that separate us.

For those who still think respect is naive and impractical in the real world, we should remind them of an important fact. When people in a community respect each other as human beings, the bonds between them become stronger, empowering them to overcome significant challenges. At West Point every freshman has to memorize a passage from a speech Major General John M. Schofield gave there in 1879. The passage, which explains the practical value of respect, reads: "The discipline which makes the soldiers of a free country reliable in battle is not to be gained by harsh or tyrannical treatment. On the contrary, such treatment is far more likely to destroy than to make an army . . . He who feels the respect which is due to others cannot fail to inspire in them regard for himself, while he who feels, and hence manifests, disrespect toward others, especially his inferiors, cannot fail to inspire hatred against himself."[5]

3. Don't Be Hypocritical: The Third Element of Universal Respect

West Point taught me that one of the most powerful leadership principles is *leading by example.* What does it mean to lead by example? In his book *Legacy of Love,* Arun Gandhi, grandson of Mahatma Gandhi, tells a story about his grandfather that illustrates what it means to lead by example:

> I became friends with a boy named Anil, who was my age. Anil had a weakness for sweets that verged on obsession. He consumed more than was good for him. One day he became ill, and his parents took him to the doctor. The doctor's advice was that Anil must drastically reduce the amount of sweets that he consumed. Anil's parents tried to enforce the doctor's orders . . . Both parents would nag Anil about not eating sweets while they themselves continued to eat sweets every day. Several weeks went by and the parents found that Anil was continuing to eat sweets when no one was looking. They brought him to Grandfather [Mahatma Gandhi] with an appeal to drum some sense into him.
>
> "Anil will not listen to us," his mother told Grandfather. "The doctor has said he should not eat any sweets, but he still consumes them on the sly. He refuses to obey us. Please speak to him."
>
> Grandfather heard the complaint patiently, and just as patiently told Anil's mother, "Come back with Anil after fifteen days."

Anil's mother was perplexed. All she believed Grandfather had to do was tell the boy not to eat sweets. They were bad for him. Why did she have to wait for fifteen days? She could not fathom this, but she was not prepared to argue with Grandfather.

On the fifteenth day she returned. Grandfather took Anil aside and whispered into his ear. Anil's eyes sparkled. Grandfather asked him for a high five to seal their private deal, and they left.

Anil's mother had no idea what had transpired, but she was skeptical. A few days later both parents came back to Grandfather utterly amazed and asked him, "How could Anil obey you so readily, and not us? Tell us the secret."

Grandfather explained, "It was no miracle. I asked you to come back after fifteen days because I had to first give up eating sweets before I could ask him to do so. I simply told Anil that I had not eaten sweets for fifteen days, and that I would not eat any until the doctor allowed Anil to eat sweets."

It was a simple lesson in the power of correcting by example, but how many of us practice this? We are quick to use our authority or superior physical strength to force others to do what we want them to do, and as a result, even if we are obeyed, we have not effected the kind of change that makes our lessons permanent.[6]

Hypocrisy occurs when we do not practice what we preach. Recognizing how dangerous hypocrisy is to the health of any military unit, the army encourages its soldiers to "lead by example." The army's Drill Sergeant Creed states: "I will lead by example, never requiring a soldier to attempt any task I would not do myself." By not asking Anil to stop eating sweets unless he did so first, Gandhi led by example.

Not only do Gandhi and the army both condemn hypocrisy. So did Jesus, saying, "Why do you look at the speck of sawdust in your brother's eye and pay no attention to the plank in your own eye? How can you say to your brother, 'Let me take the speck out of your eye,' when all the time there is a plank in your own eye? You hypocrite, first take the plank out of your own eye, and then you will see clearly to remove the speck from your brother's eye."[7]

If a person you admire who has enormous integrity gives you advice on being honest, it can be accepted with a feeling of mutual respect. But if a dishonest person lectures you on honesty it comes across as disrespectful and can make your temper boil. Few things make us angrier than hypocrisy. That is why being respectful not only involves listening and speaking to someone's potential, but also looking at our own behavior to ensure we are not being hypocritical. We can listen and speak to someone's potential all day long, but our words will sound disrespectful if we don't first practice what we preach.

The army taught me that respect is my shield. No matter how disrespectful someone is to me, responding in a respectful way serves as a shield by allowing me to maintain my moral authority. As soon as I become disrespectful I lose my moral authority, which is my true power base as a leader. To support this idea, the army taught me that the best leaders seldom have to rely on rank, because the moral authority they gain through giving respect and leading by example is so strong that many soldiers will follow them out of admiration. Gandhi showed how influential moral authority can be. He led 390 million people on the path to freedom, yet he was not a general or a president and had no official power. Martin Luther King Jr. said this was one of the most significant things that ever happened in world history.

I call respect the *infinite shield*, because it not only protects us but everyone around us. It prevents dangerous situations from escalating and serves as a first line of defense against violence. Another reason I use the word "infinite" to describe the shield of respect is because we cannot truly measure where it ends. It can extend beyond our local community. It can even extend far into the future. A husband and wife who treat each other with respect will make a positive impression on their children, passing the shield of respect on to future generations. Like the ripples that emanate from a pebble dropped in a pond, the respect we give to others ripples out into the world and through the ocean of time.

The infinite shield is only the first line of defense. It is not impenetrable and can be breached, as it was when King was assassinated. Accordingly, we must have a second, third, and even fourth line of defense as backups when people break through the infinite shield. Before I describe the other lines of defense later in this book, let us not underestimate the power of the infinite shield as a first line of defense. When we bring the infinite shield into any room we create a safer environment for everyone in that room. The more people around the world who embrace the infinite shield, the safer our world will be.

Although King was assassinated, I and countless others have better lives today because he respected the white people who opposed him. By embracing the infinite shield, he helped prevent a race war that nearly erupted as tensions mounted during the civil rights era. While imprisoned in a Birmingham, Alabama, jail for conducting a peaceful protest in 1963, he wrote: "If this [peaceful] philosophy had not emerged, by now many streets of the South would, I am convinced, be flowing with blood . . . If [African Americans'] repressed emotions are not released in nonviolent ways, they will seek expression through violence; this is not a threat but a fact of history. So I have not said to my people: 'Get rid of your discontent.' Rather, I have tried to say that this normal and healthy discontent can be channeled into the creative outlet of nonviolent direct action."[8]

Respect is an infinite shield that can help us protect ourselves and those around us. As I will discuss later in this book, the infinite shield can also help us protect our country and planet in the twenty-first century. When we learn how to wield the infinite shield with the skill of a peace warrior, however, it offers more benefits than just protection. The ability to convey respect improves our relationships with other people, and it unlocks many of our human powers such as empathy, love, and calm.

CHAPTER 4

The Power of Calm

Wielding the Infinite Shield

You cannot go wrong if you assume nothing and treat everyone with respect and compassion.

—Lieutenant Colonel Dave Grossman[1]

Martial arts taught me that we must first learn defense before we can truly learn offense. This timeless principle also applies to waging peace. Waging peace attacks the hatred, greed, deception, apathy, ignorance, and misunderstandings that permeate our society and hold people's minds hostage. But before we can attack someone's hatred, we must first learn to defend against it by knowing how to deescalate hostile situations.

Trying to attack hatred by being hateful in return is like trying to put out a fire by throwing gasoline on it. If I have a conflict with someone and kill that person out of hatred, the problem doesn't necessarily go away. It could even escalate and become worse, because the person's friends and family may decide to take revenge. This can be seen in countless examples of gang violence, feuds between families, and wars throughout history.

In this book I will describe four lines of defense that can stop violence in its tracks. The first line of defense is the infinite shield, while the second line of defense is *the sword that heals,* a term coined by Martin Luther King Jr. He said, "Nonviolence is a powerful and just weapon. It is a weapon unique in history, which cuts without wounding and ennobles the man who wields it. It is a sword that heals."[2]

What is the difference between the infinite shield and the sword that heals? The infinite shield consists of the respect expressed through our composure, attitude, and behavior. It speaks loudly not only with words, but also through actions, leading by example, and the respectful way we treat others. Sometimes the respect we give to others is all it takes to prevent and deescalate conflict on both a personal and societal level, but sometimes it is not enough. As I mentioned in the previous chapter, the infinite shield is certainly powerful, yet it is not impenetrable and can be breached. When the respect we give to others is not enough to ensure peace and justice, the sword that heals uses strong ideas and persuasive dialogue to transform how people think, along with nonviolent tactics such as protests, boycotts, and other methods to apply political and social pressure. (In the second part of this book, I more thoroughly explore the sword that heals.)

When a conflict escalates to a point where you have to use your sword, the last thing you should do is drop your shield. When King used the sword that heals to nonviolently struggle for a more just and peaceful society, he did not abandon the respect he gave to others. He said:

> The nonviolent resister does not seek to humiliate or defeat the opponent but to win his friendship and understanding. This was always a cry that we had to set before people that our aim is not to defeat the white community, not to humiliate the white community, but to win the friendship of all of the persons who had perpetrated this system in the past. The end of violence or the aftermath of violence is bitterness. The aftermath of nonviolence is reconciliation and the creation of a beloved community . . . Then we had to make it clear also that *the nonviolent resister seeks to attack the evil system* [emphasis added] rather than individuals who happen to be caught up in the system. And this is why I say from time to time that the struggle in the South is not so much the tension between white people and Negro people. The struggle is rather between justice and injustice, between the forces of light and the forces of darkness. And if there is a victory it will not be a victory

merely for fifty thousand Negroes. But it will be a victory for justice, a victory for good will, a victory for democracy.[3]

Because waging peace is such a deep and complex art form, a person could write a very long book about the subject and still only scratch the surface. Therefore a central question I had to ask myself when writing this book was, since there is so much to say about waging peace, how can I best offer a thorough explanation of waging peace, describe the obstacles that prevent us from achieving peace, and refute the myths of war in a relatively short book? To keep this book accessible I decided to write with the following principle in mind: *focus on the basic building blocks.* The purpose of this book is not to explain every tiny detail about waging peace, which would require thousands of pages, but to instead explain the basic building blocks of waging peace. By doing this I hope to offer you a *foundational understanding* that you can build on through your own personal study.

So far we have explored the basic building blocks of the infinite shield, but we could easily explore the infinite shield for several hundred more pages because there are so many ways to use it. Just as ancient Greek shields were made primarily of bronze, I have explained how the infinite shield is comprised primarily of respect. But I have not yet described the many ways we can use the infinite shield and the countless situations where it can be effective. Just as the ancient Greeks had to develop their skill at using a bronze shield and learn how to wield it in combat, we must learn how to wield the infinite shield and use it for maximum effectiveness.

One way to wield the infinite shield is in the realm of leadership. An entire book could be written just on how the respect we give to others significantly improves our overall leadership ability, and how different ways of conveying respect can be used to solve numerous leadership challenges. Lieutenant Colonel Dave Grossman offers some insights into how being respectful and professional makes us much better leaders and mentors:

> A warrior trainer is a sensei—a professional—who has confidentiality standards like a priest or a doctor. Say a doctor conducts a physical examination where he checks a police officer from top to bottom. Do you think at night

over a beer he tells other doctors about the officer and laughs about the poor man's droopy butt? No, because he is a professional . . .

Friends tease each other. SWAT teams tease each other; it comes with the territory. If you are a leader, however, you are not permitted to play the teasing game. You never joke about your trainees' failures, but you do brag about their achievements. Your entire repertoire is to talk about what went right . . . When word gets out that this is the type of trainer you are, people will no longer avoid training but will want to be there because of the environment you have created.

The fundamental rule of warrior leadership is to punish in private and praise in public. Report all failures and problems up the chain of command, but report successes to everyone. Maybe you were publicly punished and embarrassed at one time and now you despise the person who did it to you. Perhaps there was a time when a leader called you into his office and told you in private that you did a great job yesterday. While you appreciated the nice comments, you wish he had said them in front of everyone. (It's only fair, if you had messed up everyone would know!) . . . Do not talk trash about your students. Punish in private, praise in public. This is the way that a warrior-trainer, a sensei, creates a training environment in which the warrior spirit is nurtured and his warriors want to train."[4]

When a Greek soldier wielded his bronze shield with the right techniques he could block spears and arrows on the battlefield. When we wield the infinite shield with the right techniques we can block avoidable misunderstandings and unnecessary hostility not only in the workplace, but in our friendships and relationships. One technique I would like to discuss is the way we can wield the infinite shield to calm people down. One of the most important life skills we can have is the ability to calm people down, because if people are not calm they cannot think clearly. Grossman explains:

Have you ever tried to have an argument or a discussion with a truly frightened or angry person? It cannot be done, because the more frightened and angry the person is, the less rational he is. This is because his forebrain has shut down and his midbrain, the one like a dog's, is in control. In fact, you might as well try to argue with your dog; he might be intrigued by the experience but it will not accomplish much. Nor will you accomplish much when trying to talk to a human being in this heightened condition. To connect with him, you must first calm him down.[5]

How to Calm People Down

There are three steps for calming people down. The first is to *be calm*. Martin Luther King Jr. explains: "That Monday I went home with a heavy heart. I was weighted down by a terrible sense of guilt, remembering that on two or three occasions I had allowed myself to become angry and indignant. I had spoken hastily and resentfully. Yet I knew that this was no way to solve a problem. 'You must not harbor anger,' I admonished myself. 'You must be willing to suffer the anger of the opponent, and yet not return anger. You must not become bitter. No matter how emotional your opponents are, you must be calm.'"[6]

King's technique of being calm works a lot better than telling someone to calm down. Has anyone ever told you to calm down when you were really upset? It probably made you even more upset, because when people tell us to calm down it often comes across as condescending. Being calm influences others not with words but through our composure, attitude, and behavior. Psychiatrist Bruce Perry tells us, "Because of the mirroring neurobiology of our brains, one of the best ways to help someone else become calm and centered is to calm and center ourselves first—and then just pay attention."[7]

If you discuss peace or any controversial issue with people who passionately disagree with you, they might start yelling at you. How can we be calm when people are angry and disrespectful toward us? First, when we increase our respect for the humanity of others we can also increase our empathy for them. Empathizing with people allows us to connect with them on a deeper human level and see the fear, pain, or misunderstanding that is causing their anger. If you want to learn more about empathy, my book *Peaceful Revolution* has an entire chapter on empathy, its higher expression of unconditional love, and its highest expression of solidarity.

Psychologist Erich Fromm explains how empathy and love allow us to see the humanity beneath people's anger:

> There are many layers of knowledge; the knowledge which is an aspect of love is one which does not stay at the periphery, but penetrates to the core. It is possible only when I can transcend the concern for myself and see the other person in his own terms. I may know, for instance, that a person is angry, even if he does not show it overtly; but I may know him more deeply than that; then I know that he is anxious, and worried; that he feels lonely, that he feels guilty. Then I know that his anger is only the manifestation of something deeper, and I see him as anxious and embarrassed, that is, as the suffering person, rather than as the angry one.[8]

Remaining calm when others yell at us does not mean we allow them to walk all over us and treat us like dirt, because when we have self-respect we are willing to stand up for ourselves. Gandhi and King had a great deal of self-respect and certainly stood up for themselves against those who tried to oppress and exploit them. But they realized being calm allows us to stand up for ourselves more effectively, because when we become hostile and disrespectful in return we lose our moral authority along with our reason and compassion.

Frederick Douglass saw many women's rights activists strengthen their moral authority by conducting themselves with calm dignity. He witnessed how a calm yet firm demeanor is very effective when confronting injustice, because when we come across as hysterical and irrational it is too easy for the opponents of justice to call us crazy and not take us seriously. When we are calm, composed, and rational we are not as easily dismissed. Speaking about the extraordinary ability of Antoinette Louise Brown, he said, "The calmness, serenity, earnestness, ability and dignity with which Miss Brown advocates this right, compels the serious and respectful attention of all whom she addresses on the subject."[9]

When discussing the controversial issue of peace activism in particular, another way to remain calm when someone becomes angry and disrespectful toward you is by imagining you are talking to me. This will help remind you that human beings have the potential to change. When I was eighteen years old I was a firm believer in the war system. If you had talked to me about peace activism back then I might have also become angry and disrespectful toward you. During the years that followed I saw through the myths of war, deepening my commitment to waging peace. This does not mean everyone hostile to peace activists will have a transformation in their way of thinking. But it does mean we should never dismiss someone as hopelessly ignorant or beyond the potential to change.

The second step for calming people down is to listen and be respectful. As I explained earlier, in all of human history I don't think anyone has ever seriously said, "I hate it when people listen to me! I hate it when people respect me!" So much human hostility arises from people simply not feeling listened to or respected. When we genuinely listen to and respect others, it can have a profound calming effect.

The third step for calming people down is to show care and concern. This is an important yet often neglected aspect of calming people down, because if you are upset with me because I borrowed and wrecked your car, and I respond to your anger by simply being calm, you might mistake my calmness for indifference. When people are calm yet do not show care and concern, they can come across as cold and uncaring.

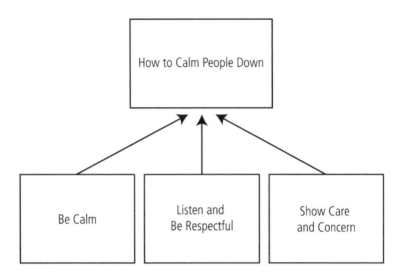

Figure 4.1 How to Calm People Down

To better explain this, when I first moved to Santa Barbara I had a prob-lem with my apartment that made me pretty angry. When I spoke with the apartment manager about it, she became outraged on my behalf and seemed more upset than I was. She said, "What happened to you is completely unac-ceptable, and I will fix this!" This immediately calmed me down. I had walked into her office with my temper boiling, and hearing how upset she was over my problem actually made me want to console her, causing me to say, "Well, maybe it's not so bad. These things happen sometimes and I understand."

Moral outrage on behalf of someone else's dilemma is a powerful expres-sion of care and concern. In *Peaceful Revolution* and *The End of War* I refer to moral outrage as *moral fury*. When people tell us about a truly unjust problem they are having, the moral fury within us can erupt like a burning flame. A flame is calm, but also intense. It is soothing, but also fierce. The flame of moral fury can be calm and soothing to those treated unjustly, while intensely and fiercely opposing the forces of injustice.

Another important way to show care and concern is to *say it with sin-cerity*. People are not mind readers. If we accidentally insult someone and did not mean to, we should say it with sincerity: "I didn't mean to offend you. I apologize if you felt disrespected in any way." As I said earlier, martial arts taught me that no technique works every single time, but by being calm, listening and being respectful, and showing care and concern, we will have the best chance of calming people down.

The power of calm is an invaluable tool that can improve our personal lives, communities, and capacity to wage peace. Gandhi, King, martial arts philosophy, West Point, and the U.S. Army all agree that the ability to remain calm is one of the most crucial life skills a human being can have, because it allows our brain to function at its optimal level. Military and martial arts training taught me that the more turbulent a situation becomes, the more important it is to be calm. Grossman explains, "As a warrior, your concern is always to help others, and to do that you must be the rock of calm. When the whole world is coming unglued and all about you are losing their heads and blaming it on you, your job is to be that rock that others can anchor themselves to . . . Panic can be contagious, and so is calm. As a warrior, you must be an example of calm."[10]

CHAPTER 5

The Three Forms of Deflection

Social Norms

To create societal change we don't have to convince every single person that a cause is justified, fair, and reasonable. We only have to convince *enough* people. For example, was every single man in America convinced women should have the right to vote? No, and there are still men in America who don't think women should have the right to vote. Was every single white person in America convinced slavery and segregation should go away? No, and there are still white people in America who want slavery and segregation to come back.

When any form of positive change is concerned, it is impossible to convince everyone it should happen. As I explain in *Peaceful Revolution*, many people have not developed their empathy, conscience, reason, and the other muscles of our humanity that encourage us to work for positive change. And as I explain in *The End of War*, the human brain is the most complex thing we know of in the universe, and our extremely complex brains make us vulnerable to a wide variety of mental disorders that can inhibit our empathy, conscience, and reason.

During my lectures around the country I often talk to diverse groups. When I speak with a group of fifty people and mention how the women's rights movement greatly inspires me, I realize there might be one or two people in the audience who wish women never gained the right to vote. Two out of fifty is only 4 percent of the audience. That might seem like a tiny percentage, but what if 4 percent of the American population believed women should not have the right to vote? How many would that be? As I write this the American population is around 300 million, and 4 percent of that is a whopping 12 million. In fact, if just one out of every thousand Americans believed women should not have the right to vote, that would still be 300,000.

Many people today who oppose women's and civil rights would never say it in public, because women's and civil rights have now become *social norms*. What is a social norm, and how does it work? A social norm occurs when a new idea has persuaded enough people to create a new public consensus. To better understand this, imagine a white man who works in a typical office in America—one that has women and people of various racial backgrounds. Now imagine him standing up and yelling, "No woman should be allowed to vote! All niggers should be slaves!" He would not only alienate the women and African Americans in his office, but also most of his white male coworkers because our society has begun to view racists and sexists as ignorant, closed-minded, and hateful. In addition to alienating his coworkers, he would probably get fired and might even get beaten up.

Now imagine if two hundred years ago in America someone shouted in public, "No woman should be allowed to vote! All niggers should be slaves!" This statement would have received little opposition and a lot of applause, because the modern social norms of women's and civil rights did not exist back then. To understand how influential social norms are, do you know what President George W. Bush considers the worst moment of his presidency? Was it when our country was attacked on September 11? Was it when the torture committed by American soldiers at Abu Ghraib prison in Iraq was exposed? Was it when Hurricane Katrina devastated New Orleans and other cities? No. President Bush said the worst moment of his presidency was when rapper Kanye West called him a racist. President Bush explains:

> At an NBC telethon to raise money for Katrina victims, rapper Kanye West told a primetime TV audience, "George Bush doesn't care about black people . . . " Five years later, I can barely write those words without feeling disgusted . . . The more I thought about it, the angrier I felt. I was raised to believe that racism was one of the

greatest evils in society. I admired Dad's courage when he defied near-universal opposition from his constituents to vote for the Open Housing Bill of 1968. I was proud to have earned more black votes than any Republican governor in Texas history. I had appointed African Americans to top government positions, including the first black woman national security advisor and the first two black secretaries of state . . . The suggestion that I was a racist because of the response to Katrina represented an all-time low. I told Laura at the time that it was the worst moment of my presidency. I feel the same way today.[1]

I am including this story from President Bush for one reason only: to illustrate how the worst thing we can call somebody today is a racist. Several hundred years ago the idea of being a racist didn't really exist. Imagine if time travel were possible and you went back to the eighteenth century. If you called a white person back then a racist, he would likely ask, "What does that mean?" If you said, "It means you think all white people are superior to black people just because they're white," he would probably reply, "Of course we're superior to black people! We're white!" Today the public consensus toward racism has changed, and it is simply not cool to openly be a racist anymore.

Because calling someone a racist is such a serious insult in modern America, many people today do not realize that the concept of racism appeared relatively recently in history. In their book *Racism*, Robert Miles and Malcolm Brown say, "Although the word 'racism' is now widely used in common-sense, political and academic discourse, readers may be surprised to learn that it is of very recent origin. There is no reference to the word in the *Oxford English Dictionary* of 1910 (although there are entries for 'race' and 'racial') . . . The *OED Supplement* of 1982 . . . records its first appearance in the English language in the 1930s."[2]

I am certainly not saying racism and sexism in America have vanished. Instead, I am saying these societal ills are different than they used to be. The new social norms of women's and civil rights have reduced the power of overt racism and sexism in America, but as a consequence the forms of racism and sexism that continue to persist have become more covert. Two hundred years ago racism was most dangerous in the daylight, like a massive army that intimidates by showing off its numerous soldiers with their sharpened spears shining beneath the sun. Racism back then gained immense public support and legal protection for the enslavement and brutal treatment of an entire race, and through sheer intimidation in the public sphere the slavery system could not only make slaves afraid to run away, but also frighten conscientious white people who wanted to oppose slavery.

Today racism is most dangerous under the cover of night, like an assassin hiding in the darkness. Racism today is not powerful because of its ability to intimidate people in the public sphere but because of its stealth. Racism today is most dangerous when we do not realize it is there, or when we make the kind of hyperbolic statements that cause people to not take us seriously, such as saying African Americans are no better off today than they were two hundred years ago.

There are still some overt forms of racism in America today, such as the prejudice against people of Middle Eastern descent. And although I use African Americans as an example of racism in America's past, many groups in America have also been subjected to racism, such as Native Americans, Asians, Hispanics, Jews, Italians, and even groups of white people such as the Irish. Many people today incorrectly assume that only those with darker skin tones have suffered from racism, but Eugene McLaughlin explains how the Irish were also treated as racially inferior subhumans:

> In both Britain and North America the Irish endured anti-Catholic hostility and were accused of taking jobs, undercutting wages, creating slums, and being political troublemakers. Anti-Irish cartoons in magazines such as *Punch*, supported by respectable writers such as Charles Kingsley, Thomas Carlyle and Elizabeth Gaskell, depicted them as being a less evolutionarily developed race. Kingsley stated that, "to see white chimpanzees is dreadful; if they were black, one would not feel it so much, but their skins, except where tanned by exposure, are as white as ours." [After visiting the United States in 1881, Oxford

professor] Edward A. Freeman commented that "This would be a grand country if only every Irishman would kill a Negro and be hanged for it." It is in this context of Irishophobia that the racist caricature of the unpredictable, drunken, violent, ignorant "Paddy" was established. Their supposed wildness meant that writers questioned whether the Irish could ever be assimilated into civilized society. Anti-Irish riots occurred in many towns in Britain and the USA during the nineteenth century.[3]

As the first two lines of defense against injustice and violence, the infinite shield and the sword that heals attack hatred and ignorance at their root by transforming how people think for the better. This has reduced racism and sexism in America, and waging peace gives us the means to continue winning battles against these and other forms of injustice. In order to win these battles, waging peace empowers us to create societal, spiritual, and ideological change on a personal, national, and global level.

Although the infinite shield and the sword that heals are very effective at transforming how people think, *deflection* is a third line of defense that is useful whenever hatred is able to breach the shield and dodge the sword. Why do I use the word "deflection?" Unlike the infinite shield and the sword that heals, deflection does not directly confront the underlying causes of people's hatred. Instead, deflection misdirects their hatred by giving them other concerns to think about, such as the serious consequences that might result if they decide to turn their hostile thoughts into hostile actions. This can deflect unjust and violent acts, just as martial artists use evasive techniques to deflect attacks.

Laws

Social norms are the first form of deflection, but sometimes not even the most entrenched social norms can dissuade a hostile person with violent intentions from committing an unjust act. This is why we need laws, which are the second form of deflection. Martin Luther King Jr. used the infinite shield and the sword that heals to dramatically transform how people think for the better, yet he never underestimated the need for laws. He also realized that every large society must have a way of enforcing its laws, which he called "the intelligent use of police force."

When the Supreme Court Case *Brown v. Board of Education* ruled that segregated schools were unconstitutional, the attempt to integrate black and white students at Central High School in Little Rock, Arkansas, was met with heavy resistance. In addition to a mob that tried to prevent nine black students, who became known as the "Little Rock Nine," from entering the school, Arkansas governor Orval Faubus decided to use armed National Guard soldiers to keep the black students out. Journalist David Margolick describes what happened:

> In the fall of 1957, [fifteen-year-old Elizabeth Eckford] was among the nine black students who had enlisted, then been selected, to enter Little Rock Central High School. Central was the first high school in a major southern city set to be desegregated since the United States Supreme Court had ruled three years earlier in Brown vs Board of Education that separate and ostensibly equal education was unconstitutional . . . Lots of white people lined Park Street as Elizabeth headed towards the school. As she passed the Mobil station and came nearer, she could see the white students filtering unimpeded past the soldiers. To her, it was a sign that everything was all right. But as she herself approached, three Guardsmen, two with rifles, held out their arms, directing her to her left, to the far side of Park. A crowd had started to form behind Elizabeth, and her knees began to shake . . .
>
> She steadied herself, then walked up to another soldier. He didn't move. When she tried to squeeze past him, he raised his carbine. Other soldiers moved over to assist him. When she tried to get in around them, they moved to block her way. They glared at her. Now, as Elizabeth continued walking south down Park, more and more of

the people lining the street fell in behind her. Some were
Central students, others adults. They started shouting at
her. The primitive television cameras, for all their bulki-
ness, had no sound equipment. But the reporters on the
scene scribbled down what they heard: "Lynch her! Lynch
her!" "No nigger bitch is going to get in our school!" "Go
home, nigger!" Looking for a friendly face, Elizabeth
turned to an old white woman. The woman spat on her.[4]

As the mob threatened to lynch the black students, the NAACP kept
them home for several weeks due to safety concerns. A court ordered Governor Faubus to withdraw his National Guard soldiers who were preventing
the integration of the school. He complied. The Little Rock Nine returned
to school on September 23, but outside the building local police tried to
control at least a thousand angry white segregationists. When the mob
threatened to storm the school, the police took the children out a back door.
The mob beat up several black journalists, including a World War II combat
veteran.[5]

In response, President Eisenhower sent federal soldiers from the 101st
Airborne Division to Little Rock. The armed soldiers arrived by dawn the
next day, escorting the nine black students through the front door and into
their classrooms. The federal soldiers remained at the school throughout the
year, but were unable to protect the students from all acts of violence. Elizabeth Eckford was pushed down a flight of stairs, and the three black male
students had to deal with physical assaults.[6] During a television interview
later that year, Martin Luther King Jr. was asked how he could advocate
nonviolence, yet support the use of armed federal soldiers to integrate a
school. He replied:

I think it is quite regrettable and unfortunate that
young high school students have to go to school under the
protection of federal troops, but I think it is even more
unfortunate that a public official, through irresponsible
actions, leaves the President of the United States with no
other alternative. So I did back [President Eisenhower] and

I sent him a telegram commending him. Now your main question is . . . how does this jibe with my whole philosophy of nonviolence? I believe firmly in nonviolence as I have already said, but at the same time I am not an anarchist. Now some pacifists are anarchists following Tolstoy, but I don't go that far. I believe in the intelligent use of police force. I think one who believes in nonviolence must recognize the dimensions of evil within human nature, and there is a danger that one can indulge in a sort of superficial optimism thinking man is all good. Man does not only have the greater capacity for goodness, but there is also the potential for evil. And I think of that throughout my whole philosophy and I try to be realistic at that point. So I believe in the intelligent use of police force, and I think that is all we have in Little Rock. It's not an army fighting against a nation or a race of people. It is just police force, seeking to enforce the law of the land.[7]

When King said he supported "the intelligent use of police force," he realized law enforcement officers can use many techniques other than killing to keep us safe. To mention a few examples, law enforcement officers stopped terrorists such as Ted Kaczynski (the "Unabomber") and Timothy McVeigh, along with numerous serial killers, without killing a single person. The police have the ability to conduct investigations and arrest people, who are then supposed to receive a public trial by a jury of their peers.

However, King was not naive about abuses committed by the police, and as a black man living under segregation in the South he saw firsthand how law enforcement officers can be used for evil. He often felt threatened by police officers in the South. As I mentioned earlier, before the Civil War federal marshals had been legally required to return escaped slaves to their slave masters. But King realized the behavior of law enforcement officers reflected the society they were protecting, and he wanted to shape social norms and laws in a way that would allow the police to do more good than harm. Waging peace gives us the power to defeat the social norms and laws that are unjust, and create ones that are just.

Social norms and laws deflect violent and unjust behavior by making people consider the consequences. This can deter them from turning their hostile intentions into hostile actions, because the consequences could include public ridicule, harm to one's career and reputation, physical injury, being arrested, and going to jail. Unlike deflection, however, the infinite shield and the sword that heals *do not deter* people from turning their hostile intentions into hostile actions. Instead, these forms of waging peace *strive to transform* their hostile intentions into understanding and compassion. King believed that many white people in the South were good while many more had the potential for goodness. To unlock their vast potential for goodness, King thought Jesus was wise when he commanded us to "love our enemies." King said, "Love is the only force capable of transforming an enemy into a friend."[8]

Although I experienced some racism in Alabama, I am proud to be from Alabama for many reasons. To help me survive in the dangerous world he knew, my father taught me to think like him and previous generations of African Americans who lived in terror, yet a lot has changed since he grew up during segregation and the days when his father was raised by former slaves. Whenever I return to visit the South, I can see how far it has come since my father grew up during segregation, and I am proud of the progress it has made. King showed that hostile intentions could in fact be transformed into understanding and compassion, because today in Alabama there are many more people who treat African Americans as human beings rather than subhumans.

Nevertheless, there are still some people in Alabama and other states who want to kill human beings because of the color of their skin, so I am glad we have laws. Waging peace does not seek to demonize these or any other people, but to understand them. Later in this book I will explore the depths of human nature to explain why new ideas are often met with so much hostility.

Outsmarting Violence

Sometimes people are so determined to murder someone that even social norms and laws cannot deter them. When people are willing to break the law to commit violence, a third form of deflection is available. Before I can discuss what it is, however, I must first discuss the differences between waging war and waging peace.

Waging war and waging peace have a lot in common. They both require courage, commitment, determination, teamwork, discipline, camaraderie, strategic thinking, selflessness, sacrifice, and many more similarities. But there are two major differences between waging war and waging peace. The first is the use of violence. Waging war tries to turn the human beings who oppose you into corpses, while waging peace tries to turn the human beings who oppose you into friends. That's a big difference, but there's an even bigger difference.

Sun Tzu said it best: "All warfare is based on deception. Hence, when able to attack, we must seem unable; when using our forces, we must seem inactive; when we are near, we must make the enemy believe we are far away; when far away, we must make him believe we are near."[9] When I studied boxing I learned it is based on deception. If you want to punch your opponent with your left hand, you should trick him into thinking you're going to punch him with your right hand. The better a boxer is at deceiving his foe, the more easily he can defeat him. Like boxers, the best chess players are also very skilled at using deception to bluff, confuse, bait, and ambush their opponents.

It is unfortunate our society sees the fundamental nature of war as violence, when its fundamental nature is really deception. Sun Tzu taught that the art of war is in many ways the art of deception, and many religions and mythologies acknowledge that deception is a deeper evil than violence. For example, Satan in Christianity, Loki in Nordic mythology, and Mara in Buddhism are not evil because they are masters of brute force and violence, but because they are masters of cunning and deception.

The god of war in Greek mythology is Ares. Just as all war is based on deception, Ares is a liar who is despised by his father Zeus. In the *Iliad*, Zeus tells Ares he hates him more than any of his other children, and if they were not father and son he would banish the god of war to the bottom of the dark pit where the cursed Titans are imprisoned. Zeus says, "No more, you lying, two-faced . . . I hate you most of all the Olympian gods . . . You have your mother's uncontrollable rage . . . You are *my* child [but] to me your mother bore you. If you had sprung from another god, believe me . . . long ago you'd have dropped below the Titans, deep in the dark pit."[10]

Waging peace on the other hand is based on the truth, and the art of waging peace is in many ways the art of truth-telling. Some people who believe in moral relativism have told me there is no such thing as truth, but I have evidence that proves otherwise. To offer a couple of examples, it is true that women are not intellectually inferior to men, and it is also true that African Americans are not subhuman. These statements express as much scientific truth as Copernicus and Galileo when they claimed the earth revolves around the sun. The underlying purpose of the women's rights movement was to expose the truth about women's equality, and the underlying purpose of the civil rights movement was to expose the truth that African Americans are human beings.

Our most cherished ideals—such as liberty, justice, and fairness—cannot exist without the ideal of truth. Unless our society is built on a foundation of truth-telling, we will never truly have liberty, justice, and fairness. Peace is another ideal that requires the ideal of truth. The war system, on the other hand, requires deception. When a military commander masters the art of deception, he can easily gain the element of surprise in war. This gives any military commander a significant advantage over his opponent, but Gandhi realized waging peace requires us to replace the element of surprise with the element of honesty.

Every effective army in history kept secrets to maintain the element of surprise, and today militaries around the world have extensive top-secret files. But Gandhi did not have any top-secret files, because he knew that peace requires trust, mutual understanding, and transparency. In fact, when he conducted his Salt March to the Sea, a nonviolent protest against the oppressive British salt tax, he sent a letter to the British viceroy, Lord Irwin, telling him exactly what he planned to do. In the letter Gandhi explained why the salt tax was unjust. He then outlined his plan to oppose the tax and invited the viceroy to arrest him. Gandhi said in his letter:

If you cannot see your way to deal with these evils and my letter makes no appeal to your heart, on the 11th day of this month, I shall proceed with such coworkers of the Ashram as I can take, to disregard the provisions of the salt laws. I regard this [salt] tax to be the most iniquitous of all from the poor man's standpoint. As the [Indian] independence movement is essentially for the poorest in the land the beginning will be made with this evil. The wonder is that we have submitted to the cruel monopoly for so long. It is, I know, open to you to frustrate my design by arresting me. I hope that there will be tens of thousands ready, in a disciplined manner, to take up the work after me . . . This letter is not in any way intended as a threat but it is a simple and sacred duty peremptory on a civil resister.

He ended the letter by saying, "I remain, your sincere friend, M. K. Gandhi."[11] Later in this book I will explain why Gandhi's approach was so revolutionary from a strategic perspective. Many people today would call Gandhi stupid for telling the viceroy his plan, but later I will explain why Gandhi was more innovative than any general I have ever studied.

If the ideal of truth that Gandhi was loyal to creates the foundation not only for ideals such as liberty, justice, and fairness, but also waging peace itself, is it ever all right to lie in pursuit of peace? To understand why this question is so challenging, take a moment to consider the following moral dilemma. Imagine you were living in Germany during World War II and hiding Jews in your attic. Several Nazi soldiers come to your house, knock on your door, and rigorously question you about the whereabouts of any Jews hiding in the area. Is it all right to lie to them?

This is not a far-fetched hypothetical scenario, because situations similar to this occurred many times during the brutal reign of the Nazis in Germany. According to historian Johannes Tuchel, the head of the German Resistance Memorial Center in Berlin, an estimated 20,000 to 30,000 Berliners actively hid Jews from Nazis. Tuchel says, "The number of Berlin rescuers might sound impressive at first, but compared to the 4 million who lived in Berlin at the time and didn't help, 20,000 are not a lot at all."[12]

Situations such as this also occurred when the Hutus massacred the Tutsis in Rwanda and conscientious people tried to hide the survivors. This happens wherever there is genocide, and it might be happening somewhere in the world as I write this.

This is not an easy question for some peace activists, because it causes them to question their most cherished ideals, such as the ideal of truth. I know peace activists who are unwilling to lie, even when confronted with the scenario I just presented. One peace activist told me, "Instead of telling them where the Jews were hiding or lying about it, I would try to distract the Nazis by pointing somewhere off in the distance and saying, 'Look over there!'" I replied, "I don't think most Nazis were that stupid, and realistically speaking it would probably only make them more suspicious of you."

The question of when to lie to deflect violence troubled me for a long time, but then a peace activist and peace studies professor named Barbara Wien told me a story that gave me new insights into the question. Shortly after the September 11 attacks, Barbara, who was seven months pregnant at the time, went into a subway station and saw several neo-Nazis bullying an Arab American. They were taunting him with racial slurs, pushing him, and becoming very aggressive. Although the station was mostly empty, Barbara immediately went around and pleaded with the few people waiting for the next subway train. She said, "We have to help him! We have to stop this!"

Nobody wanted to get involved and risk getting hurt, so they turned away or hid their faces behind their newspapers. Unable to recruit any allies and concerned she would not be able to convince the neo-Nazis to back down without the help of others, Barbara needed another plan. She thought about calling 911 because some aggressive people will back down when they realize the police are on the way, but she could not get cell phone reception in the subway tunnel. Just when it seemed like no options were left she suddenly had a radical idea, but in order for it to work she would have to time it just right.

When the next subway train pulled in and the doors opened, she ran up to the Arab American and said, "Mohammed! It's so great to see you! It's been so long!" The Arab American and neo-Nazis all had confused looks on their faces. Not giving them time to react, she quickly grabbed the Arab American's arm and pulled him onto the subway train. As the doors closed, the neo-Nazis suddenly had realized what happened. Enraged, they started pounding on the door and shouting as the subway train began to speed away.

Did you notice what Barbara did? When she called the Arab American "Mohammed" and acted like she knew him, she used deception. She had never met him before and had no clue who he was. Her creative and brilliant plan was an example of the third form of deflection: *outsmarting violence.*

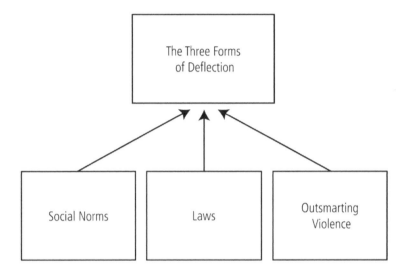

Figure 5.1 The Three Forms of Deflection

Gavin de Becker, widely regarded as the nation's leading expert on violence prediction and prevention, says that of all human behavior violence is the easiest to predict, because it gives off the most warning signs. His book *The Gift of Fear* explains how we can recognize the warning signs of violence. He also explains how we can predict and prevent violence, because as human beings we have the ability to outsmart it. There are many ways to outsmart violence, and using deception is one way. If you would like to learn more about how we can outsmart violence, I highly recommend *The Gift of Fear.*

Barbara was in a situation where the neo-Nazis were so hateful and enraged that the infinite shield and the sword that heals seemed unlikely to work, unless she could recruit allies willing to stand with her. When people refused to join her, she moved onto the third line of defense: deflection. But it is difficult to enforce social norms (the first form of deflection) without the support of others, and laws (the second form of deflection) also seemed unlikely to work because she could not contact the police and the neo-Nazis were so blinded by rage that the consequences of breaking the law did not seem to matter to them. Barbara's next option was outsmarting violence (the third form of deflection), and it worked.

In a similar way, if Nazis came to your house looking for Jews and the infinite shield, the sword that heals, social norms, and laws could not protect the people you were hiding, another option would be to outsmart violence by telling the Nazis a very convincing lie. Like every technique, outsmarting violence does not always work. If the Nazis were not fooled by your lie, the aftermath could be deadly. Historian Klaus Fischer describes how one Nazi reacted when he realized a woman was withholding information from him: "In one town the Jews had gone into hiding and when the SS swept through the town they discovered a woman with a baby in her arms. When the woman refused to tell them where the Jews were hiding, one SS man grabbed the baby by its legs and smashed its head against a door. Another SS man recalled: 'It went off with a bang like a bursting motor tire. I shall never forget that sound as long as I live.'"[13]

The purpose of this chapter is not to tell you what to do in every situation, but to let you know what your options are so that you can make the best decision. Every hostile situation is different, and you must assess the unique circumstances you are in, consider your options, and do what you think will work. When the option of outsmarting violence as a way of deflecting hostile actions is concerned, I must make a crucial point that I cannot emphasize enough. *Lying should not be used when waging peace, but only in the rare situations when the infinite shield and the sword that heals seem unlikely to work and deception is needed to protect someone in imminent physical danger.* I have seen too many activists tell exaggerated stories and outright lies in order to draw more attention to their cause, rationalizing their deception by saying it's serving the mission of peace. But as long as we believe we can lie our way to peace, we will never truly achieve peace.

Human memory is not perfect, but we must be committed to honoring the truth the best we can. When we try to wage peace by exaggerating our stories and twisting the facts, we are no longer waging peace. When waging peace in our personal lives, a lot of skill is required to deal with people honestly yet gently and compassionately. Being honest does not give us a license to be rude. In other words, being honest does not give us a right to insult people and disregard their feelings.

Japan's *Code of the Samurai*, written over three hundred years ago, emphasizes the importance of balancing truth with tact:

> Expressing your opinions to others, or objecting to their views, are also things that should be done with due consideration . . . Anything a warrior says must be tactful and considerate. How much the more so when speaking with friends and colleagues; tact is even more appropriate under those circumstances . . . Once you have become someone's confidant, it shows a certain degree of dependability to pursue the truth and speak your mind freely even if the other person doesn't like what you say. If, however, you are fainthearted and fear to speak the truth, lest you cause offense or upset, and thus say whatever is convenient instead of what is right, thereby inducing other people to say things they shouldn't, or causing them to blunder to their own disadvantage, then you are useless as an advisor.[14]

There is also a practical reason for balancing truth with tact, because the more disrespectful and condescending you are when speaking the truth the more difficult it is for people to hear it. A highly trained peace warrior is not just a truth teller, but a *skilled* truth teller. To illustrate the differences between deflection and the truth telling of waging peace, the following diagram depicts the four lines of defense:

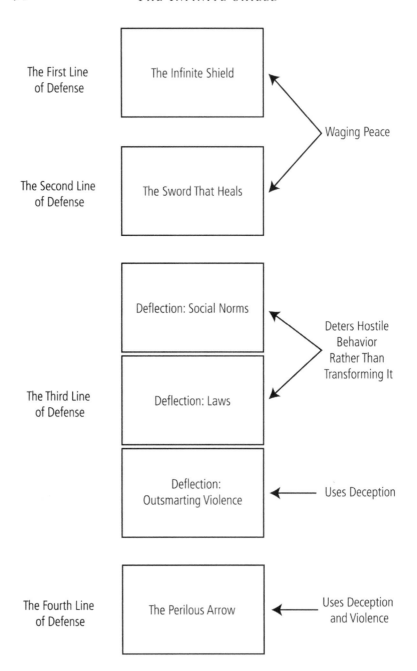

Figure 5.2 The Four Lines of Defense

To protect us from violence and injustice, the infinite shield and the sword that heals are the first two lines of defense. *They are waging peace.* The third line of defense is deflection. It is not waging peace, because the first two forms of deflection (social norms and laws) deter hostile behavior rather than transform people's ignorance and hatred into understanding and compassion, and the third form of deflection (outsmarting violence) permits deception. The fourth line of defense, which I call the *perilous arrow*, permits not only deception but also violence. The fourth line of defense is the furthest thing from waging peace, because the perilous arrow is violence itself.

CHAPTER 6

The Perilous Arrow

The Gandhi Myth

If the capacity for non-violent self-defense is lacking, there need be no hesitation in using violent means.
—Mahatma Gandhi[1]

Although I developed the infinite shield because I wanted to control my rage, I am not the only person who can benefit from the infinite shield in this way. I have met many activists who avoid talking to those who disagree with them because they are worried more about their own temper than the hostility of other people. When I speak with activists around the country about waging peace, one of the most common questions they ask me is, "How do you remain calm and not get angry when dealing with hateful and ignorant people?" A female peace activist once told me, "I'm usually a very peaceful person, but sometimes the people who support war say things that sound so offensive and ignorant to me that I want to punch them."

The infinite shield can help us live peacefully with our friends, coworkers, family members, and significant others by preventing disagreements from turning into destructive shouting matches. But the infinite shield is also vital when waging peace on a larger scale. If we encourage people to take action for a just cause but don't prepare them to deal with their own anger or a hostile person who disagrees with them, we are not giving them the practical tools they need to maximize their effectiveness. When we revile instead of respect those who disagree with us, it not only weakens our ability to create positive change. It can also have deeper consequences, because despising others can suck the joy out of our lives, draining our energy to work for peace and justice during challenging times, and putting us at risk of becoming bitter and cynical people.

By increasing our respect for the humanity of others, the infinite shield can protect us from becoming bitter and cynical. This is one of the many ways the infinite shield benefits us, along with everyone we interact with. A bronze shield protected Greek soldiers, but not beyond its edges. Anyone standing beyond its edges was excluded from its sanctuary. Also, a bronze shield was designed to defend only those standing behind it, not those in front. But unlike the bronze shield of the ancient Greeks, the infinite shield has no edges, no borders, no front, no back. The infinite shield does not exclude anyone. When human beings oppose us, the infinite shield guards them from our disrespect and hostility as much as it guards us from theirs.

So far in this book I have explored the basic building blocks of the first line of defense: the infinite shield. Later in this book I will explore the basic building blocks of the second line of defense: the sword that heals. The infinite shield influences people by conveying respect through our words, composure, attitude, and behavior. The sword that heals influences people by using strong ideas, persuasive dialogue, and strategic actions to transform how they think. This book creates a foundation you can build on through your own study, and I hope these pages inspire you to learn more about the incredibly deep and complex art of waging peace.

If we truly want to wage peace effectively, strengthening the infinite shield within us and learning how to wield it for the benefit of all is the first step. Many believe the idea of respecting all people as human beings is naive, but this book shows it has practical survival value, because respecting others makes us less likely to have conflicts with them and more successful at resolving the conflicts that do arise. Many also do not realize how important the ability to remain calm truly is, but Roman philosopher Seneca tells us, "The power of wisdom is better shown by a display of calmness in the midst of provocation, just as the greatest proof that a general is mighty in his arms and men is his quiet unconcern in the country of the enemy."[2]

However, is there ever a situation where the first line of defense (the infinite shield), second line of defense (the sword that heals), and even third line of defense (the three forms of deflection) don't work? What happens when someone breaches the infinite shield, dodges the sword that heals, and prevents us from deflecting an attack? What happens when people are filled with so much berserker rage that their forebrain—the part of our brain capable of thinking and listening—shuts down? What happens when the siren song of rage drowns out a person's ability to hear the voices of reason, compassion, and conscience? In his book *On Combat,* Lieutenant Colonel Dave Grossman shares a letter written to him by Keith Nelson Borders, a police officer he trained. The letter describes what happens when all hell breaks loose and the only option left to protect people is violence:

> On April 28, 2001, at [8:38 p.m.], I was involved in my sixth officer-involved shooting with a man intent on killing his wife, daughter, and four-year-old granddaughter. His plan was to shoot them, and he had armed himself with a .357 mag., 9mm, and a 12-gauge pump shotgun.
>
> When I arrived, the suspect immediately began firing at me with the handguns while I evacuated the daughter and granddaughter. While attempting to evacuate the wife, the suspect aimed the shotgun at us. I pushed the lady on the ground and covered her with my body. The suspect fired and four pellets struck me in the head, two entered my brain.
>
> The blast of the shotgun flipped me over, and I got up off the ground and pulled the lady behind cover. I engaged the suspect in a running gun battle wounding him seven times (five fatal wounds), but he would not go down. As with most head wounds, I was bleeding profusely and felt as though I would soon lose consciousness, when I saw the suspect coming towards the lady and me. I had fired 39 of the 40 rounds that I carry. So, using the breathing technique that you teach, and that I learned in the U.S. Army Infantry [marksmanship training] 15 years ago, I slowed myself down, got a good sight picture, and fired the fatal headshot.

The bullet struck him in the left eye, my exact point of aim, and ended the threat. I was wounded, bleeding profusely, and firing with only one hand, as I had to hold the lady down behind cover.

This was my sixth officer-involved shooting, all have been fatal for the bad guys. I have been shot in three of those six shootings, and my body has seven bullet holes in it. I have been stabbed once and have lost a partner in the line of duty—but we must fight the good fight.[3]

Would Gandhi approve of police officer Keith Nelson Borders using violence to protect the innocent from a berserking man? When Gandhi's son asked him if violence should ever be used to protect those being attacked, he responded:

I do believe that where there is a choice only between cowardice and violence, I would advise violence. Thus when my eldest son asked me what he should have done had he been present when I was almost fatally assaulted in 1908, whether he should have run away and seen me killed or whether he should have used his physical force which he could and wanted to use, and defend me, I told him it was his duty to defend me even by using violence. Hence it was that I took part in the Boer War, the so-called Zulu rebellion and the late war [World War I]. Hence also do I advocate training in arms for those who believe in the method of violence. I would rather have India resort to arms in order to defend her honor than that she should in a cowardly manner become or remain a helpless witness to her own dishonor. But I believe non-violence is infinitely superior to violence.[4]

Most people in our society view Gandhi as a naive pacifist who fully rejected all uses of violence, but this portrayal of Gandhi is a myth. Many peace activists also believe in this mythical portrayal of Gandhi. During my lectures I often ask peace activists to raise their hands if they knew that Gandhi served as a military recruiter four different times, volunteered as a medic for the British army in the Boer War and Second Zulu War (also known as the Zulu Rebellion), received the War Medal from the British Empire for his military service, and supported Britain's violent resistance against Germany in World War I and Poland's violent resistance against Germany in World War II. Very few raise their hands.

Gandhi was certainly committed to nonviolence. But when people were being harmed by injustice, he would rather see them become disciplined soldiers trained to fight back violently than be helpless victims too afraid to resist. According to Gandhi, the worst thing a person can do when being abused or witnessing abuse is remain passive and impotent. He said, "Violence is any day preferable to impotence. There is hope for a violent man to become nonviolent. There is no such hope for the impotent."[5] Gandhi thought it was easier to get conscientious, disciplined soldiers to embrace nonviolence than it was to transform passive, undisciplined people into peace warriors. I offer my own life journey as evidence to support his claim, because as a soldier I used to believe strongly in violence but found much in his philosophy that appealed to me.

Even at the end of his life, Gandhi maintained a nuanced view of violence and nonviolence. Gandhi scholar Peter Brock said: "Indeed [Gandhi] had never ceased to maintain that, while nonviolent resolution of conflict was preferable to the use of violence, himsa [violence] employed to right a wrong was preferable to tame submission to injustice or aggression. A follower of ahimsa [nonviolence], he believed, had to reckon with that fact."[6] Thomas Merton, a Trappist monk and peace activist, said: "Those who cannot practice a really dedicated non-violence should defend their rights and justice by force, if no other means are available. Gandhi does not preach the passive surrender of rights or of human dignity. On the contrary, he believes that nonviolence is the noblest as well as the most effective way of defending one's rights."[7]

Gandhi said: "Non-violence is not a cover for cowardice, but it is the supreme virtue of the brave . . . Cowardice is wholly inconsistent with non-violence . . . Non-violence presupposes ability to strike . . . He who cannot protect himself or his nearest and dearest or their honor by non-violently facing death may and ought to do so by violently dealing with the oppressor. He who can do neither of the two is a burden."[8]

Gandhi believed nonviolence is "the supreme virtue of the brave," and this book supports his viewpoint by showing that courage is necessary to effectively wield the infinite shield. For example, Gandhi and Martin Luther King Jr. risked their lives when waging peace, exhibiting impressive courage in the midst of enormous danger. Although Gandhi understood the power of waging peace, he realized violence may sometimes be necessary to defend our rights, those we love, and justice itself. To better understand how a person can advocate waging peace without fully rejecting violence, consider a medical doctor who advocates antibiotics without fully rejecting amputation.

If a man gets an infection in his foot, most doctors believe a proactive method of treatment such as antibiotics is preferable and far superior to a method of last resort such as amputation. Likewise, when a conflict arises between human beings, I think a proactive method of conflict resolution such as waging peace is preferable and far superior to a method of last resort such as violence. Two hundred years ago, medical technology was very limited, and little was known about preventative medicine. When a person had an infected foot back then, doctors would often amputate because they did not know how to cure the infection. Our way of violently resolving conflicts is limited in the same way medical technology was two hundred years ago.

The use of amputation and violence have a lot in common, because they are both more reactive than proactive, often waiting until a situation has escalated to a dangerous point before taking action. But using antibiotics and waging peace are both proactive, dealing with the problem early before it spirals out of control. Furthermore, just as preventative medicine aims to prevent infections from happening in the first place, waging peace aims to prevent conflicts before they arise.

Although amputation and violence are both sometimes necessary, this book will show that people in our world rely too heavily on violence because they have not been trained in the art of waging peace, just as doctors two hundred years ago relied too heavily on amputation because they did not know about antibiotics such as penicillin. In this chapter I will discuss the rare situations when violence might be effective as a last resort, and later in this book I will explain from a strategic perspective why violence should *never* be used in a social movement.

Like Gandhi and many other peace advocates, I struggled for many years to reconcile my commitment to waging peace with my understanding that violence as a last resort might sometimes be necessary. This led me to develop the four lines of defense, which show that violence, like amputation, has its place. The four lines of defense also show that the skillful use of waging peace, like the skillful use of preventative medicine and antibiotics, is always preferable and usually more effective than a destructive last resort. As the first two lines of defense, the infinite shield and the sword that heals are the preventative medicine for human conflict. They are the penicillin for evil.

Martin Luther King Jr. said human beings have a "greater capacity for goodness" but also the "potential for evil."[9] If we want to create a more peaceful world we must not lose sight of this reality. Although my books show that human beings are not naturally violent by citing abundant evidence from military history and other sources, my books also explain the many ways people can become violent. For example, I have had a violent temper, but I was not born this way. Rather, I was conditioned to be violent. Similarly, the vast majority of people in the violent criminal population were abused as children in ways that hindered their greater capacity for goodness and nurtured their potential for evil.

Many peace activists understand our greater capacity for goodness but underestimate how violent a person can become through trauma, abuse, and conditioning. I have met some activists who believe the world doesn't need police officers or even laws. The rage within me disagrees. Because I have experienced the berserker mindset firsthand, I realize how extremely dangerous people can become when they are seduced by the siren song of rage. One reason I became obsessed with studying peace was because I wanted to learn how to protect society from people who have experienced violent tendencies like myself.

I have had many life-changing realizations during my journey on the road to peace. Although our psychological wounds can urge us to lash out violently, I learned we can heal our trauma, abuse, and conditioning through the process of spiritual change. I also learned there are so many peaceful ways to resolve conflict, and when we are trained in these nonviolent methods we almost never have to resort to violence. Not only did Gandhi and King understand this, but so have other warriors.

Kaibara Ekken was born into a samurai family in Japan during the seventeenth century, serving as a samurai scholar for the Kuroda Han clan.[10] Trained as a physician, he later became a philosopher who wrote about many subjects, including the warrior code. In the following excerpt, his description of proper warrior behavior sounds very similar to the nonviolent philosophy of Gandhi and King. In addition, Ekken explains the importance of avoiding violence not from a moralistic viewpoint, but a practical and realistic perspective:

> If you are insulted in the presence of others, you shouldn't get angry even if it happens twice. You should respond with the truth. If the person doesn't accept the truth, then rebuke him sternly. Don't insult him back . . . You shouldn't contemptuously insult people yourself, because no matter how timid they may be, if they get angry they may go ahead and fight . . .
>
> A man of courage is not outwardly rough. He should be, as Xunzi says, "able to be calm, then able to respond." That means that when facing an opponent you can win by calming your mind and not letting it stir. If you get excited at the drop of a hat, you have no internal basis for responding to opponents, so you won't be able to overcome people . . .
>
> Superior warriors consider it best to win without fighting. If a fight is unavoidable, a good commander is skilled in the ways of war and has strategy, so he doesn't get a lot of people killed, whether enemies or allies . . . Even if they become generals, humane men do not kill a lot of people . . . When battling opponents, if you are excessive in beating them, they'll lash back and fight powerfully . . . Even in an argument between ordinary men, if one vilifies the other too much and is excessive in beating him down, he'll wind up the loser if the other man can't

put up with it and retaliates vehemently . . . When dealing with people, it is imperative to be polite in speech and manner, avoiding discourtesy.[11]

The Unpredictable Nature of Violence

At West Point I studied "just war theory," which is an argument developed by Saint Augustine and other thinkers that provides moral justification for war. Western culture has been obsessed with the morality of war and the question of when violence is justified. But many Eastern thinkers take a more useful approach by instead focusing on the practicality of war and the question of when violence is effective.[12] According to many Western just war theorists, if you can justify using violence then it is acceptable to attack someone. But according to martial arts philosophy, even if you can justify using violence it is often not the best way to solve a problem, and can actually put you in greater danger.

For example, if someone pulls a knife on me I am certainly justified in punching him. But martial arts taught me that attacking a person with a knife is not the most effective way to protect myself. If someone threatens me with a knife, martial arts taught me to first consider other options such as talking my way out of the situation or running away, because violence escalates conflict and should therefore be my last resort. Rick Wayman, one of my coworkers at the Nuclear Age Peace Foundation, was held at knifepoint in London. He explains what happened:

> I decided to hit up the shops on Brick Lane in East London . . . I lost myself in the thought of a Bangladeshi curry dish or a fresh-baked bagel, both specialties of Brick Lane. I was shaken from my delicious daydream by a swift blow to the head. Out of nowhere, an angry, raging young man appeared with a flurry of fists. His intoxicated stumble allowed me time to make a brief getaway, but the next thing I knew I was between a brick wall and a chain-link fence on the sidewalk with a knife pressed against my wool

sweater, poised to plunge into my stomach. "You're another one of those white racist sons of bitches who come down to Brick Lane thinking you own the fucking place, aren't you? I'm just another no-good Paki—that's what you think, isn't it? Isn't it? What the fuck are you and your people doing to my brothers in Iraq?"

He doesn't ask for my wallet; he doesn't demand the passport I'm carrying in my bag. He has lived the oppressed life of a Pakistani teenager in Britain, and chose me as the outlet for his anger. This random act of violence, fuelled by alcohol and probably years of being bullied and ignored by most of British society, put me in a bit of a quandary. Do I punch and run? Do I knee-in-the-balls-grab-the-knife-throw-it-down-the-sewer? Do I tell him to drop the knife and "fight like a man with your hands"?

All of these are options that may have ended the confrontation and led to my safe escape. But my reaction was to look him in the eyes. I asked him questions about himself. I told him what I do in London and about the people I work with. I told him about the Pablo Neruda book I checked out from the library yesterday. I told him I would rather have a cup of coffee with him than fight him. He asked me questions: "So you were trying to prove Saddam Hussein had nuclear weapons? So you support Tony Blair?" and later . . . "How long have you lived in London?"

Aha! There's hope! Active nonviolence can work! Knife in pocket, he invites me to his uncle's restaurant (one building down) for a cup of coffee. Out of another, deeper pocket, he pulls out a longer knife. He hands it to someone in a nearby doorway. Along the way, I ask him why he carries a knife—is it for protection? "I'm not afraid of nobody on this street but God." He opens the door to the restaurant for me. It's a nice place—crisp white table-cloths, napkins folded in the shape of roses, wine glasses and shiny silverware on all the tables. Three steps in, he

cries "You motherfucker!" and lands a right hook to my
jaw. I grabbed both his arms so he couldn't punch me anymore, but somehow he did. A few older men came in and
started speaking to him in their common language. Two
guys in their 20s managed to grab one of his arms each,
leaving me free to go. So I went.

What does this all mean? Where did I go right, and
where did I go wrong? When does my desire to live exceed
my desire to reach the humanity of the other person? Is
nonviolence the answer? What would I do if I could do it
all over again?[13]

As I mentioned earlier, every hostile situation is different, and whether
you are being yelled at by a loved one or held at knifepoint by a stranger,
you must assess the unique circumstances you are in and do what you think
is best. During life-threatening confrontations you must use your reason and
intuition to decide whether you should rely on the infinite shield, use the
sword that heals, try to deflect the attack, or resort to the violence of the
perilous arrow.

Did Rick handle the situation the right way? Martial arts philosophy
focuses on protection and survival, and if you walk away from a life-
threatening situation with only a couple of bruises it is considered a victory.
Perhaps Rick could have handled the situation differently, but the important
thing is that he survived and nobody was seriously injured. If I had gone
berserk in that situation I might have maimed or killed the attacker, but I
also might have been seriously wounded or killed in the process. Kaibara
Ekken said, "Superior warriors consider it best to win without fighting," and
I think Rick's way of resolving the conflict without resorting to violence
would have made Ekken and even Sun Tzu proud.

In *The Art of War*, written over two thousand years ago, Sun Tzu says,
"Attaining one hundred victories in one hundred battles is not the pinnacle
of excellence. Subjugating the enemy's army without fighting is the true pinnacle of excellence."[14] Studying Eastern thinkers and martial arts philosophy
taught me that violence is not the best option for solving problems because
it escalates conflicts and is extremely unpredictable. By contrasting chess and

poker, we can better understand why violence is so dangerous.

A street fight is less like chess and more like poker, because in chess you can see what your opponent has on the board, but in poker you don't know what cards the other person is hiding. Perhaps your opponent has a high probability of beating you because his cards contain a flush, straight, full house, or royal flush. There are many unknowns in a poker game, and the same is true in a street fight. Perhaps the person you are about to fight has a concealed weapon, is stronger and more skilled than he appears, likes to fight dirty by gouging the eyes and attacking the groin, or easily goes berserk. What if someone intervenes on his behalf during the fight and hits you on the back of the head? Or what if he knocks you out with a lucky punch? Even if you are bigger, stronger, and a much better fighter, you could still lose due to any of these reasons.

Just as two poker players raise the stakes by betting more and more money, trying to make the other person give up by "folding," two people in a street fight raise the stakes with every punch they throw, hoping the other person will fold. Perhaps the person will fold after you throw the first punch, or maybe the person will go berserk and be willing to bet his life. Rage differs from anger, because people filled with rage care more about hurting you than their personal safety. That is not the kind of person you want to gamble with.

Most people do not like getting punched and are afraid of fighting. As a result, when they feel terrified and desperate after getting hit, their behavior becomes extremely unpredictable. They might beg for mercy, curl up in the fetal position and protect their head, try to run away, kick you in the groin, or rip off your ear. I call violence the *perilous arrow* for two reasons. First, the word "perilous" refers to the *escalating nature of violence*. The respect we convey through the infinite shield does not always get through to people, but it's difficult to imagine a scenario where a genuine show of respect would escalate a conflict or backfire. If people attack us after we show them genuine respect, it is probably because they already intended to assault us. The perilous arrow, on the other hand, can easily escalate conflicts and backfire because it requires us to raise the stakes with violence, like a poker player making larger and larger bets.

The second reason I use the term "perilous arrow" is because the metaphor of an arrow represents the *unpredictable nature of violence*. Unlike a shield and sword, which are in your grasp and safely under your control, once you shoot an arrow across a long distance you lose control of it and cannot predict with certainty where it will land. Just as an arrow can be blown off course by an unexpected gust of wind, violence is so unpredictable and difficult to control because chance often decides who wins and who loses. Military strategist Carl von Clausewitz said, "There is no human affair which stands so constantly and so generally in close connection with chance as war. But together with chance, the accidental, and along with it good luck, occupy a great place in war."[15]

Every hostile situation is unpredictable, no matter what line of defense we use. But of the four lines of defense, the perilous arrow (violence) is the most unpredictable. Why? The infinite shield and the sword that heals work effectively only when we remain calm and control our aggression. Calm reduces the chaos, confusion, and unpredictability in a situation. But for the perilous arrow to work I must take violent actions that escalate aggression. Aggression increases the chaos, confusion, and unpredictability in a situation. Calm and aggression are both also contagious. Calm people can transform a hostile situation into a peaceful and productive discussion, whereas aggression can have a domino effect, causing the situation to spiral out of control.

Furthermore, the perilous arrow forces you to abandon your other lines of defense, because you cannot shoot an arrow while holding a shield and sword. In other words, you must temporarily discard the infinite shield and the sword that heals when resorting to the perilous arrow, because you cannot practice the art of waging peace while punching someone in the face. To better explain the risks and uses of the perilous arrow, I must discuss how the perilous arrow comes in three varieties.

1. Personal Self-defense

I have seen pro-war advocates argue that if people are against war, they must also be against the use of violence for personal self-defense. This is simply not true. I for one am adamantly opposed to war, yet I do not reject the use of violence for personal self-defense. How can this be?

If a man breaks into my apartment and attacks me, he is *choosing* to put himself in an illegal and very dangerous situation. But in modern wars the majority of people killed have been innocent civilians who were never given a choice. Using violence for personal self-defense is therefore very different from modern war, because if a person chooses to invade my apartment and attack me I can defend myself without killing any innocent people. In addition, I don't have to kill an aggressor invading my apartment in order to protect myself, because I can begin by threatening him with violence. If he does not back down and assaults me, I can knock him unconscious, wrestle him to the ground and apply a submission hold, or stab him with a knife until he loses the ability to fight, then immediately call 911 so he receives emergency medical care that might keep him alive. If the aggressor ends up dying, then I have killed one person who chose to invade my apartment and attack me.

When personal self-defense is concerned, we have various ways of using violence to protect ourselves, many of which are nonlethal. The Shaolin monks in China, who developed a form of martial arts to defend their Buddhist monasteries from bandits, used the bo staff as a personal self-defense weapon because it allowed them to subdue an attacker without inflicting lethal wounds. They were also trained to use swords in case a situation required a deadlier weapon. But when modern war is concerned, even the countries that try to minimize civilian casualties kill many civilians due to the chaos and confusion of war. During the past seventy-five years there have been many wars where tens of thousands, hundreds of thousands, and even millions of civilians have died from the intended and unintended effects of war. There are so many examples that I cannot list them all in this short section.

Because war kills so many innocent civilians, using violence in war is much different from using violence against one person who chooses to invade my apartment and attack me. Journalist Tony Dokoupil describes just one of the countless ways war kills innocent civilians:

> Lu Lobello, a machine gunner with the Saints and the
> Sinners in 2003, traveled to Washington, D.C., to speak
> to a panel at the *Newsweek* and The Daily Beast Hero

Summit. To an audience of mostly civilians in business casual, he revived his memories of that battle in Baghdad. By way of introduction, the moderator, Wolf Blitzer, said that Fox Company had killed three civilians in the crossfire. "Well," said Lobello, "first off, there were about 20 innocent civilians, not three." He then limned the rest of the raw story: many of the cars in the intersection held families, not fighters. When the Marines realized this, they tried to help, but often it was too late. Another car would come, and they would shoot it, because what if this one was the enemy. "We were shooting at civilians," his superior officer explained to a reporter in 2008. "We were taking out women and children because it was us or them." The image that stays with Lobello is one of the first from that day, of a fellow Marine walking in tight circles, talking to himself. "We shot a baby!" he screamed, turning to Lobello. "Lobello, we shot a baby!"[16]

In addition to protecting ourselves from home invasion, personal self-defense also refers to the act of protecting our loved ones from a violent attack, because in most cases we can defend them by confronting the aggressor and not hurting any innocent people. I am a strong advocate for personal self-defense, and that is why I am also a strong advocate for waging peace. *The infinite shield and the sword that heals are the most effective forms of personal self-defense*, followed by the three forms of deflection. The perilous arrow is a dangerous last resort.

2. Police Force

Law enforcement officers have many options other than violence. As I mentioned earlier, they stopped terrorists such as Ted Kaczynski and Timothy McVeigh, along with numerous serial killers, without killing a single person. Law enforcement officers have the ability to conduct investigations and arrest people, who are then supposed to receive a public trial by a jury of their peers. Also, when the police came to my apartment after I broke the window, they didn't kick the door down and attack me. Instead, they used nonviolent techniques to calm me down.

Not all police officers are trained in nonviolent techniques, and some rely far too much on violence. Psychologist Abraham Maslow said, "I suppose it is tempting, if the only tool you have is a hammer, to treat everything as if it were a nail."[17] In a similar way, if a person is trained only in violent techniques then physical force will seem like the best way to solve a problem. Our society also conditions us to view violence as an effective way to solve problems. I have seen countless television shows and movies that portray violence in a glamorous and unrealistic way.

I am well aware of the fact that police officers have often abused their power, but Lieutenant Colonel Dave Grossman is doing incredible work to help strengthen the ethical code of law enforcement officers who are supposed to "serve and protect." Grossman is also helping to improve their training so that when they must resort to violence, innocent bystanders are less likely to be injured. According to Grossman, the human brain does not function well in combat, and that is why people need high-quality training in order to perform effectively in combat. Human beings are not natural predators of their own species, and that is why people need thorough combat training to become proficient fighters.

In fact, combat is such a chaotic and confusing environment for the human brain that soldiers often kill their own comrades accidentally in what are known as "friendly fire" or "fratricide" incidents. According to the U.S. Army, 12 to 14 percent of the American soldier deaths during World War II were due to friendly fire. During the Vietnam War it was 10 to 14 percent, and in Operation Desert Storm it was 12 percent.[18] In June 1993 after the first Gulf War, the House Armed Services Committee prepared a study stating that a "15 to 20 percent fratricide rate may be the norm, not the exception [as] past rates of fratricide have been systematically and substantially underestimated."[19]

The chaos and confusion of combat, in addition to unethical behavior, can cause police officers to harm the innocent. But police officers, like Japanese samurai and European knights before them, are supposed to live up to a high ethical code. The warrior class in any society is often required to obey an ethical code—also known as a warrior code—because when a group of people are armed with weapons they can do immense harm to the population they are supposed to protect. Although many samurai behaved more like thugs and criminals than virtuous warrior protectors, the *Code of the Samurai* clearly states that a samurai should never abuse someone who cannot fight back. A common theme in warrior codes around the world is that warriors have a duty to protect the innocent, vulnerable, and helpless. The *Code of the Samurai*, written over three hundred years ago, states:

> If the conduct of a warrior's wife displeases him in some way, he should explain the reason and admonish her in such a way that she will understand . . . If you don't follow this advice but instead shout at your wife . . . abusing her with foul language, that may be the way of back-alley [workers] of the business district, but it is certainly not appropriate to the behavior of a knightly warrior. How much the more objectionable it is to brandish your sword or punch her with your fist—this is unspeakable behavior, characteristic of a cowardly warrior . . . *To abuse someone he sees cannot fight back is something a valiant warrior simply does not do.* [emphasis added]"[20]

Will our society always need police officers trained in the perilous arrow to protect it? Or is it possible to reduce violent crime to such a large extent that police officers will no longer be needed in the future? As I write this the American population is around 300 million. If only one out of every ten thousand Americans had a propensity for committing violent crimes as a "repeat offender," this would amount to 30,000 violent criminals in our country—quite a large number. And since those 30,000 people can join each other to create small violent groups, we can understand why Martin Luther King Jr. believed in "the intelligent use of police force."

In a small tribe ranging from a dozen to several hundred people, it is easy to imagine a situation where law enforcement officers are not needed and people can settle disputes among themselves. But when a society contains hundreds of millions of people—any of which could be affected by the serious mental disorders that can cause people to endanger others—there will always be some murderers, child molesters, con artists, and others who want to take advantage of the vulnerable. It is the duty of police officers to protect the vulnerable.

In addition, as long as there is alcohol in the world we will need police officers. I am certainly not arguing in favor of prohibition, nor am I trying to be moralistic. Instead, I am simply being realistic. It is a fact that a small percentage of people become aggressive when they drink alcohol, and that people are more likely to commit violent crime when drunk. The *Code of the Samurai* understood the dangers of alcohol, warning us to be careful around those in drunken rages: "It is not impossible that on the road, or at your destination, you may run into someone in a drunken rage, or some kind of fool, and get into an unexpected duel."[21]

As King said about the use of federal soldiers in Little Rock, "So I believe in the intelligent use of police force, and I think that is all we have in Little Rock. It's not an army fighting against a nation or a race of people. It is just police force, seeking to enforce the law of the land."[22] By refining the warrior code to help us meet new challenges in the twenty-first century and holding law enforcement officers accountable for their wrongdoings, we can ensure the perilous arrow does more to protect rather than harm humanity.

3. War

War is a master of deception. The war system has convinced most people that it is effective at keeping us safe, but in the second part of this book I will reveal what the war system doesn't want us to know. We are living during a fragile time in human history when war is no longer an acceptable way of using the perilous arrow. Now that I have introduced the four lines of defense and discussed the basic building blocks of the infinite shield, I can explain in the pages ahead why war is so dangerous and counterproductive in the twenty-first century. In order to solve our national and global problems, we must realize that our greatest enemy today is not a particular group of people in a far-off country. Our greatest enemy is war itself.

PART II

The
Sword That Heals

CHAPTER 7

West Point and World Peace

How West Point Trained Me for Peace Activism

My training as a peace activist began in an unlikely place: the United States Military Academy at West Point. During my four years there I learned the timeless ideals and essential skills that can make us all more effective at waging peace. Many people are surprised to hear that West Point armed me with the tools to wage peace. In fact, when I give talks around the country I often meet peace activists who have a negative stereotype of West Point and the military, saying things such as, "Didn't West Point discourage critical thinking and train you to be closed-minded? Doesn't military leadership rely on bullying and other abusive techniques to keep soldiers in line?"

How did West Point train me to be a peace activist? Before I can explain this I must first discuss General Douglas MacArthur. No single person had a greater influence on West Point than MacArthur. He was not the founder of West Point, but in many ways he is its father.*

The United States Military Academy at West Point was established by President Thomas Jefferson in 1802. Many assume the university was founded to train soldiers to fight, but it is actually the oldest engineering college in the United States. West Point's original focus was training engineers, and Jonathan Williams, grandnephew of Benjamin Franklin, became its first superintendent. Historian Jennings L. Wagoner explains:

---

* Although Sylvanus Thayer is often called the "Father of West Point," I think MacArthur had a larger impact on shaping West Point than Thayer. MacArthur's biographer, D. Clayton James, calls MacArthur the "Father of the New West Point."

The grandnephew of Benjamin Franklin, [Jonathan] Williams had lived with and served as his [great] uncle's research assistant while abroad. On their return voyage from Europe in 1785, Franklin and Williams had conducted experiments on the relationship between water temperature and ocean currents. Williams extended his research on later voyages and in 1799 published his findings as a book to aid in navigation. He also contributed essays to the *Transactions* of the American Philosophical Society and was serving as its secretary when Jefferson became the society's president . . . By selecting Williams [to be West Point's first superintendent], Jefferson not only entrusted West Point to the care of a man with at least moderately acceptable political views, but he also made a practical-minded scientist the academy's first superintendent.

Official provisions and expectations for the new military academy were modest at the outset. As initially established by the 1802 Military Peace Establishment Act, the United States Military Academy (USMA) was not created to train officers for all branches of the regular army or militia, or even the nucleus of a general officer corps. Instead, [West Point] was to prepare a small number of cadets for duty in a narrow branch of technical service, the Corps of Engineers . . . Williams' hope that [West Point] might become an important national scientific establishment clearly outdistanced the funds available for the project. Williams wanted the American ministers to England and France to seek the opinion of "the most eminent professional Men in London and Paris" regarding books and equipment and to purchase for the academy "every Book of merit that is extant, so far as is connected with the Profession . . ."

In spite of the [Jefferson] administration's stringent financial policies and the vagaries of the act of establishment, Williams, who was promoted to lieutenant colonel in July 1802, endeavored to do whatever he could to advance the academy as a scientific institution. His desire to transmit to the cadets a spirit of scientific inquiry and an awareness of the broad horizons their new profession offered was perhaps best exemplified by his establishment of the United States Military Philosophical Society (USMPS). "Our guiding star," Williams wrote, "is not a little mathematical school, but a great national establishment . . . We must always have it in view that our Officers are to be men of Science, and as such will by their acquirements be entitled to the notice of learned societies."[1]

For many years West Point emphasized engineering, math, and science in addition to military studies. But when MacArthur became the academy's superintendent in 1919, he wanted West Point to also emphasize liberal arts. Today many people say students need to focus on studying math and science, and subjects such as history, psychology, philosophy, social studies, and the humanities have little importance in the modern world. Columnist Michael Adkins tells us:

> Scores of universities are cutting Liberal Arts programs. Analysts argue that disciplines such as classical studies, philosophy, history, cultural anthropology and sociology have no real value within the modern workforce. Many of these programs are seen as frivolous or nonessential and they are among the first to be cut from a university budget. This trend reflects a disturbing change within higher education. The value of critical thinking skills has diminished. The ability to operate the latest computer software is often seen as more important than the ability to engage in critical thinking or make ethical decisions.[2]

MacArthur's academic philosophy helped me see the importance of having a well-rounded education. An education that helps us understand math and technology is critical, but MacArthur realized building a more peaceful and prosperous future requires us to also understand something far more complex than calculus equations and electronic components: the human mind. When we are students of humanity we can hone many crucial leadership skills. These skills include how to motivate people to work together toward a shared goal, how to inspire them to remain determined and never give up during difficult times, and how to help them unlock their full potential as human beings.

By developing an academic curriculum that would help cadets understand man as well as machine, MacArthur wanted to create military officers with the educational background and critical thinking skills necessary to solve a wide variety of problems. Because wars are intertwined with deeper societal conflicts, he realized future officers must not only be able to solve military problems, but also political and social ones. He wanted to mold warriors who were powerful leaders, capable of inspiring people to overcome serious challenges in order to achieve the highest goals. He wanted to create West Point graduates who could not only fulfill their duties as soldiers, but also uphold their responsibilities as active citizens and conscientious human beings.

MacArthur said he wanted West Point to produce officers who "[possess] an intimate understanding of the mechanics of human feelings, a comprehensive grasp of world and national affairs, and a liberalization of concept which amounts to a change in [the] psychology of command."[3] Criticized as a "liberal innovator"[4] by the academic board at West Point, he encountered severe opposition during his efforts to reform the educational system. Historian D. Clayton James explains:

> An early and lasting dispute developed when MacArthur told the members of the academic board that more stress must be placed on the social sciences. In line with his aim to produce officers who understood human motivations and were knowledgeable about national and foreign affairs, he urged the introduction of courses in political science, economics, sociology, and psychology; enlargement of the offerings in English and history; and creation of a department of economics, government, and

history. Professor Holt had been crusading for these changes since 1911, but most of the faculty believed that greater attention should be given to improving and extending the courses in military and technical subjects . . .

One of his characteristics which some professors found shocking was his periodical visiting in classes. In an unprecedented action for a superintendent, MacArthur would suddenly appear in a classroom, take a seat in the rear, and start making notes. Afterward he would visit the particular professor or instructor in his office and offer suggestions on ways to improve his teaching methods. His presence and counsel were obviously abhorred by some teachers, but he was able to persuade several men to introduce new methods. He induced Holt, for example, to place more emphasis on training in oratory and debate and to require cadets in history and government sections to study two newspapers daily and discuss current events in class."[5]

West Point upholds engineering and liberal arts as two important pillars of education. When I was at West Point cadets had to minor in engineering[6] regardless of their major, and take several math courses including statistics, a full year of physics, and Calculus I and II. Cadets also had to take a wide variety of mandatory courses such as poetry, philosophy, psychology, international relations, English, leadership, political science, world and military history, environmental science, computer science, economics, chemistry, a foreign language, law, exercise physiology, swimming, gymnastics, wrestling, boxing for men, and self-defense for women.

I have met some people who are surprised to learn I received such an excellent education at West Point. I have even met some peace activists who assumed the only things West Point taught me was how to kill people and blindly follow orders. It did not surprise me to hear them say this, because even I will admit that West Point's focus on engineering and liberal arts at first sounds really odd. After all, when most people hear the words "military academy," engineering and liberal arts are among the last things that usually come to mind.

Although West Point never fully became the scientific institution its first superintendent, Jonathan Williams, hoped it would be, the spirit of scientific inquiry lives on at the academy and helped shape my growth as a human being. This is reflected in my writing, because in all of my books I question the most basic assumptions about war, peace, and human nature. By questioning these assumptions I have been able to dispel the myths of war. And although many of MacArthur's changes to West Point took a long time to be implemented, West Point gave me many tools that help me wage peace, such as public speaking skills, leadership training, a warrior ethos that encourages me to serve others, a deeper understanding of human behavior, and a well-rounded and excellent education.

MacArthur wanted military officers to be warrior philosophers and soldier scholars. The idea that warriors should be highly educated is not new, but a timeless warrior principle. Japan's *Code of the Samurai* states: "If you are [a warrior] in public service, when off duty you do not simply lounge around; you read, practice calligraphy, contemplate ancient stories or ancient warrior codes. Whether you are walking, standing still, sitting down, or reclining, in your conduct and manner you carry yourself in a way that exemplifies a genuine warrior."[7]

Nakae Toju, a seventeenth-century Japanese philosopher who wrote extensively about the warrior code, explained the practical reasons soldiers should be educated in a wide variety of subjects. According to Toju, a general who masters military science may win battles, but if he is not educated in culture and ethics he may become a threat to his own people:

> Warriorhood without culture is like the shade of autumn and winter without the sun of spring and summer . . . Literature, music, manners, writing, and mathematics, as arts, are outgrowths of the virtue of culture . . . Uniting culture and warriorhood . . . you are a genuine cultured warrior . . . One who has mastered cultural and martial arts on the basis of fundamental humaneness and justice is a noble man of many talents . . . People born with the capacity to be great generals may master military science and achieve military successes without the polish of [ethical]

psychology, but without that quality of character they get deluded by their ability and come to like killing. Since they act unjustly and immorally, the populace sorrows, having been injured by their poison.[8]

Why did MacArthur make radical changes to West Point that reflected timeless warrior ideals? The reasons were based largely on his own life experience. Graduating from West Point in 1903 as valedictorian and the highest-ranking cadet in his class, he had an insider's perspective on how West Point could be improved. He later served in World War I, where he received six silver stars and a distinguished service cross, becoming the most decorated American officer during the war.[9] While serving in World War I he learned many lessons that shaped the rest of his life.

One lesson MacArthur learned was that military leaders who bully and demean their soldiers create an unstable unit, and the most effective leaders treat their soldiers with empathy, fairness, and respect. He explained, "There were officers overseas shot in the back by their own men simply because they had been brought up with the mistaken idea that bullying was leadership."[10] As a consequence, when he became West Point's superintendent in 1919 he was determined to end hazing, a practice where higher ranking cadets bully and demean lower ranking cadets. Hazing has spread beyond the military and is common in many fraternities around America today, but MacArthur realized hazing teaches people to be disrespectful, ineffective, and dangerous leaders.

Alexander the Great, Gandhi the Greater

In this book I want to debunk stereotypes. A common stereotype is that effective military leadership is based on cruelty and that army leaders must control their subordinates by abusing them. When I give talks around the country I often ask the audience, "Since combat is a terrifying experience and most people would rather run away than suffer a violent and painful death, what is the most reliable way for military commanders to get their soldiers to fight?" The most common answer I hear is, "Threaten to execute the soldiers if they run away."

But death threats are actually one of the least reliable ways to get soldiers to fight, and soldiers are far more likely to risk their lives on the battlefield if their leaders instead treat them with compassion and respect. Although many armies throughout history have used death threats to keep their soldiers from retreating, it has usually been as a last resort. From a practical perspective, when military commanders kill their own men they end up with fewer soldiers to fight the enemy with.

Many people incorrectly assume that effective military leaders must bully, threaten, and demean their soldiers to keep them in line, but this could not be further from the truth. In chapters 2 and 4 of *Peaceful Revolution* I thoroughly explain why the most effective military leaders treat their soldiers with empathy, respect, and fairness. The idea that soldiers function best when their leaders treat them well is a fact of human nature; it is true in every culture and time period. In *The Art of War*, Sun Tzu says, "Regard your soldiers as your children, and they will follow you into the deepest valleys; look upon them as your own beloved sons, and they will stand by you even unto death."[11]

According to Liu Ji, a fourteenth-century Chinese military strategist, "What makes soldiers in battle prefer to charge ahead rather than retreat even for survival is the benevolence of the military leadership. When the soldiers know their leaders care for them as they care for their own children, then the soldiers love their leaders as they do their own fathers. This makes them willing to die in battle."[12]

In the U.S. Army the highest-ranking soldiers are supposed to eat last so the lowest ranking can eat first. The highest-ranking soldiers are also expected to lead by example, put the well-being of their subordinates above their own, and sacrifice for those under their command. These ideals of warrior leadership are timeless. Liu Ji* explains how the Chinese general Wu Qi demonstrated these ideals in the fifth-century BC: "During the Warring States era, when the Wei general Wu Qi was military governor of West River, he wore the same clothes and ate the same food as the lowest of his soldiers.

---

* Liu Ji also discusses fear tactics for making soldiers fight, such as publically executing those who don't obey orders and killing one's own soldiers if they try to flee during the battle. These "negative" techniques that rely on threats have been used in armies throughout history as a last resort, but they are not as effective as "positive" techniques that persuade soldiers to fight for a cause they believe in, because it is very inefficient to have an army killing itself. As a general you want all of your army's energy focused on fighting the other side. Also, the immediate fear of a massive army running toward you can be greater than the fear of possible punishment for retreating.

He did not use a mat to sit on, and he did not ride when traveling. He personally carried his own bundle of provisions and shared the toil and hardships of the soldiers."[13]

Zhuge Liang, born in AD 181 and widely regarded as one of China's most brilliant generals, added:

> Good generals of ancient times took care of their people as one might take care of a beloved child. When there was difficulty they would face it first themselves . . . They would tearfully console the wounded and sorrowfully mourn the dead. They would sacrifice themselves to feed the hungry and remove their own garments to clothe the cold. They honored the wise and provided for their living; they rewarded and encouraged the brave. If generals can be like this, they can take over anywhere they go . . .
>
> According to the code of generalship, generals do not say they are thirsty before the soldiers have drawn from the well; generals do not say they are hungry before the soldiers' food is cooked; generals do not say they are cold before the soldiers' fires are kindled; generals do not say they are hot before the soldiers' canopies are drawn . . . They do as everyone does . . . Do not look down on others because of your own elevated rank . . . Do not sit down before the soldiers sit; do not eat before the soldiers eat. Bear the same cold and heat the soldiers do; share their toil as well as their ease. Experience sweetness and bitterness just as the soldiers do; take the same risks that they do. Then the soldiers will exert themselves to the utmost.[14]

Warrior leaders around the world have embodied these ideals, especially in ancient history. However, in recent times there have been many politicians who avoided military service like it was the plague, but became the most zealous pro-war advocates when they gained political power, sending young people to die in battles overseas. This has caused many peace activists to describe war as the old sending the young to die. This is largely true today, but in ancient wars it was not the case, because the rulers often fought in battles and it was not uncommon for them to die in combat. The leaders of Greek city-states frequently risked their lives on the front lines in war. For example, Spartan men served in the military until age sixty, and many Spartan kings died in battle, such as Areus I, Archidamus III, Cleombrotus I, Leonidas, and Agis III.

The Greek historian Diodorus described the death of the Spartan king Agis III, who ordered his Spartan soldiers to retreat and then sacrificed himself to allow their escape:

> [Agis] had fought gloriously [at a battle near Megalopolis] and fell with many frontal wounds. As he was being carried by his soldiers back to Sparta, he found himself surrounded by the enemy. Despairing of his own life, he ordered the rest to make their escape with all speed and to save themselves for the service of their country, but he himself armed and rising to his knees defended himself, killed some of the enemy and was himself slain by a javelin cast; he had reigned nine years.[15]

Furthermore, politicians from Greek city-states such as Athens and Thebes also fought on the front lines. The prominent Athenian politician Themistocles led the Athenian navy toward victory when it defended Greece against an invading Persian fleet in 480 BC at the Battle of Salamis. When the Persians had tried to invade Greece ten years earlier at the Battle of Marathon, Themistocles and Aristides (another prominent Athenian politician) fought at the most dangerous point on the battlefield. The Greek historian Plutarch said, "In the battle [of Marathon] the Athenian center was the hardest pressed . . . There, then, Themistocles and Aristides fought brilliantly, ranged side by side."[16]

Epaminondas was a Theban statesman who fought on the front lines at the height of his political power. It would be unimaginable for a leading American politician to do this today, especially in an era when civic and military life are no longer intertwined. Epaminondas's willingness to risk his life to protect others was demonstrated in his youth, when he and other Thebans fought with the Spartans against the Arcadians. A young man who had not yet become a leader of his nation, he saved the life of his wounded friend Pelopidas during the battle. Plutarch recounts:

> Pelopidas, after receiving seven wounds in front, sank down upon a great heap of friends and enemies who lay dead together; but Epaminondas, although he thought him lifeless, stood forth to defend his body . . . and fought desperately, single-handed against many, determined to die rather than leave Pelopidas lying there. And now he too was in a sorry plight, having been wounded in the breast with a spear and in the arm with a sword, when Agesipolis the Spartan king came to his aid from the other wing, and when all hope was lost, saved them both.[17]

When the Spartans tried to invade Thebes, Epaminondas—who was now in his late forties and one of the most powerful politicians in Thebes—personally led an army that defeated the Spartans at the Battle of Leuctra. Even though the Spartan army outnumbered the Thebans, Epaminondas and his soldiers forced the Spartans to retreat. At the age of fifty-six, Epaminondas defeated the Spartans a second time at the Battle of Mantinea in 362 BC, again forcing them to retreat.

During the Battle of Mantinea, when Epaminondas saw his soldiers struggling against the mighty Spartans, he realized he had to take action. The Greek historian Diodorus described what happened:

> After the battle had continued long, and none were able to judge who would be the conquerors, Epaminondas resolved to decide the matter, with the hazard of his own life. To that end taking a choice band of the most able men he had with him, and, drawing them up in close order, he forthwith charged at the head of them, and was the first that cast his javelin, and killed the [Spartan] general, and then broke into the midst of his enemies . . . The fame of Epaminondas, and the strength of that body he then had

with him, struck such a terror into the [Spartans], that they turned their backs, and began to make way.[18]

What happened next reveals how ferociously soldiers will fight to protect a commander they love and respect. As Epaminondas and his soldiers pursued the retreating Spartans, he was seriously wounded when a javelin struck him in the chest. The Spartans tried to capture him, but the Theban soldiers fought furiously to protect him, again forcing the Spartans to retreat. The Thebans pulled Epaminondas to safety, and the fifty-six-year-old politician died from his chest wound soon after the battle ended.

Perhaps the most striking example of a ruler fighting on the front lines was Alexander the Great, a Macedonian king born in 356 BC who was wounded eight times in combat. He embodied all the leadership ideals listed in the previous quotes from Sun Tzu, Liu Ji, and Zhuge Liang. As a young king prior to his conquest of Persia, Alexander's leadership style reflected West Point's leadership philosophy of sacrificing for one's subordinates, treating them with respect, and leading by example.

In his book *Leadership: The Warrior's Art*, Colonel Christopher Kolenda, a West Point graduate and former professor at the academy, describes Alexander's willingness to risk his life for his soldiers: "Alexander's genius on the battlefield was matched by his personal courage. He was always at the most dangerous point on the battlefield, showing a disregard for his own personal safety and inspiring, through the force of personal example, the same bravery in his soldiers. As [historian Nicholas] Hammond observes, Alexander's courage 'added a special dimension to his power of leadership; for he was the first to do whatever he asked his men to do.'"[19]

Alexander led by example in many ways. During the siege of a Mallian town during the winter of 326–325 BC, the Macedonian soldiers were afraid to scale the city walls where Mallian soldiers waited on the other side. So Alexander grabbed a ladder and climbed the wall with a handful of bodyguards trailing behind him. This gave his soldiers the courage to follow his example. But as they rushed forward to climb the ladders, Alexander and his bodyguards leapt down from the wall and began fighting the Mallians alone. During the fight Alexander was nearly killed when an arrow struck him in the chest.[20]

Military historian J. F. C. Fuller says, "According to Plutarch, this was Alexander's eighth and most dangerous wound. The other seven he lists as follows: In the Illyrian campaign he was wounded in the head by a stone and suffered a neck injury from a cudgel; at the Granicus a head wound from a dagger; at Issus a sword wound in the thigh; at Gaza an arrow wound in the ankle and a dislocated shoulder; at Maracanda a leg bone was split by an arrow; among the Aspasians an arrow wound in the shoulder; and among the Gandridae an arrow wound in the leg."[21]

But as Mahatma Gandhi, Martin Luther King Jr., and countless other peace activists have demonstrated, some of the most courageous acts occur off the battlefield. The same was true of Alexander. Colonel Kolenda explains:

> While Alexander's battlefield exploits were remarkable, two of his finest acts of personal courage occurred away from the battlefield. In August 333 B.C. Alexander fell ill after bathing in a cold spring near Mount Tarsus, so Alexander's physician and long-time friend, Philip, had prepared a purge for the king. As Alexander was about to drink, he received a letter from [his general] Parmenion warning that Philip might try to poison him. According to [the historian] Arrian, Alexander read the letter and while drinking the purge, handed the letter over to Philip. Through this act "Alexander showed Philip that as his friend he trusted him . . . that he was resolute in refusing to suspect his friends and steadfast in the face of death."
>
> Perhaps Alexander's most celebrated act of personal courage occurred during the grueling march through the Gedrosian Desert in October 325 B.C. . . . The march took an enormous toll on his army and the mass of camp followers that accompanied him. Water was a precious commodity, and at one point the supply of it was nearly exhausted. Some of Alexander's soldiers had found a small spring of water and gathered it into a helmet which they offered to the King. According to Arrian, Alexander "took it and thanked them, but then poured it out in the sight

of everyone; and at this action the army was so much heartened that you would have guessed that all had drunk what Alexander had poured away." Alexander never asked his men to do what he himself was unwilling to do, nor did he allow himself material goods which his soldiers were denied.

Another hallmark of Alexander's leadership was the care he showed for his soldiers. Alexander no doubt realized that his success was dependent upon the goodwill and spirit of his men, but it would be incorrect to regard this caring as merely a ploy for future self-aggrandizement. Soldiers, then as now, can spot a hypocrite fairly quickly and will rarely follow one. This was especially true in the Macedonian army which prided itself on a culture of respect between leader and led. Alexander's care for his soldiers was genuine and it motivated his entire army. After his first great battle with the Persians at Granicus (334 B.C.), Alexander, according to Arrian, "took great care of the wounded, visiting each man himself, examining their wounds, asking how they were received, and allowing them to recount and boast of their exploits." After taking Halicarnassus that same year, Alexander decided to send home his recently married soldiers so they could spend time with their new families in Macedonia over the winter. Arrian tells us that Alexander gained as much popularity by this act among the Macedonians as by any other . . .

After the battle [of Issus], despite a sword wound in his thigh, Alexander again went around to see the wounded. He then collected all of the dead and gave them a splendid military funeral . . . Through his care of the wounded and dead, Alexander demonstrated a genuine regard for his soldiers, and they in turn trusted him to make his plans for battles and campaigns which assured their victory with a minimum loss of life.[22]

Alexander demonstrated many of the positive leadership qualities West Point taught me, but after he conquered Persia he exhibited many characteristics of bad leadership. Prior to his conquest of Persia, Alexander was renowned for treating his soldiers with empathy, fairness, and respect. During this time his soldiers never mutinied or attempted to kill him, and were willing to die for him. But after he conquered Persia he started acting like a bully and tyrant, behaving in ways his soldiers found dangerous and disrespectful. As a result his soldiers mutinied and conspired to overthrow him.

How did Alexander get Greeks and Macedonians to support his invasion of Persia? Seeking to expand its empire, Persia twice attempted to conquer Greece and failed. Consequently, many Greeks and Macedonians wanted to invade Persia to protect the Greek homeland from future invasions and to punish the Persians for destroying Greek cities and holy sites. Alexander channeled their desire toward a military campaign.

When Alexander invaded Persia he tried to destroy the Persian army while winning over the common people. To show his respect for their culture he even started to dress like them. To understand how strange Alexander's soldiers found it when he started wearing Persian clothing, imagine if President Lyndon Johnson had attempted to win over the Vietnamese by wearing their traditional clothing during the Vietnam War, or if President George W. Bush had tried to win over the Iraqis by wearing traditional Muslim clothing. Many of Alexander's soldiers were far more troubled by other Persian customs he adopted, such as his increasingly despotic leadership style and extravagant displays of wealth in his royal court. They were also disturbed when they saw Persians treating him like a god. Colonel Kolenda explains:

> While the aim of Alexander's tactics was to win great battles, the aim of his strategy was to pacify and not antagonize his enemy, thereby hoping to limit the number of battles he had to fight. According to [the historian] Justin, when "marching forward in quest of the enemy, he kept the soldiers from ravaging Asia, telling them that they ought to spare their own property, and not destroy what they came to possess." Alexander wished to achieve a bloodless conquest as much as possible, and thus drew a distinction

between the Persian army and the Persian people: his aim was to defeat the former and win over the latter . . .

To bridge the gap between the [Greeks] and Persians, Alexander began to adopt Persian customs and dress. Persian flatterers were welcomed into the court and Alexander's personal attire reflected a mixture of Macedonian and Persian. With this change in appearance, according to Arrian, came a change in Alexander's conduct. "Alexander was carried away into imitation of Median and Persian opulence and of the custom of barbarian kings not to countenance equality with subjects in their daily lives."

These developments were alarming to the Macedonians who began to resent the king's growing "orientalism." Rifts began to grow between the "new" Alexander and the "old" Macedonians . . . The problem came to a head in the autumn of 328 B.C., when a drunken argument developed between Alexander and Cleitus [an officer who had saved Alexander's life at the Battle of the Granicus] at an evening banquet. Cleitus, alienated by the increasing trend toward oriental despotism at the court, gave expression to the general unrest by condemning the eastern practices of Alexander and claiming that the king's lust for glory was becoming parasitical. Outraged, Alexander ran Cleitus through with a spear in what Balsdon regards as a typical act of a story-book tyrant.

Deeply troubled by this murder, Alexander reportedly brooded in sorrow for three days. Anaxarchus, one of the court flatterers, visited Alexander and informed him that as all acts of the gods were considered just, so all the acts of the great king should be held as just. Whether Alexander actually believed this specious line of argument is difficult to tell . . .

By 330 B.C. the breakdown of trust between Alexander and his officers was rapidly becoming apparent, ultimately setting the stage for Alexander's only "defeat" at the

Hyphasis and the subsequent mutiny at Opis . . . The first of these problems was an attempt on Alexander's life, the alleged "Philotas plot" of 330 B.C. The conspiracy failed, resulting in the execution of Philotas, the commander of the Companion Cavalry, and the assassination of his father, Parmenion. To prevent a recurrence, the increasingly despotic Alexander reorganized the command of his army by splitting up the leadership of the Companion Cavalry into two parts so no one single man would have the command and loyalty of such a large and potent force . . .

The strategy worked for a time among the soldiers, but the next conspiracy came from an unlikely source: the sons of the Macedonian nobles who traveled with Alexander's entourage . . . These "Pages" were afforded the honor of accompanying Alexander on hunting expeditions and guarding the king's tent at night. Apparently during one such hunting expedition, one of the pages, Hermolaus, violated protocol by killing the first boar before Alexander had a chance to do so. This apparently outraged the king who ordered the young page to be beaten in the presence of his peers.

This precipitated a plot by Hermolaus and some of the pages (327 B.C.) to murder the king at night when it was their turn to guard his tent. The plot, which was foiled when Alexander failed to return to the tent after yet another night of feasting and drinking, was revealed to Alexander the next day. In confessing his guilt Hermolaus claimed that "no free man could longer endure Alexander's hubris" and inveighed against the unjust deaths of Philotas and Parmenion, the drunken murder of Cleitus . . . and Alexander's excessive drinking and strange sleeping habits. Hermolaus claimed he could bear it no more and sought to liberate himself and the other Macedonians. Significantly, this plot was not about power but about concerns over Alexander's *arete*: his arrogance, orientalism, and alleged barbarism. Hermolaus evidently saw his act as a sacrifice for freedom for himself and the Macedonians in the face of a tyrant. Hermolaus and his fellow conspirators no longer believed in Alexander's character or vision and were probably not alone in this belief (Hermolaus and the other conspirators were stoned to death) . . .

When analyzing the leadership of Alexander, what rapidly becomes apparent is the manner in which the convergence and divergence of fundamental, core interests help shape the relationship between leader and led. The young Alexander was never troubled by conspiracy and revolt. While there were certainly many differences of opinion over plans and policies, both military and administrative, between the king and his generals and the Greek allies, Alexander was generally able to persuade them to believe in the direction he wanted to pursue. Their interests in the early years were seemingly convergent. They wished to avenge the sacrilege of [the Persian King] Xerxes and eliminate the perceived threat posed by the Persian empire to the Greek world . . . While Alexander's trustworthiness as a battlefield commander was unquestionable, his trustworthiness as a king in the eyes of his followers became suspect . . . For this reason they revolted at the Hyphasis and again at Opis and finally rejected his vision altogether after his death.[23]

Why am I discussing a conqueror such as Alexander the Great in a book about waging peace? Because he is the reason I became so fascinated with Gandhi. When I first began reading about Gandhi on my own at West Point, I was amazed by how much he resembled an ideal military leader. I thought, "Here is a person who has all of Alexander's good qualities as a leader, but lacks his most destructive vices." As a young general Alexander led by example, put the well-being of his soldiers above his own, and treated them with respect and compassion.

Gandhi also led this way, but he did not limit it to his followers. Unlike Alexander, who was ruthless at times toward his enemies, Gandhi behaved respectfully and compassionately toward all human beings. Many people attach the word "great" to Alexander's name because of his courage, leadership ability, strategic genius, and impact on the world. But in all the ways someone could argue that Alexander was great, this book will show that Gandhi was greater.

Sergeant Major Gandhi

As a war veteran, Gandhi was not a stranger to the military. He served in the British army as a medic during the Boer War in 1899 and Second Zulu War in 1906, holding the rank of sergeant major (the same rank as my father). During the Boer War he was also awarded the War Medal by the British army for his courage in retrieving the wounded on the front lines. The British were known for their racism toward the Indians, but Gandhi saw how strong bonds of affection among soldiers in a military unit caused camaraderie to replace racism. During Gandhi's war service we can also witness him treating the enemy with the same compassion an ideal general would treat his own soldiers, and we can see the beginning of his mission to change the world. In the book *Gandhi: The Man, His People, and the Empire*, Gandhi's grandson and biographer Rajmohan Gandhi explains:

> [Gandhi and his Indian stretcher bearers were] requested by General Buller . . . to fetch the wounded from the front [lines]. On some days Gandhi and his fellows on the corps carried the [British] wounded on stretchers for 20 miles or more; among those carried was General Woodgate. Camaraderie quickly replaced color prejudice. On a hot and exhausting day, Gandhi and some other Indians marched toward Chievely Camp, where Lieutenant Roberts, son of Lord Roberts, had received a mortal wound. When, trudging together, thirsty Indians and whites eventually reached a tiny brook, *the Indians*

asked the whites to drink first, while the whites asked the Indians to do the same [emphasis added] . . .

[During the Zulu rebellion against the British] Gandhi and his colleagues were on active service in the Zulu terrain for four weeks in June-July 1906, carrying on stretchers Zulu friendlies mistakenly shot by British soldiers and nursing them as well as Zulu suspects whose wounds received from British lashes had festered for days . . . But Gandhi quickly saw that the military campaign supported by him was only a man-hunt. Whatever his head may have advised, his heart was with the unfortunate Zulus, and "every morning" he was assailed by bitter qualms as he heard "rifles exploding like crackers in innocent hamlets."

His conscience was somewhat eased by the fact that he and his corps nursed innocent Zulus who would otherwise not have been cared for. Dr. Savage, the "very humane" doctor in charge of the ambulance, had told him that white nurses were not willing to attend to the wounds of the Zulus. In fact, white soldiers tried to dissuade the Indians from doing so. When the Indians did not heed them, the [British] soldiers "poured unspeakable abuse on the Zulus." . . . With or without the wounded, Gandhi and his colleagues marched long distances, at times 40 miles a day. In his treks "through these solemn solitudes," Gandhi "often fell into deep thought." The horrors of war were "brought home" to him with "vividness," and Gandhi's conscience pricked him for being on the side of those who had practiced great brutality . . .

In the Zulu country Gandhi sensed that he himself would fight well and on a large canvas. "A mission . . . came to me in 1906 [during the Zulu rebellion], namely, to spread truth and non-violence among mankind in the place of violence and falsehood in all walks of life," he would say in 1942. He may not have used these exact words in 1906, but the sense of a calling was present . . . Concluding justly that "the turning point in Gandhi's personal life came in 1906" in Zululand, Jonathan Schell notes equally correctly that whereas in both East and West, holy vows have usually been accompanied by a withdrawal from the world and from politics, "Gandhi proceeded in exactly the opposite direction." His vows had freed him not from, but for, action.[24]

I have met countless people who see Gandhi as a naive idealist in a loincloth, but studying leadership at West Point allowed me to realize how impressive Gandhi truly was. West Point taught me how to recognize a great leader when I saw one, and Gandhi as a leader was greater than Alexander. As the leader of a nonviolent campaign to remove British colonialism from India, Gandhi emulated the qualities of an ideal general, but did not draw a distinction between his followers and his opponents. He treated everyone with empathy, fairness, and respect.

At first glance Gandhi might seem naive for treating those who wanted to destroy him not as foes but as friends and potential allies, but this humane approach actually demonstrates his strategic genius. Later in this book I will explain how studying military strategy at West Point convinced me that Gandhi was one of the most brilliant strategists who ever lived. I hope someday West Point will utilize Gandhi as an example to teach leadership and strategy.

Why Trust Matters

So far in this book I have discussed timeless military leadership principles such as leading by example, sacrificing for one's subordinates, putting their well-being above your own, and treating even the lowest ranking soldiers with empathy, fairness, and respect. By exploring these leadership principles more deeply, we can better understand human nature, the power of waging peace, and why trust is so crucial for the well-being of any human community. In order to explore these leadership principles more deeply, however, I will discuss how they can be found in an unlikely and surprising place: mercenary armies.

To show how universal and effective these leadership principles are, even some commanders of mercenary armies have behaved in ways that resembled Gandhi and ideal generals. When people hear the word "mercenary" today, they tend to think of soldiers who fight only because of greed. But this is an oversimplistic stereotype, because many mercenaries throughout history fought for a variety of reasons, of which money was only one. For example, when Alexander and his Greek and Macedonian soldiers fought against the Persians at the Battle of the Granicus, around five thousand Greek mercenaries fought with the Persians. Although the Persians paid them, the Greek mercenaries also had deeper motivations. Alexander's father, King Philip II of Macedonia, had conquered the Greeks by defeating them at the Battle of Chaeronea. Accordingly, many of the Greek mercenaries saw Alexander as a tyrant and wanted to free Greece from Macedonian rule.[25]

Some mercenaries fought because of greed alone, but many also fought due to lack of job opportunities, the need for food, and the hope of improving their station in life. Many mercenaries in the ancient world were also exiles trying to fulfill basic needs such as employment. In his book *Greek Mercenaries*, historian Matthew Trundle tells us, "Poorer men were more likely to seek service for a wage and for sustenance. Naturally the commanders, the aristocrats of mercenary service, came into service for more noble and honorable reasons and on account of their international associations with the aristocrats of other states . . . Many mercenaries had been exiled by their communities. Exiles were a problem of the fourth century [BC]. That century saw an increase in exilings . . . With exile came loss of property at home and loss of any status."[26]

The two most famous commanders of mercenary armies in military history were Hannibal, a North African general from Carthage who tried to conquer the Roman Republic, and Xenophon, a Greek general who was a student of Socrates. Hannibal invaded the Roman Republic primarily to break its growing power, and also to avenge the destruction Rome had caused to his homeland during the First Punic War. He is widely regarded as the most brilliant general who ever lived, but what kind of leader was he? It is difficult to tell, because most of what we know about Hannibal comes from historians such as Livy, who was born in Roman Italy, and Polybius, a Greek who later resided in Rome. Their accounts of Hannibal are biased, because most Romans hated Hannibal more than most Americans hated Osama bin Laden. To understand why the Romans hated Hannibal so much, imagine if instead of being attacked on a single bloody day during September 11, a foreign army had landed on United States soil and terrorized the American people for sixteen years. That is what Hannibal did to the Romans.

Hannibal maneuvered his army throughout Italy for about a decade and a half (218–203 BC). He hired mercenaries from many regions where the Romans had made enemies, including Spain, Gaul (France), and North Africa. Even though the Romans had a highly trained and well-equipped military that greatly outnumbered Hannibal's small mercenary force, they could not defeat him in a decisive battle on the Italian peninsula. To get him to leave Italy, the Romans had to invade his country of Carthage, forcing him to return to North Africa to protect his homeland. Hannibal was an underdog who kept a mercenary army in hostile enemy territory for sixteen years, and there is no recorded instance of his men ever revolting against him. One reason was because he was very skilled at keeping his soldiers alive in battle, but what were some of the other reasons? The Roman historian Livy explains how Hannibal became the commander of the army after his brother-in-law Hasdrubal was assassinated:

> Hannibal was sent to Spain where he won the hearts of the entire army immediately upon his arrival . . . There was no other officer under whom the [common soldier] had more confidence and enterprise . . .[27] There was no doubt about who would succeed Hasdrubal [after his death]. The soldiers' choice came first—the young Hannibal had been immediately carried into the general's tent where the men noisily and unanimously acclaimed him as commander—and the endorsement of the commons followed . . .
>
> Hannibal was possessed of enormous daring in facing dangers, and enormous resourcefulness when in the midst of those dangers. He could be physically exhausted or mentally cowed by no hardship. He had the ability to withstand

heat and cold alike; his eating and drinking depended on the requirements of nature, not pleasure. His times for being awake and asleep were not determined by day or night. Only the time which he had left from discharging his duties was given to sleep, and it was not brought on by a soft bed or silence . . . Many often observed him lying on the ground, amidst the sentry-posts and pickets [common soldiers], wrapped in a soldier's cloak. His dress was no better than that of his comrades . . . On horse or foot he was by far the best soldier; the first to enter battle, he was the last to leave once battle was joined.[28]

Another famous mercenary commander was Xenophon, the first westerner to write extensively about the art of leadership. Born in 430 BC, nearly a century before Alexander the Great, he was a Greek who fought for the Persian prince Cyrus the Younger against Cyrus's older brother King Antaxerxes II of Persia. When Cyrus was killed by a spear at the Battle of Cunaxa, the Greek mercenaries—known as the "Ten Thousand"—became stranded deep within hostile territory. The mercenaries elected Xenophon to be one of the generals to lead them on the dangerous path back to Greece. David Sears, a historian who served as a lieutenant commander in the U.S. Navy, describes how Xenophon created a foundation of trust between him and his soldiers:

[Historian Godfrey Hutchinson said,] "One of the strongest beliefs held by Xenophon was that a commander must inculcate loyalty in his men." Loyalty, however, does not come easily. A leader must create a foundation of trust, a prerequisite for loyalty, through his actions . . . One's followers expect that their leadership will always act in their best interest. Trust, is not only a keystone to loyalty, but is also the bedrock of cooperation . . .

Xenophon placed a high priority on meeting his follower's needs in order to achieve the goal of high morale. For instance, while trapped in a blizzard in the mountains of Western Armenia, Xenophon personally visited each of his men to ensure that they were taking necessary precautions against the cold . . . Rather than continue on to the nearest village with the rest of the commanders, Xenophon chose to remain behind with his soldiers of the rearguard who were unable to move. He denied himself food, warmth and comfort that could rightfully have been his, to ensure that in the morning his men were out of danger and able to continue the journey.

[According to Godfrey Hutchinson] Xenophon perceived "the link between general and soldier [as] an unspoken contract of care." He would ensure that his men were provided for, and in return he would receive their loyalty and obedience. So long as a leader kept the interests of his men above his own he would remain the leader . . . His conviction was that a leader was obligated, first and foremost, to always place the interests of his men first . . .

The records of Xenophon give us many examples of his self-subordination. He was always the last to bed down and the last to eat. On one exceptionally cold night in the mountains of the Carduchians, while the other commanders and generals slept in the comfort of a local village, Xenophon stayed back with his men and "bivouacked without fire or food." In matters of pay, the driving incentive of the mercenary army, Xenophon hadn't "even been given what some of the company commanders [had] received, let alone the other generals." At one point, Xenophon even turned down being elected to supreme commander because he felt that it was not in the best interest of his men . . . In every case of self-subordination, his payback was more respect and loyalty from his men. [29]

Do military commanders treat their soldiers with care and compassion in a calculated way, simply to receive "payback" in the form of more loyalty? Or is their compassion genuine? Some military commanders who treat their soldiers well are certainly calculating and insincere, but Jonathan Shay explains how war causes many soldiers to genuinely treat their comrades with nurturing, compassion, and other "maternal" instincts:

> Combat calls forth a passion of care among men who fight beside each other that is comparable to the earliest and most deeply felt family relationships . . . Our culture insists upon the gender association of nurturance and compassion as maternal, whereas the ancient Greek culture understood *philia* to be equally available to both genders. Another [Vietnam] veteran described his role in explicitly maternal terms: "I became the mother hen . . . I was watching the other five guys like they was my children." . . . The terror and privation of combat bonds men in a passion of care that the word *brother* only partly captures. Men become mothers to one another in combat.[30]

Many people do not realize male soldiers can have maternal instincts in war, nor do they realize how dangerous mothers can be. A woman protecting her child, like soldiers defending their comrades, is one of the most dangerous creatures on the planet.

During an appearance on *The Oprah Winfrey Show*, Gavin de Becker told a story about a woman who was attacked by a man while she was getting into her car. He grabbed her legs and she started kicking. When he would not let go she gouged out both of his eyes with her car keys. He had made the mistake of attacking her when she had her four-year-old daughter in the back seat. Gavin de Becker said, "The reason I tell you this story, not to scare you at all, but to know that there's a reason men do not attack women who have their kids with them. Too damn dangerous. I asked her afterwards, 'Are you sorry about what happened to that man?' She said, 'You know what? He got into something really dangerous. He attacked me when I was with my little girl.'"[31]

Gandhi also noticed that the bonds of brotherly and maternal love between soldiers lead to bravery on the battlefield. He said, "War is an unmitigated evil. But it certainly does one good thing. It drives away fear and brings bravery to the surface."[32] As I explain in my other books, human beings have an instinctual fear of lethal violence, but the bonds of brotherly and maternal love between soldiers make them willing to die for each other. In my other books I also offer abundant evidence showing that human beings are not naturally violent, but I am certainly not saying we cannot become violent. When our loved ones are in danger, we might do whatever it takes to keep them safe, even if we must use violence as a dangerous last resort. And when people bully us to the point where we become desperate, we might do whatever is necessary to stop them.

Bullies usually target vulnerable people who cannot fight back. It is common to see several bullies attacking a smaller person, but I have never seen a lone person trying to bully several larger individuals who are carrying weapons. So you can imagine what might happen when a military commander tries to bully thousands of soldiers who are trained to kill. In *Peaceful Revolution* I describe three methods of getting people to accept being oppressed. Although these three methods work in a variety of situations, bullying trained killers who outnumber you, from a practical perspective, is usually not a wise thing to do. Furthermore, effective military units require strong bonds of trust between leader and led, similar to the bond between mother and child, because soldiers must place their most precious possession in their leader's hands—their very lives.

There are many ways of building trust within an army. When military commanders lead by example by never asking their soldiers to do what they are unwilling to do, soldiers are encouraged to trust their leaders with their lives. Leading by example is also important because military commanders can enforce strict discipline if they are not hypocritical and apply the same standards of strict discipline to themselves (Xenophon was very strict with his soldiers). Other ways of building trust include sacrificing for one's subordinates, putting their well-being above your own, and treating them with empathy, fairness, and respect. When trust breaks down between soldiers and their commanders, the results can be deadly. Alexander was not the first military commander whose soldiers revolted because they lost their trust in him, nor was he the last.

Most military commanders in history have fallen far short of these ideals. As I mentioned earlier, General MacArthur said, "There were officers overseas shot in the back by their own men simply because they had been brought up with the mistaken idea that bullying was leadership."[33] This also happened during the Vietnam War. Many American soldiers in Vietnam distrusted not only their military commanders, but also the politicians they believed were lying to them. In his book *Achilles in Vietnam*, Jonathan Shay says:

> Fragging is Vietnam slang for assassination of one's military superior . . . Among Vietnam combat veterans, however, fragging has been a widely acknowledged impulse. How many Vietnam combat veterans daydreamed of executing General Westmoreland, or the whole U.S. Congress, or Secretary of Defense McNamara, or Presidents Johnson and Nixon for the deaths and suffering of their friends? More to the point is the actual murders or attempted murders of officers and NCOs in Vietnam. Richard Holmes cites an estimate that 20 percent of American officers who died in Vietnam were assassinated by their own men. Richard Gabriel, who served twenty-two years in the U.S. Army, writes . . . "At least 1,013 documented killings of superiors or attempted killings . . . were reported [for the Vietnam War]."[34]

Regarding the hypocrisy of politicians who avoid military service in their youth but become zealous pro-war advocates when they gain political power, I have met veterans and even many peace activists who wish they could force these politicians to fight on the front lines. To many peace activists this would not be cruel, but simply fair.

I am certainly not advocating that we should meld political and military life as the ancient Greeks and Romans did. In *The End of War* I discuss why the military must be subservient to civilian authority. It would be extremely dangerous to live in a country where the politicians are also generals, because rulers are rarely like Cincinnatus. When Rome was attacked by invaders in 458 BC, the general Cincinnatus was plowing his farm when a government official informed him that he had been elected to serve as military dictator. Within sixteen days Cincinnatus not only defeated the invaders but gave up his authority, returning control of the government to the Roman people. After giving up absolute power, Cincinnatus went home to tend his farm. But for every figure in history like Cincinnatus there are many like Julius Caesar, who used his military service to hoard political power and overthrow the government.

Although it is extremely dangerous for a democracy to have politicians serving as generals like the ancient Greeks and Romans did, it is equally dangerous when the vast majority of national politicians and their immediate families are not required to make any sacrifices in war, because being immune to the risks of war makes them more likely to rush to war. When the Theban politician Epaminondas argued in favor of fighting the Spartans, at least people knew he was willing to be the first one to die.

Smedley Butler, a Marine general twice awarded the Medal of Honor, had firsthand experience about the dangers that result when people in a society are not required to risk anything in war. In his book *War Is a Racket*, published in 1935, he said:

> War is a racket . . . A racket is best described, I believe, as something that is not what it seems to the majority of people. Only a small "inside" group knows what it is about. It is conducted for the benefit of the very few, at the expense of the very many. Out of war a few people make huge fortunes . . . At least 21,000 new millionaires and billionaires were made in the United States during the [first] World War . . . How many of these war millionaires shouldered a rifle? How many of them dug a trench? How many of them knew what it meant to go hungry in a rat-infested dugout? How many of them spent sleepless, frightened nights, ducking shells and shrapnel and machine gun bullets? How many of them parried the bayonet thrust of an enemy? How many of them were wounded or killed in battle?[35]

As long as the vast majority of American politicians do not have to risk anything when our country goes to war, how can we truly trust them with such a critical decision that has the potential to end countless lives? When wealthy people are able to make vast profits from war, it gives us even more reason to not trust our politicians with the decision to go to war.

Trust is the key. What do West Point, General Douglas MacArthur, and Alexander the Great have in common with peace activists working toward world peace? What do Eastern military strategists such as Sun Tzu, Liu Ji, and Zhuge Liang have in common with Gandhi? And what do mercenary commanders such as Hannibal and Xenophon have in common with Martin Luther King Jr.? They all taught me that the foundation of every human community is trust. And respect, empathy, selflessness, and fairness are reliable ways of building trust. A solid foundation of trust can help any community become more effective, whether it is a community of activists, citizen-soldiers, mercenaries, the community of fifty states we call America, or our global human community.

Trust within a military unit is so important that General MacArthur instituted a formal honor code at West Point. The honor code states, "A cadet will not lie, cheat, steal, or tolerate those who do." The ideals of West Point, like the ideals of the peace movement, include honesty, respect, empathy, selflessness, and fairness. But unlike ruthless generals such as Alexander, Hannibal, and Xenophon, who harnessed these ideals to kill their enemies, Gandhi and King harnessed these ideals to win over their enemies. Instead of using these ideals to destroy an opponent's army on the battlefield, Gandhi and King used these ideals to destroy the ignorance, hatred, and misunderstandings that divide us as human beings.

At West Point I saw enormous power in the warrior ideals. But how could we channel these warrior ideals toward waging peace? Just as panning for gold allows people to separate gold from dirt, how could we separate the golden warrior ideals from the filth of war? As I studied Gandhi more deeply I was surprised to learn that he wondered the same thing. Gandhi scholar Peter Brock explains: "Gandhi showed here another trait that appears constantly in his later writings: his respect for the positive qualities war can bring out in men alongside the evil ones, for the heroism, comradeship and sense of duty it engenders among ordinary men . . . he would seek to create a technique that could preserve the virtues of the warrior while eliminating the negative aspects of warfare . . . [Gandhi believed people] must regain the martial qualities of the Kshatriyas [warriors] of old before qualifying to become true disciples of nonviolence."[36]

Gandhi called himself a "soldier of peace." Just as soldiers in war must be willing to die for a cause or their comrades, Gandhi said nonviolent activists must also be willing to die: "We should learn to dare danger and death . . . and acquire the capacity to endure all manner of hardships."[37] Martin Luther King Jr. said, "A man who won't die for something is not fit to live."[38] There aren't many professions where people must risk being killed by their fellow human beings. The profession of military service and the profession of waging peace are among the few.

Alexander and Hannibal led by example in combat, by being among the most daring and skilled soldiers on the battlefield. But Gandhi and King led by example in waging peace, by being among the most compassionate, understanding, and persuasive activists in their movements. Alexander and Hannibal inspired their armies by not surrendering to physical discomforts and hardships during their military campaigns, while Gandhi and King inspired others by not surrendering to cynicism and hopelessness during their campaigns of peace. Gandhi and King possessed other warrior ideals such as discipline, courage, determination, selflessness, strategic thinking, and a sense of duty. These warrior ideals create stronger people and greater trust within communities, but can they also create stronger citizens and greater trust within American society?

The U.S. military is unique, because although most conservatives greatly admire it as an organization, it possesses many ideals admired by liberals. Nicholas D. Kristof, an op-ed columnist for the *New York Times*, ponders how military ideals could benefit our society:

> You see, when our armed forces are not firing missiles, they live by an astonishingly liberal ethos—and it works. The military helped lead the way in racial desegregation, and even today it does more to provide equal opportunity to working-class families—especially to blacks—than just about any social program. It has been an escalator of social mobility in American society because it invests in soldiers and gives them skills and opportunities.

The United States armed forces knit together whites, blacks, Asians and Hispanics from diverse backgrounds, invests in their education and training, provides them with excellent health care and child care. And it does all this with minimal income gaps: A senior general earns about 10 times what a private makes, while, by my calculation, C.E.O.'s at major companies earn about 300 times as much as those cleaning their offices. That's right: the military ethos can sound pretty lefty.

"It's the purest application of socialism there is," Wesley Clark, the retired four-star general and former supreme allied commander of NATO forces in Europe, told me. And he was only partly joking. "It's a really fair system, and a lot of thought has been put into it, and people respond to it really well," he added. The country can learn from that sense of mission, he said, from that emphasis on long-term strategic thinking… And while the ethic of business is often "Gimme," the military inculcates an ideal of public service that runs deep.[39]

We cannot effectively wage peace when we believe in shallow stereotypes. So far in this chapter I have tried to shatter stereotypes and preconceptions by showing that the United States Military Academy at West Point is an engineering and liberal arts college, Gandhi shares similarities with generals, male soldiers share similarities with mothers, and the U.S. military shares similarities with socialism. One of the biggest stereotypes I must shatter is the myth that General Douglas MacArthur spent his entire life as a right-wing war hawk, when the truth is that the father of West Point wanted world peace.

The MacArthur Myth

As I mentioned in the previous chapter, most people in our society view Gandhi as a naive pacifist who fully rejected all uses of violence, but this

portrayal of Gandhi is a myth. In a similar way, I have met many people
who believe that General MacArthur spent his entire life as a right-wing war
hawk, but this portrayal of MacArthur is also a myth. MacArthur is one of
the last Americans that most peace activists would ever imagine as an advocate for peace, but what did the father of West Point really think about peace?
Kenneth P. O'Donnell, one of the most powerful members of President
Kennedy's White House staff, described Kennedy's impressions after his first
two meetings with MacArthur in 1961:

> President Kennedy first began to have doubts about
> our military effort in Vietnam in 1961 when both General
> Douglas MacArthur and General Charles de Gaulle
> warned him that the Asian mainland was no place to be
> fighting a non-nuclear land war. There was no end to Asi-
> atic manpower, MacArthur told the President, and even if
> we poured a million American infantry soldiers into that
> continent, we would still find ourselves outnumbered on
> every side . . .
>
> Later the President invited the general to the White
> House for lunch. They talked for almost three hours, ruin-
> ing the whole appointments schedule for that day [July
> 20]. I could not drag them apart. The President later gave
> us a complete rerun of MacArthur's remarks, expressing a
> warm admiration for this supposedly reactionary old sol-
> dier that astonished all of us. MacArthur was extremely
> critical of the military advice that the President had been
> getting from the Pentagon, blaming the military leaders
> of the previous 10 years, who, he said, had advanced the
> wrong young officers . . . MacArthur implored the Presi-
> dent to avoid a U.S. military build-up in Vietnam, or any
> other part of the Asian mainland, because he felt that the
> domino theory was ridiculous in a nuclear age. MacArthur
> went on to point out that there were domestic problems—
> the urban crisis, the ghettos, the economy—that should
> have far more priority than Vietnam.[40]

In 1964, several months after President Kennedy's assassination, President Johnson visited MacArthur at Walter Reed hospital (MacArthur died three weeks later at the age of eighty-four). Eric Goldman, a Princeton professor who served as special advisor for President Johnson from 1963 to 1966, described what happened: "[President Johnson] told an almost incredible story about his last visit to see General Douglas A. MacArthur in Walter Reed Hospital. The aged warrior might be a world-wide symbol of American belligerence in the Far East but as LBJ repeated the conversation, the general had counseled him, 'Son, don't get into a land war in Asia.'"[41]

As a veteran of the most destructive wars in history, MacArthur had many reasons to dislike war. During a speech he gave at West Point in 1962, he said, "The Soldier above all other people prays for peace, for he must suffer and bear the deepest wounds and scars of war."[42] Immediately after World War I, he was worried another major war would happen not only in Europe, but also in Asia. Decades before his predictions came true, he advocated strengthening America's military so we would be prepared to defend ourselves and other nations. Like many World War II veterans, MacArthur truly believed Nazi Germany and imperial Japan had to be stopped. But after World War II and the Korean War, he realized war itself, rather than a specific country, poses the greatest threat to America and humanity as a whole.

During the Cold War MacArthur realized most people in America and the Soviet Union truly wanted peace, but the propaganda of political leaders made each side believe the other was evil. In a 1952 speech he said, "I say the peace-loving peoples of all of the nations, for the masses behind the Iron Curtain just as do the masses of the free world long for real peace. It is political leaders who fail this great concept."[43] He gave many more speeches that discussed the need to abolish war, and his words were reported in newspapers around the country. At the beginning of this book I included an excerpt from a speech he gave in 1955, and *Peaceful Revolution* begins with an excerpt from a 1961 speech.

As the supreme commander of Allied Forces in the Southwest Pacific Area during World War II, MacArthur even thought the use of atomic bombs in Japan was unnecessary. He later said:

Japan realized defeat was inevitable as early as September of 1944 when we initiated the recapture and liberation of the Philippines. This enabled us to interdict by sea and air her essential supplies, from the South, of oil, rubber, nickel, tin and other war materials. This blockade,* together with her air vulnerability, made her ultimate destruction a certainty. She was anxious for peace and the Pacific War should have ended several months before it did. In my opinion there was a monumental failure of statescraft on the part of the Allies in not consummating this end. My own professional views as to the weakness of the enemy were well known . . . I made daily reports to the Army Chief of Staff. I was not consulted about the use of the atom bomb. Had I been I would have expressed the view that it was unnecessary—that Japan was already prepared to surrender."[44]

I have included MacArthur's views on Japan to show how inconsistent he can seem.† How can someone who opposed the use of the atomic bomb in Japan have suggested using the atomic bomb against China during the Korean War? Going to West Point has helped me reconcile this contradiction, because MacArthur's most famous quote that every cadet has to memorize is: "[In war] there is no substitute for victory."[45]

Although MacArthur wrote that the atomic bomb was not needed to achieve victory during World War II, he thought it might be necessary during the Korean War. After being fired for insubordination by President Truman, he had trouble living with the fact that America and its allies had not won the Korean War. Believing that the North Korean government would be a threat for decades to come, he was haunted by the war's indecisive outcome. To achieve world peace, MacArthur wanted to end all current wars such as the Korean War as quickly as possible, and abolish all future wars.

When I read MacArthur's speeches that he gave after the Korean War, I

---

* MacArthur called blockades "the most effective weapon known to military science."
† As MacArthur's views changed over time, he can seem inconsistent. He also made many mistakes, such as his attack on the Bonus Marchers, who he believed were communists trying to overthrow the government.

noticed he wanted to abolish war for three reasons. First, the existence of nuclear weapons makes war a threat to human survival. Second, MacArthur thought preparation for war and war itself wasted enormous amounts of money that could be better used for other purposes, such as ending poverty. According to him, the war system creates greater poverty, damages our economy, and leads to higher taxes. And third, when politicians have the power to frighten people with the threat of war, it is too easy for them to manipulate the masses in order to advance their own selfish interests. Later in this book I will explain why MacArthur was correct on all three points.

If we define world peace as "the end of politically organized violence between countries," then MacArthur was also correct when he said the road to world peace would be very challenging. He was far from naive, understanding the immense political roadblocks that stand in the way of peace. In one of his last speeches, given at West Point in 1962, he expressed his doubts by referencing a quote misattributed to Plato: "Only the dead have seen the end of war." Like MacArthur, I do not think world peace is inevitable, only possible. But as I will explain throughout the rest of this book, we have more reasons today to think world peace is possible than MacArthur did in the early 1960s.

After MacArthur gave a nationally recognized speech in 1955 about the need to abolish war, peace activists Oscar Hammerstein II, Roger Stevens, and Norman Cousins sent him a letter expressing their admiration. Hammerstein was a famous Broadway musical director and writer who won eight Tony Awards and two Academy Awards, Stevens was an influential Broadway producer who became a founding chairman of the Kennedy Center for the Performing Arts and the National Endowment of the Arts, and Cousins was a leading journalist and close friend of Nobel Peace Prize laureate Albert Schweitzer. In their letter they wrote, "We read with excitement and gratification your Los Angeles speech of January 26. Your inspiring plea for the abolition of war is a provocative challenge. We are deeply interested in advancing your view and would be honored to have an appointment with you at your earliest convenience to discuss this important matter."

MacArthur replied:

Only the cynic will challenge the philosophy that the utter futility of war in its present scale of mass destruction dictates its abolition, but unfortunately cynicism plays a mighty, sometimes indeed a predominant role, in the fashioning of events which guide the world. But cynicism fortunately is largely confined to the upper strata of society and forms little part in the thinking of the great masses . . . And there is no doubt but that if the issue of war or peace were left to the free will of the masses they would rule out war with practical unanimity. The question is how to mobilize that will and clothe it with at least a veto control upon the madness of leaders avaricious for the personal power which springs from the threat of war.

From a life time of service in foreign lands which has given me the opportunity to assess human philosophy in its manifold influence upon divergent sectors of the human race, I have come to realize that what reaches closest to a common aspiration of all mankind is the protective shield of constitutional law—a device which has grown to be universally recognized by all peoples of all races as the ultimate safeguard against arbitrary despotism of rights and liberties of the individual. So true is this that even the despot seeks refuge behind so-called peoples' constitutions . . .

In the light of such observations and experiences, I have come to the personal conclusion that the abolition of war must ultimately rest upon a constitutionally mandated liberty guaranteed to the people—a liberty to be free of war which the people themselves will stoutly defend, and free from the confiscatory taxation to which the preparation for war inevitably leads. Therein would lie a system of universal inspection by the people themselves, whose predominant self interest would rest upon the avoidance of steps which lead to war.

The natural question which then arises is how all of this is to be brought about. To which I would repeat the axiom that there must always be a first in all things. In this, our great and powerful nation should be the first. Equipped as is no other nation or combination of nations successfully to wage modern war, it should show itself through dynamic leadership no less equipped to lead the world down the noble but highly practical road toward universal peace. In my opinion this well might be done through a ringing affirmation by a leader in public authority endowed with the necessary vision and moral courage of our readiness to abolish war by placing the issue of war or peace squarely into the hands of the people through constitutional guarantees against war or the concomitant taxation for the maintenance of war making power, subject of course to similar guarantees being accorded at least to the peoples comprising the other major nations of the earth. We would thereby challenge all other nations to meet us on so high a moral plane. By so doing our own moral position would stand out as a beacon to summon all men of good will everywhere to join with us. In due course I am confident the pressure of other peoples upon their leaders would bring about another grand alliance, but this one not joined together for the massive prosecution of war but rather dedicated to the bringing about of universal peace.[46]

Despite what MacArthur said, cynicism is no longer largely confined to the elite, but has now spread to the masses. In order to combat the cynicism that hinders progress, the rest of this book will share the practical steps we can take to make MacArthur's dream of world peace a reality. The following chapters will also reveal what many American politicians are not telling us about the true nature of terrorism, and how waging peace gives us a more effective way to protect our country and planet in the twenty-first century. Because war threatens human survival, I will also explain that when the mission of creating world peace is concerned, there is truly no substitute for victory.

CHAPTER 8

The Master of Deception

The Deceptive Beauty of War

Since my earliest memories, I was taught that violence is needed to stop violence. When I read comic books as a child, Superman, Spider-Man, and Batman protected humanity and saved the world by beating up villains. In action movies, the hero killed the bad guy, saved the world, kissed the girl, and peace was won.

In our society we are taught that we need to use war as a means to end war, and when people believe war serves the goal of peace they are more willing to fight. When America was attacked by Japan during World War II, and Nazi Germany threatened the world, Americans more willingly served in the military. During the Vietnam War, when many soldiers were not sure why they were fighting, it was more difficult to recruit people into the military. When American politicians, in response to the attacks on September 11, 2001, talked about the need to fight terrorism, make the world safer, and spread freedom and democracy around the globe through military force, more volunteers joined the military.

During my time at West Point and in the army my old belief that war is needed to end war was shattered. As I studied military history I realized that almost everything our society and the media teach us about war is a distortion of the truth. I gradually began to perceive the true nature of war, and the reality I saw behind the distortions shook the way I saw the world. If I asked you to draw a symbol that best serves as an accurate metaphor for war, what image would you choose? Would you draw a sword? A gun? A bomb? A corpse? A mushroom cloud? Take a moment to think about it.

Now what if I told you that a far more accurate symbol for war is not a sword, gun, bomb, corpse, or mushroom cloud, but a necklace?

One of the most accurate and *useful* metaphors for war is the Necklace of Harmonia from Greek mythology. When Aphrodite, the goddess of love, had an affair with Ares, the god of war, they had a daughter named Harmonia. Although Harmonia was the goddess of harmony, she soon became associated with tragedy and suffering. Aphrodite had cheated on her husband, Hephaestus, the god of fire (known as Vulcan in Roman mythology). Enraged by his wife's adultery, Hephaestus gave Harmonia a cursed necklace as a gift on her wedding day. The necklace was made of gold and covered in jewels, and it possessed the kind of beauty that could only be forged by a god. Everyone at the wedding was stunned by the divine gift Hephaestus had carefully crafted, unable to see the curse hidden beneath its sparkling surface.

The Necklace of Harmonia promises to keep its wearer young and beautiful, but there is a catch. The necklace also curses its wearer with tragedy and suffering. While possessing the necklace, Harmonia was transformed into a serpent. It then passed from wearer to wearer, causing tragedy after tragedy. The Necklace of Harmonia is an accurate and useful metaphor for war, because like war, it appears beautiful on the surface but its true nature is destructive. The Necklace of Harmonia, like war, has a deceptive appearance.

I am not exaggerating when I say war appears beautiful on the surface, and I will explain how war takes on this deceptive appearance. During my freshman year at West Point, my history professor—an army captain and West Point graduate—made all the cadets in his class watch a disturbing PowerPoint slideshow presentation. The professor dimmed the lights so we could clearly see the images as a projector displayed them on a large screen at the front of the room. The slideshow began with photos of new army recruits who enlisted to fight in World War I, not realizing how hellish the war would be. While haunting music played in the background, I saw over a dozen black-and-white pictures of young men posing proudly with their rifles. They looked enthusiastic and even excited about the war. The photos seemed to be taken in the hometown of each young man, and the proud poses made it seem like they were getting ready to depart for a grand and glorious adventure.

The slideshow then took a drastic turn. The pictures of innocent young men were replaced by black-and-white photos of corpses rotting on the battlefield. The pictures of mangled and twisted bodies seemed to go on forever, but the most disturbing part of the slideshow was the end, when images of dead bodies were replaced by pictures of soldiers who survived with severe facial injuries. Most of them had missing jaws, and their faces were so mutilated I was shocked they even survived. They had a blank and unsettling look in their eyes I cannot describe, and I wondered what horrors those eyes had seen on the battlefields of Europe.

The message behind the slideshow presentation was clear. As my history professor explained, many people volunteered for World War I because their governments convinced them the war would be short, glorious, adventurous, and even fun. War was depicted as a beautiful thing, but when World War I began the reality of the battlefield was much different.

A lot has changed since World War I, because today the horror of war has been documented in countless pictures, videos, personal testimonies, and psychological studies that confirm the damaging effect war has on the human mind. Today it has become common knowledge that war is hell, and even the advocates of war now admit "war is hell." But if the hellish nature of war is so widely known, why do wars still exist? Before I can address this question I must first describe how war has a far more deceptive kind of beauty, capable of seducing some of the kindest and most conscientious people into supporting the war system. Just as the Necklace of Harmonia has a layer of jewels mounted on a deeper layer of gold, the necklace of war also has various layers of sparkling deceit.

Many peace activists underestimate the deceptive nature of war; they do not understand how someone can say "war is hell" while being an advocate for war. But the war system is a master of deception, able to convince even those who hate its horror to be its allies. In an article titled "War Is Hell: There Is No Substitute for Victory" that appeared in the *Wall Street Journal* on October 30, 2001, Senator John McCain said:

War is a miserable business. The lives of a nation's finest patriots are sacrificed. Innocent people suffer and die. Commerce is disrupted, economies are damaged. Strategic interests shielded by years of patient statecraft are endangered as the exigencies of war and diplomacy conflict . . . Shed a tear, and then get on with the business of killing our enemies as quickly as we can, and as ruthlessly as we must . . . We must destroy them, wherever they hide. That will surely increase the terrible danger facing noncombatants, a regrettable but necessary fact of war. But it will also shorten the days they must suffer war's cruel reality . . . War is a miserable business. Let's get on with it.[1]

The preceding excerpt from John McCain's article reveals that even conscientious people can support war. Many peace activists mistakenly believe that all pro-war advocates are evil, but the first half of McCain's quote sounds exactly like the words of many peace activists I know. Similar to McCain's description of the horror of war, I have met many peace activists who also say, "War is a miserable business, [soldiers] are sacrificed, innocent people suffer and die, commerce is disrupted, economies are damaged, and war and diplomacy conflict." Although pro-war advocates are often demonized by peace activists, I have met many pro-war advocates who truly believe war is synonymous with safety, security, freedom, and peace. Some of the kindest people I have ever met were pro-war advocates, and for most of my life I supported the war system because I believed it made our country safe and free.

Throughout the rest of this book I will reveal many of the war system's most carefully guarded secrets. Before we can uncover its secrets, however, we must first explore how the war system—the master of deception—disguised its destructive nature in ancient history. Ares, the Greek god of war, and his sister Eris, the goddess of hatred and strife, were despised by many Greeks and often portrayed as ugly. In the *Iliad*, Homer says, "Hate [Eris] whose wrath is relentless, she the sister and companion of murderous Ares, she who is only a little thing at the first, but thereafter grows until she strides on the earth with her head striking heaven. She then hurled down bitterness equally between both sides as she walked through the onslaught making men's pain heavier."[2]

Malcolm Day, a scholar of religion, mythology, and ancient history, further explains why Ares and Eris were despised by the ancient Greeks:

> Eris was known as the sister of Ares (god of war), who helped him foster battles; she reveled in the anguish and bloodiness of war. She filled their hearts with animosity in the hope that they would fight to the death . . . Not surprisingly, no one loved this cruel deity, who is usually depicted in art as an ugly harridan with an unquenchable thirst for discord. Eris' ways of inveigling men into her possession were subtle, for she did not say to them, "Behold my face and my shape," for that would have disgusted them. Instead, she played on their insecurities, inflated their pride, and suggested their superiority over their neighbors . . .
>
> An unpopular god, Ares was not generally worshiped by the Greeks, who were afraid of his lust for violence and cruelty. Such a vicious deity *was not considered trustworthy* [emphasis added], so Ares did not receive the reverence shown by the Romans to Mars. Along with Jupiter, Mars was the favorite god of the Romans.[3]

As I mentioned in chapter 5, Sun Tzu said all war is based on deception, and the *Iliad* portrays Ares as a liar who is despised by his father Zeus. But Ares was not the only major god of war in Greek mythology. There was another major deity the ancient Greeks worshipped as a symbol of war, but most of us who learned about Greek mythology in elementary school do not associate her name with war. The war system in ancient Greece hid behind this beloved goddess. Unlike Ares, she was beautiful, wise, and intelligent.

The war goddess I am referring to is Athena. She was not only the goddess of war, but also wisdom and intelligence. Ares represented the horror, mistrust, and violence of war, while Athena represented just war, strategy, and tactics. Although Ares was widely despised, Athena was widely worshipped and loved. She was one of the most popular deities in ancient Greece. The Greek city-state Athens was named after her, and she was also a patron goddess of Sparta.[4]

According to Greek mythology, Athena was born wearing full armor, signifying she was born ready for battle. In the fifth century BC, the Athenian sculptor Phidias created a massive bronze statue called *Athena Promachos* (*promachos* means "fighting on the front rank in battle"). The largest statue in Athens, it was thirty feet high and located on a hill where sailors miles away could see her glistening shield, armor, helmet, and spear shining in the sun.[5] Athena's spear served two symbolic purposes. It was a symbol of protection to comfort the Athenian citizens and a symbol of intimidation to frighten adversaries. Although Athena was a fierce and brave goddess, she was worshipped not as a warmonger, but as a beautiful protector.

Historian Leonhard Schmitz explains: "[Athena] seems to have been a divinity of a purely ethical character, and not the representative of any particular physical power manifested in nature; her power and wisdom appear in her being the protectress and preserver of the state and of social institutions. Everything, therefore, which gives to the state strength and prosperity, such as agriculture, inventions, and industry, as well as everything which preserves and protects it from injurious influence from without, such as the defence [sic] of the walls, fortresses, and harbours, is under her immediate care."[6]

Many ancient Greeks saw the goddess of war Athena as a protector, and today many people see the war system as a protector. In the late 1940s the U.S. Department of War was renamed the Department of Defense and the "secretary of war" became the "secretary of defense." Strategic Air Command, the military organization that controlled much of the U.S. nuclear weapons arsenal during the Cold War, had the motto "Peace is our profession."[7] During the end of the Cold War the United States deployed the Peacekeeper— an intercontinental ballistic missile armed with a nuclear weapon. Because Americans see war in much the same way as the ancient Greeks, it is no coincidence that the central feature on the West Point crest is Athena's helmet.

Just as war today has become synonymous with safety and security, Athena was seen as a goddess of safety and security. According to Malcolm Day, "From earliest times, Athena was connected with citadels. During the chaotic period after the fall of the Myceneans (c. 1100 BCE), only the stronghold of Athens, the Acropolis, was able to withstand the onslaught. Not surprisingly, then, Athena was adopted as the protectress of the city."[8]

Ares was a warmonger who represented bloodlust and chaos. But Athena was a guardian who represented protection and just war. She did not possess Ares's maniacal lust for senseless slaughter, and since she was considered a stronger and more trustworthy deity than Ares, the Greeks preferred to have her on their side. In the *Iliad*, the god of war Ares sided with the Trojans, and the goddess of war Athena sided with the Greeks. The Trojans lost the war, and the Greeks won.

In Roman mythology, the god of war Ares was called Mars, but Mars was more similar to the wise Athena than the homicidal maniac Ares. Just as the Greeks saw Athena as a protector, the Romans saw Mars as a bringer of peace. This is one reason Mars was such a popular god in Rome. Although many people claim humanity is naturally violent, General MacArthur disagreed, noticing throughout his life that human beings have an immense desire for peace. He said, "Our ideal must be eventually the abolition of war. Such is the longing hope of all of the masses of mankind of whatever race or tribe. Indeed, so well is this understood that even the despot, in order to assure a following, cloaks the threat or application of force with the hypocritical pretense that his purpose is to secure the peace."[9]

General MacArthur realized that dictators and democracies alike wage war in the name of safety, security, and peace. Herman Goering, a Nazi leader and military commander later executed for war crimes, also realized this. Goering said:

> Why, of course, the people don't want war. Why would some poor slob on a farm want to risk his life in a war when the best that he can get out of it is to come back to his farm in one piece. Naturally, the common people don't want war; neither in Russia nor in England nor in America, nor for that matter in Germany. That is understood. But, after all, it is the leaders of the country who determine the policy and it is always a simple matter to drag the people along, whether it is a democracy or a fascist dictatorship or a parliament or a communist dictatorship

. . . Voice or no voice, the people can always be brought to the bidding of the leaders. That is easy. All you have to do is *tell them they are being attacked* [emphasis added] and denounce the pacifists for lack of patriotism and *exposing the country to danger* [emphasis added]. It works the same way in any country.[10]

When people do not feel safe and secure, they will often pursue peace at any cost, even if it means war. Journalist Hamida Ghafour, who was born in Afghanistan, said in an interview on BBC Radio, "Living in Europe and living in North America, one thing that people always assume incorrectly about Afghans is that all they want to do is fight . . . And living and working in that country, people desperately want peace . . . *people are desperate for security at almost any cost* [emphasis added] . . . People in the world have one basic thing in common. They want things for their families. They want safety and security."[11]

Rulers in ancient Greece and Rome manipulated people's desperation for security and desire for peace. By using propaganda to make war synonymous with security and peace, these rulers convinced many of their citizens to support wars and even oppressive government policies—all in the name of security and peace. Pax, the Roman goddess of peace, was engraved on Roman coins to depict Rome as a symbol of peace, even though in reality it was an aggressive empire. Furthermore, Mars was also engraved on Roman coins. He often held a weapon as a symbol of strength, military victory, and protection, but he was also portrayed on some coins extending an olive branch—a symbol of peace.[12] This reveals a lot about how the Romans saw the world.

The *Aeneid*, written by the Roman poet Virgil during the first century BC, is a mythical story about the Trojan soldier Aeneas who became a forefather of the Roman people. When Aeneas and his comrades arrive in Italy after a long journey, a character named Pallas grabs his spear and confronts the new arrivals, asking them, "Soldiers, what drives you to try these unfamiliar paths? Where are you going? Who are your people? Where's your home? Do you bring peace or war?"[13] The poet Virgil had Aeneas respond with a gesture of peace: "Then captain Aeneas calls from his high stern, his hands extending the olive branch of peace."[14]

The olive branch is a famous symbol of peace that derives from ancient times. The Romans referred to the goddess of war Athena as Minerva. Like Mars, she was also portrayed on Roman coins holding an olive branch. However, Mars was more popular than Minerva among the Romans and was more often depicted on coins, including a coin where he is extending an olive branch in peace while placing his foot on the helmet of a defeated enemy.[15] The symbolism clearly linked the god of war Mars to peace, revealing that many Romans saw Mars in much the same way many Americans see the Department of Defense—as a protector and bringer of peace.

Many Romans also saw their government and emperor as symbols of protection and peace. Archeologist Neil Faulkner explains:

> Propaganda is considered to be a modern political art, but the Romans were masters of 'spin.' . . . All empire-builders have to justify what they do—to themselves, to their own people, and to those they dominate . . . Perhaps the most important [theme] was the idea that Rome represented peace, good government, and the rule of law. The societies with which Rome was in conflict were caricatured as barbaric, lawless and dangerous . . . This concept, of a tough but essentially benevolent imperial power, was embodied in the person of the emperor . . . His image was stamped on every coin, and thus reached the most remote corners of his domain . . . How did the spin-doctors of ancient Rome represent the great leader to his people? Sometimes . . . he was depicted as a warrior and a general; an intimidating implicit reference to global conquest and military dictatorship. At other times, he wore the toga of a Roman gentleman, as if being seen in the law-courts, making sacrifice at the temple, or receiving guests at a grand dinner party at home. In this guise, he was the paternalistic 'father of his country,' the benevolent states-man, the great protector. The message was clear: thanks to the leadership of the emperor, the frontiers are secure, order reigns at home, and we can all go safely about our business and prosper.[16]

Military history shows that every powerful nation has equated war with safety, security, and peace. Ata-Malik Juvaini, a Persian historian who was alive when the ruthless Mongol conqueror Genghis Khan created the largest empire on earth, wrote the following propaganda about the Mongol warlord: "In the latter part of his reign he had brought about complete peace and quiet, and security and tranquility, and had achieved the extreme of prosperity and well-being; the roads were secure and disturbances allayed."[17]

In 1933 Nazi Germany published a book of Adolf Hitler's speeches titled *The New Germany Desires Work and Peace*. In the introduction, propaganda minister Joseph Goebbels says, "But just as this New Germany desires *work*, it also desires *peace*. It has announced to the whole world, through the mouth of the Chancellor [Adolf Hitler] himself, speaking in the Reichstag, that it has *no aggressive intentions whatever*, that it does not wish to provoke anyone nor to stir up unrest. It wishes to pursue its work in peace and in a spirit of deep moral conviction, in order to make sure of its daily bread . . . The speeches delivered by Adolf Hitler since the 30th January 1933 are eloquent proofs of Germany's desire for work and peace."[18]

Like many conquerors, Hitler seduced people into supporting war by deceiving them with an eloquent message of peace. In some of his 1933 speeches he said, "In our relations to the world we wish, having clearly before our eyes the sacrifices of the War, to be the champions of a peace which shall finally heal those wounds from which all are suffering . . . It has always been my idea that there can be nothing finer than to be the advocate of those who cannot defend themselves . . . There is today only one great task: to safeguard the peace of the world."[19]

Just as the Necklace of Harmonia uses a beautiful illusion of gold and jewels to hide its destructive nature, even Hitler disguised his destructive intentions with a beautiful illusion of peace. Throughout military history, powerful nations often used war as a symbol of peace, and sometimes the word "war" was literally replaced with words such as "defense" and "peace." Some Roman coins depicting the god of war Mars had the inscription MARS PACATOR, meaning "Mars the Peacemaker."[20] There was even a Roman coin depicting the violent demigod Hercules with an olive branch in one hand and a club and lion's skin in the other. The inscription next to his name read

PACIFERO, meaning "to keep peace.* The Romans saw Mars and Hercules as heroes who used violence to create peace. Perhaps we are not so different from the Romans, because our society admires modern-day mythic heroes such as Superman, Spider-Man, and Batman, who also use violence to create peace.

For the most part, modern superheroes reflect our human yearning for justice, and these superheroes are largely seen as metaphors for the triumph of justice over evil. The depiction of modern superheroes as peacemakers is the least of our worries, because it is far more dangerous when governments try to equate war with peace. Martin Luther King Jr. used a violent symbol— a sword—as a symbol of waging peace. But the Romans used a peaceful symbol—the olive branch—as a symbol of waging war. King used the symbol of the sword because he thought it truthfully captured the struggle inherent to waging peace, but the Romans used the olive branch as a form of deception.

Every powerful country has tried to equate its own wars, even the wars it started, with peace. General MacArthur realized that no nation, whether dictatorship or democracy, wants to see itself as a warmonger. And Noam Chomsky said, "Every society perceives itself, or tries to make its public perceive itself, as benevolent.[21] Accordingly, military history shows that George Orwell was indeed correct when he said rulers in power often replace the word "war" with "peace." In 1964 when President Johnson announced to the American people that the U.S. military had bombed targets in North Vietnam, he mentioned the word "war" only once by saying "we still seek no wider war." And when he referred to the United States attacking North Vietnam he did not use the word "war," but called it "the struggle for peace and security in southeast Asia" and the "determination to take all necessary measures in support of freedom and in defense of peace in southeast Asia." He ended the speech by saying, "It is a solemn responsibility to have to order even limited military action by forces whose overall strength is as vast and as awesome as those of the United States of America, but it is my stated conviction, shared throughout your government, that firmness in the right is indispensible today for peace; that firmness will always be measured. Its mission is peace."[22]

* When I asked a Latin professor whether pacifero meant either "peace" or "to pacify," she said the words basically meant the same thing to Romans because they saw peace primarily as the security that resulted from military conquest.

Like many Americans who do not blindly believe everything our politicians say, Martin Luther King Jr. was not fooled by President Johnson's illusions. King later said, "What was woeful, but true, was that my country was only talking peace but was bent on military victory. Inside the glove of peace was the clenched fist of war."[23] We must question what our politicians say rather than blindly believe the illusions they present to us, because war—like the Necklace of Harmonia—can cause immense tragedy and suffering.

The Necklace of Harmonia promises to give us harmony in the form of youth and beauty, but its harmony is tainted. In a similar way, the necklace of war promises to give us harmony in the form of security and peace, but its harmony is also tainted. As an example, Alexander the Great's wars of conquest possessed a beautiful surface illusion of human brotherhood that hid a tainted core. Military historian J. F. C. Fuller describes the beautiful surface of Alexander's military campaigns:

> But it is known that immediately after his visit to the shrine of Ammon at Siwah, in his conversation with the philosopher Psammon, like St. Paul on his way to Damascus, "suddenly there shined round about him a light from heaven." It was that God was not only the ruler of mankind, but also the common father of mankind. Therefore all men were brothers, and consequently, Homonoia, which Tarn translates as "a being of one mind together," or negatively, "to live without quarrelling," was the linchpin which, as it held each family together, could hold together his empire, a family of many races, in a state of peace . . .
>
> It was this aspiration which he expressed in his prayer at Opis, and, according to Tarn, it had little to do with his so-called policy of fusion which was "a material thing," but with an idea, "an immaterial thing." It was firstly, that all men are brothers; and secondly, that he had "a divine mission to be the harmonizer and reconciler of the world, to bring it to pass that all men, being brothers, should live together in Homonoia, in unity of heart and mind."[24]

In *Peaceful Revolution* I describe the complex nature of the human conscience, and explain how self-deception allows people to believe their own propaganda. The war system is such a master of deception that it can even cause us to deceive ourselves. We do not know what Alexander's true intentions were or whether he believed his own propaganda. What we do know is that his original "war of self-defense" to prevent future invasions from Persia became a war of aggression that had no end in sight. We also know that the reality of his military conquests was much different than his dream of harmony.

Just as the harmony provided by the Necklace of Harmonia is tainted, the harmony provided by Alexander's ruthless conquests was also tainted. Alexander's empire fell apart after his death from a sudden illness (which might have been poisoning) at the age of thirty-two, and in addition to the suffering he inflicted on those he conquered, many Greeks and Macedonians also suffered. In his book *Leadership: The Warrior's Art*, Colonel Christopher Kolenda explains:

> Although the disaffection in the army was approaching the breaking point, Alexander continued to campaign towards the Indus over the next year. One campaign seemed to lead to another. Alexander never articulated at what point he considered the empire "secure" and when the Macedonians could expect to return home. He merely offered the worn out and vague explanation of reaching the "Ocean" which was supposedly just beyond yet another "next" river . . . At the Hyphasis River in 326 B.C. his soldiers had had enough . . .
>
> When [his soldiers] demanded that Alexander define for them the purpose of continuing, the king invoked the familiar nebulous themes of reaching the mythical Ocean, and securing the empire against internal revolt and external conquest . . . The campaign, instead of being a necessary means to a logical end, had become an end in itself. Alexander's explanations were no longer good enough. With no clear direction from their king and no attainable

or discernible end to the campaigning in sight, Alexander's soldiers simply refused to go on unless Alexander forced them . . .

After initially informing his officers that he would go on himself with whomever would volunteer, Alexander retired to his tent and kept to himself for three days hoping for a change of heart from the soldiers. When none was forthcoming, Alexander found the only way out of the dilemma possible. Sacrificing to the gods and seeing that the omens were unfavorable, Alexander informed his soldiers that he would turn back. Despite their elation at the prospect of returning home, Alexander's resolution of the dilemma had most likely left some lingering doubts among his soldiers . . . Trust still remained an unresolved issue in the eyes of the Macedonians . . .

The tragedy of Alexander can be seen in [his hubris]. In Alexander's self-conception he was also the agent of civilization . . . conquering the world not for himself (Alexander never hoarded the wealth he attained) but for his Macedonians and Greeks . . . Alexander [saw] himself as a bestower of great gifts, but [was] perceived by the Greeks and Macedonians as one who, despite the gifts, had failed to deliver the good life.[25]

Just as the Necklace of Harmonia promises to keep its wearer young and beautiful, the necklace of war promises to keep us safe and secure. Just as the Necklace of Harmonia disguises its tragic nature with a deceptively beautiful appearance, the tragic nature of war wears a disguise of freedom and peace. Is there anything more beautiful than safety, security, freedom, and peace? War is also equated with other beautiful things such as wealth and prosperity. Malcolm Day says, "When Athens later developed into a commercial center, the Greeks believed that Athena protected its craftsmen, the source of the city's wealth, and so she became the patroness of the arts and crafts." [26] The god of war Mars was also the god of agriculture, and Romans prayed to him hoping for an abundant harvest. Just as Athena and

Mars were violent deities who symbolized peace, freedom, security, and prosperity, later in this book I will explain why the American military budget is widely seen as the "peace, freedom, security, and prosperity" budget.

General MacArthur was not the only military strategist who recognized that aggressive war is often portrayed as a beautiful thing such as peace. Naganuma Muneyoshi, a seventeenth-century Japanese samurai and military scientist, realized that aggressive war is also portrayed as another beautiful thing: humanitarian intervention. Thomas Cleary, a scholar and translator of Eastern philosophy, says Muneyoshi was known for "condemning predatory warfare in pursuit of reputation or profit . . . He criticizes a popular tendency to admire the power of violence without question of ethical probity or purpose."[27] Muneyoshi said:

> In later ages, rulers and commanders largely employed arms to usurp territory and profit economically. This is unnatural and inhumane, but they had no shame. Killing countless innocents, ending countless lives, they cared for nothing but to expand their territory and increase their power. How are they different from bandits in this? Their conduct of affairs was entirely dependent on what power could accomplish, without considering where justice lay . . .
>
> When later people don't criticize these crimes but go along with them and praise them, this is of the gravest concern to good generals and wise rulers. This is using instruments of ill omen* for violence and disruption, starting a dangerous business that destroys both soldiers and civilians. The cruelty and viciousness in that is impossible to express in words. When the corruption of latter-day militarists verge on this, we should not fail to take a warning . . .
>
> *When a pretense of humanity and justice is used for profiteering, that is treacherous warfare* [emphasis added]. Those who arm out of greed will perish, because this is unnatural and inhuman. In latter days this type of treachery is not

---

* Chinese philosopher Lao Tzu called weapons "instruments of ill omen."

rare. There are those who outwardly claim to have a just cause in executing usurping assassins, while inwardly harboring a scheme to set themselves up . . . People of the world do not discuss whether they are just or unjust but simply praise the cunning who take by aggression and have won battles repeatedly, calling them heroes and good commanders. Noble men despise prestige that is wrongly acquired.[28]

To learn whether love or hate is the more powerful instinct in human beings, we can examine the way war propaganda has functioned throughout history. According to political leaders, wars are always about self-defense, protecting our families, fighting for freedom, defending our way of life, or liberating oppressed people. There has never been a war where the war propaganda told a population, "We are fighting for money, gold, or oil. We are fighting so the rich can get richer." Although wars are often about greed and profit, most people aren't willing to die for greed and profit. What most people *will* die for is their family, country, freedom, and ideals.

War propaganda tells people they are fighting for a noble cause in defense of their family, country, or an ideal. As I explain in *Peaceful Revolution*, war propaganda also hides the enemy's humanity by portraying them as non-human. The Necklace of Harmonia is a metaphor not only for war propaganda, but the entire war system. In a later chapter I will discuss the truths and illusions of American foreign policy, which will further reveal why the war system is so dangerous and must be abolished.

The Curse of Empire

Has there ever been a necessary war? During an interview David Pakman asked me, "[Do people ever say] Paul Chappell is clearly just a pacifist and he is against war on kind of a theoretical level, and he's not really connected with the realities that sometimes war is necessary—so I guess my question to you is, are you against war, period?"

I replied, "There were some necessary wars in the past. And that's why the war propaganda is so hard to refute . . . It's hard to argue from the perspective of the Greeks that they shouldn't have fought against the Persians when they were being invaded. It's hard to argue from the perspective of the British that they shouldn't have defended themselves against the Nazis. And Gandhi said if you have to choose between violence and doing nothing, you should not hesitate to use violence. And Gandhi supported Poland's violent resistance against Nazi Germany . . . There have been wars where if you are being attacked you have to defend yourself. And that again is why the war propaganda is so persuasive, because they [war propagandists] can make every modern war seem like World War II, or they can make every modern war seem like the [American] Civil War [that claimed to be freeing the slaves], or a fight for freedom . . . But I've found that nonviolent techniques in this era, in the twenty-first century, are just more effective. In terms of a way of combating these problems, nonviolence is just a more effective method, or as Gandhi would call it a more powerful 'weapon' than violence."[29]

There have certainly been justified wars of self-defense in the past, such as when ancient Athens defended itself against two Persian invasions. But after winning military victories against Persia, Athens became an aggressive empire that refused to abandon the necklace of war. Just as the Necklace of Harmonia curses its wearer with tragedy, the necklace of war led to the ruin of Athens during the Peloponnesian War, when the nations oppressed by the Athenian Empire rebelled.

In fact, every single empire in human history has collapsed, often due to military overexpansion. Thomas Cleary explains, "In the strategic science of [Sun Tzu's] *The Art of War*, prolonging or expanding hostilities unnecessarily is regarded as one of the major causes of self-destruction."[30] In the ancient world, the empires of the Persians, Athenians, Spartans, Carthaginians, and Romans were ruined by extending their militaries too far. And in the twentieth century alone, the empires of Germany, Japan, and the Soviets (who invaded Afghanistan) were ruined by waging too much aggressive war. Also during the twentieth century, the European empires lost most of their colonies when the people they were oppressing rebelled in the form of nonviolent movements and violent uprisings. Martin Luther King Jr. said, "Oppressed people cannot remain oppressed forever. The yearning for freedom eventually manifests itself."[31]

Unlike the British who were proud to say they were members of the British Empire, most Americans don't like seeing our country as an empire. Why don't we like seeing ourselves this way? Our country was born when American patriots resisted the largest empire in the world—the British Empire. More recently, Ronald Reagan called the Soviet Union the "Evil Empire," and the villain in the famous film series *Star Wars* is "The Empire." In addition, many Americans know enough about the horrors of colonialism to realize that the European empires were not as benevolent as they claimed to be.

Although Americans have many reasons to despise the word "empire," the fact of the matter is that the United States currently has a more expansive military presence across the world than any other country in human history. Is the United States an empire or not? Have American politicians not been telling us the truth about America's role around the world? Is our country on the precipice of tragedy as Athens and Rome were, and if so, what can we as American citizens who love our country do about it? Rather than giving you easy answers to these questions, I will give you enough information throughout the rest of this book to help you draw your own conclusions. I will also describe the weapon we can use to defeat the master of deception.

CHAPTER 9

The Sword of Truth

The Truth Will Set Us Free

Growing up in Alabama as a descendant of slaves, I am able to write these words today because people who came before me used the sword of truth to defeat deception. When people said racial segregation in America must end, those who supported segregation controlled the society, government, military, corporations, many universities, and most of the money. What did the advocates of desegregation have on their side? The truth. Contrary to widely believed myths, it was not true that African Americans were subhuman and inferior to whites. It was not true that racial harmony was impossible.

I have met cynical people who say, "All truth is relative. We cannot really know what is true and what is untrue, because there is no such thing as truth." *But there is such a thing as truth.* For example, it is a scientific fact that African Americans are not genetically subhuman or inferior to white people. It is a scientific fact that women are not intellectually inferior to men. And it is a scientific fact that the earth and other planets in our solar system revolve around the sun. Not long ago, people were imprisoned, beaten, and even killed for promoting these truths.

In the seventeenth century, Galileo Galilei published scientific evidence demonstrating that the earth revolved around the sun. Threatened by the evidence, the Roman Catholic Church allowed him to choose between recanting his ideas or facing execution. But even if he recanted, Galileo's books would be banned and he would be put under house arrest for the rest

of his life. At this time the church was a superpower that controlled governments, societies, militaries, religious beliefs, educational systems, and much
of the wealth worldwide. If you think the world looks hopeless today, imagine how it must have looked to Galileo, who was almost killed for saying
the earth revolved around the sun and spent the rest of his life under house
arrest after recanting his ideas.

In 2000, Pope John Paul II issued a formal apology on behalf of the
Roman Catholic Church for its treatment of Galileo and other mistakes it
had made. His apology reveals a lot about the power of truth to overcome
deception. Truth has achieved many more victories against deception. As I
mentioned earlier in this book, for most of recorded history women around
the world had virtually no rights.[1] During the eighteenth century they were
not only forbidden from voting or owning property, but in most places they
were property. Those who advocated women's rights were ridiculed and
threatened for challenging the oppression of women, but today if an American politician were to suggest that women be denied the right to vote or
own property, many would consider him insane.

Today it would be political suicide for any American politician to say,
"We should bring back slavery and segregation, and women should not be
allowed to vote or own property." But two hundred years ago nearly all
American politicians openly supported slavery and the oppression of women,
and the vast majority of Americans also supported these unjust policies.
Many men thought women were just not smart enough to vote intelligently
or own property responsibly. The *New York Herald*, which became the most
popular and profitable newspaper in the United States in 1845,[2] editorial-
ized: "How did woman become subject to man, as she now is all over the
world. By her nature [of being inferior to men], just as the negro is and
always will be, to the end of the time, inferior to the white race."[3]

Frederick Douglass was an escaped slave who lived during this oppressive era, but he saw through the illusion of gender inequality. Just as Galileo
revealed timeless truths about our solar system, Douglass realized that
women's intellectual equality with men was also a timeless truth. In 1848
he said women are "fully equal in moral, mental and intellectual endowments
[with men], in short, entitled to an equal participancy in all the designs and
accomplishments allotted to man during his career on earth. May the accu-

mulated evils of the past, and those of the present, which superstition and bigotry have prescribed for them as a test of inferiority, be buried forever."[4]

The idea of women's equality does not mean men and women are exactly identical. Instead, women's equality means it is scientifically incorrect to say women are less intelligent than men, and therefore women should have the same rights and freedoms as men. A number of scientific studies show there may be some cognitive differences between the ways most men and women process information, but this does not mean women are less intelligent than men. Because more men than women are mathematicians, physicists, and scientists, I have heard both men and women say, "It's difficult to say women are intellectually equal to men, because men are a lot better than women at math and science." However, a January 2008 article in the magazine *Scientific American Mind* explains why it is inaccurate to say women are less intelligent than men in math and science, even though there seem to be differences in how they process information:

> There was not much public discussion about the reasons more women are not pursuing careers in these fields [of science, math, and engineering] until 2005, when then Harvard University president Lawrence Summers offered his personal observations. He suggested to an audience at a small economics conference near Boston that one of the major reasons women are less likely than men to achieve at the highest levels of scientific work is because fewer females have "innate ability" in these fields . . . One reason Summers' comment upset many people was its implication that any attempt to close this gap was futile. If most women are naturally deficient in scientific ability, then what could be done? But this seemingly simple interpretation contains two misconceptions.
>
> First, there is no single intellectual capacity that can be called "scientific ability." (For simplicity, we will often use the term "scientific" to refer to skills important to work in the fields of science, technology, engineering and mathematics.) The tools needed for scientific achievement

include verbal abilities such as those required to write complex journal articles and communicate well with colleagues; memory skills such as the ability to understand and recall events and complex information; and quantitative abilities in mathematical modeling, statistics, and visualization of objects, data and concepts.

Second, if women and men did demonstrate differences in these talents, this fact would not mean these differences were immutable. Indeed, if training and experience did not make a difference in the development of our academic skills, universities such as Harvard would be accepting tuition from students under false pretenses.

One of the confusing things about the field of sex differences is that you can arrive at very different conclusions depending on how you decide to assess abilities. Women clearly have the right stuff to cut it academically. They have constituted the majority of college enrollments in the U.S. since 1982, with the attendance gap widening every year since then. Similar trends are occurring in many other countries. Furthermore, women receive higher average grades in school in every subject—including mathematics and science.

Despite their success in the classroom, however, women score significantly lower [than men] on many standardized tests used for admissions to college and graduate school . . . Females get higher grades in math classes at all grade levels and also do slightly better on international assessments in algebra, perhaps because of its languagelike structure. But boys shine on the math part of the Scholastic Aptitude Test (SAT)—resulting in a difference of about 40 points that has been maintained for over 35 years . . . [5]

Around the time school begins . . . the sexes start to diverge. By the end of grade school and beyond, females perform better on most assessments of verbal abilities. In a 1995 review of the vast literature on writing skills,

University of Chicago researchers Larry Hedges (now at Northwestern University) and Amy Nowell put it this way: "The large sex differences in writing . . . are alarming. The data imply that males are, on average, at a rather profound disadvantage in the performance of this basic skill." There is also a female advantage in memory of faces and in episodic memory—memory for events that are personally experienced and are recalled along with information about each event's time and place.

There is another type of ability, however, in which boys have the upper hand, a skill set referred to as visuospatial: an ability to mentally navigate and model movement of objects in three dimensions. Between the ages of four and five, boys are measurably better at solving mazes on standardized tests.[6]

This scientific research is intriguing, but it mostly amounts to generalizations. The research can cause us to assume that men are better than women at navigating three-dimensional spaces, but I met some women in the military who had far better navigational skills than most men. And although the research shows that men on average get higher scores on the math portion of the Scholastic Aptitude Test (SAT), a girl in my high school received a perfect score on both the math and verbal sections of the SAT in 1997. According to an article in the *New York Times*, nearly 1.5 million college-bound seniors took the SAT in 2005, and only 238 received a perfect score. Of the students who received perfect scores on all three sections of the test—including math, reading, and writing—131 were boys and 107 were girls.[7] That is a minor difference, and these results show that men and women should be assessed based on their own abilities; they should not be stereotyped as being more or less intelligent than an opposing gender.

Furthermore, the research shows that women tend to have better writing skills than most men, but there have been many men in history who were brilliant writers. So there are exceptions to every piece of research, and it is possible for a woman to be a mathematical genius, just as it is possible for a man to be a literary genius. Although discussion continues about when a woman might join the ranks of great physicists like Isaac Newton and Albert Einstein, we should not underestimate the mathematical and scientific potential of women, because many boys in our society receive more encouragement than girls to excel at math and science. As a result, we must recognize how society shapes the development of men and women. There is a reason all the generals, historians, military scientists, and philosophers I quote from ancient history are men. It is because women were oppressed and forbidden from excelling in these pursuits.

For much of American history women were forbidden from voting, owning property, and even attending college, but today we know with certainty that women are as capable as men when it comes to voting intelligently, owning property responsibly, and excelling academically in college. During the early nineteenth century most people thought women would never get the right to vote or own property, and would always be seen as less than human. Most people in the nineteenth century believed women were not only intellectually inferior to men, but also morally inferior.[8] This misinformation was so deeply embedded in American society that it caused many women to view themselves as inferior.

The illusion of gender inequality was so powerful during the nineteenth century that even Charles Darwin echoed this illusion by claiming women were intellectually inferior to men. In the *Descent of Man*, published in 1871, Darwin said, "The chief distinction in the intellectual powers of the two sexes is shewn [*sic*] by man attaining to a higher eminence, in whatever he takes up, than woman can attain—whether requiring deep thought, reason, or imagination, or merely the use of the senses and hands. If two lists were made of the most eminent men and women in poetry, painting, sculpture, music (comprising composition and performance), history, science, and philosophy, with half-a-dozen names under each subject, the two lists would not bear comparison . . . The average standard of mental power in man must be above that of woman."[9]

But Frederick Douglass did not believe the illusion of gender inequality. Since women comprised roughly half the human population, Douglass said the oppression of women robbed society of half its moral and intellectual power. In 1881 he said:

If intelligence is the only true and rational basis of government, it follows that that is the best government which draws its life and power from the largest sources of wisdom, energy, and goodness at its command . . . [When men prevent women from participating in democracy] one-half of the moral and intellectual power of the world is excluded from any voice or vote in civil government. In this denial of the right to participate in government, not merely the degradation of woman and the perpetuation of a great injustice happens, but the maiming and repudiation of one-half of the moral and intellectual power of the government of the world.[10]

Douglass knew that if Galileo could reveal the truth about our solar system, then female activists could also reveal the truth about women's equality. For most of history women were viewed as intellectually subhuman, but for most of history people also thought the world was flat and the sun revolved around the earth. If society had been so wrong for so long about the shape of our planet and our place in the universe, wasn't it possible that society had also been so wrong for so long about its understanding of women? The Nineteenth Amendment, granting women the right to vote, was not ratified until 1920, but in 1888 Douglass said the following in a speech to the Woman Suffrage Association:

The universality of man's rule over woman is another factor in the resistance to the woman suffrage movement. We are pointed to the fact that men have not only always ruled over women, but that they do so rule everywhere, and they easily think that a thing that is done everywhere must be right. Though the fallacy of this reasoning is too transparent to need refutation, it still exerts a powerful influence. Even our good Brother Jasper yet believes, with the ancient church, that the sun "do move [around the earth]," notwithstanding all the astronomers of the world are against him.

One year ago I stood on the Pincio in Rome and witnessed the unveiling of the Statue of Galileo. It was an imposing sight. At no time before had Rome been free enough to permit such a statue to be placed within her walls. It is now there, not with the approval of the Vatican. No priest took part in the ceremonies. It was all the work of laymen. One or two priests passed the statue with averted eyes, but the great truths of the solar system were not angry at the sight, and the same will be true when woman shall be clothed, as she will yet be, with all the rights of American citizenship.

All good causes are mutually helpful. The benefits accruing from this movement for the equal rights of woman are not confined or limited to woman only. They will be shared by every effort to promote the progress and welfare of mankind everywhere and in all ages. It was an example and a prophecy of what can be accomplished against strongly opposing forces, against time-hallowed abuses, against deeply intrenched error, against world-wide usage, and against the settled judgment of mankind, by a few earnest women, clad only in the panoply of truth, and determined to live and die in what they considered a righteous cause . . . When a great truth once gets abroad in the world, no power on earth can imprison it, or prescribe its limits, or suppress it."[11]

During an era when women were not allowed to vote or own property, Frederick Douglass became one of the most vocal advocates for women's rights. Reflecting on his life, he said: "When I ran away from slavery, it was for myself; when I advocated emancipation, it was for my people; but when I stood up for the rights of woman, self was out of the question, and I found a little nobility in the act."[12]

In his book *Frederick Douglass on Women's Rights*, Philip Foner says:

In their long, continuing struggle for equality, American women have had to rely primarily on their own resources. This is not to say, however, that men have not helped advance their cause. Throughout our history they have had the vigorous support of a group of men who lent their names and voices to the woman's movement in the face of ridicule and even violence . . . According to woman's [sic] own testimony, foremost among them was Frederick Douglass. For when the American women who led the early movement were asked later in their lives to suggest the names of men who should be placed on an honor roll of male supporters, the list was invariably headed by this man who, having been born a slave in Maryland, had known oppression first-hand. "He was the only man I ever saw who understood the degradation of the disfranchisement of women," said Elizabeth Cady Stanton, the pioneer of the American woman's rights movement. On July 25, 1919, the *Atlanta Constitution* reported that in opposing the Georgia legislature's ratification of the Nineteenth Amendment granting woman suffrage, white supremacist representative J.B. Jackson climaxed his argument with the statement: "Frederick Douglass is the father and Susan B. Anthony, who received the Negro in her home, is the mother of this amendment!"[13]

Waging peace is more than opposing problems that personally affect us. German citizen Albert Schweitzer healed the sick in Africa and advocated for the humane treatment of animals. White men such as Henry David Thoreau and William Lloyd Garrison spoke against slavery, and Martin Luther King Jr. tried to improve the lives of poor white people. King said:

Many poor whites, however, were the derivative victims of slavery. As long as labor was cheapened by the involuntary servitude of the black man, the freedom of white labor, especially in the South, was little more than a myth . . . To this day the white poor also suffer deprivation and the humiliation of poverty if not of color. They are chained by the weight of discrimination, though its badge of degradation does not mark them. It corrupts their lives, frustrates their opportunities and withers their education . . . It has confused so many [poor whites] by prejudice that they have supported their own [rich white] oppressors. It is a simple matter of justice that America, in dealing creatively with the task of raising the Negro from backwardness, should also be rescuing a large stratum of the forgotten white poor.[14]

Today there is a widely believed myth that white men in America have never suffered injustice, but King knew this myth was false and wanted to help lift poor white men and women out of poverty. Frederick Douglass also explained how slavery created an unjust economic system not only for black slaves, but poor whites: "The white laboring man was robbed by the slave system of the just results of his labor, because he was flung into competition with a class of laborers who worked without wages . . . A white man holding no slaves in the country [Maryland] from which I came, was usually an ignorant and poverty-stricken man. Men of this class were contemptuously called 'poor white trash.'"[15]

Waging peace is a calling to help others, even if a problem does not personally affect us. Because people heeded that calling in the past I am able to write these words today. I, along with every other African American, owe a great debt to white women such as Susan B. Anthony, Elizabeth Cady Stanton, Lucretia Mott, Lucy Stone, and countless other female activists who struggled for the abolition of slavery. Today white women are allowed to vote and own property because of black men like Frederick Douglass, and black men have benefitted from the sacrifices of many white female activists. That is the beauty of waging peace.

Women activists played a leading role in two of the greatest underdog stories in history: the struggle to gain human rights for African Americans and the struggle for their own human rights. When women tried to gain equal rights with men, the men who opposed women's rights controlled the society, government, military, corporations, many universities, and most of the money. What did the advocates of women's equality have on their side? The truth. Contrary to widely believed myths, it was not true that women were intellectually inferior to men. It was not true that women were less than human.

How did women and African Americans use the sword of truth to defeat deception, injustice, and oppression? Before I can discuss this, I must first explain why the symbol of a sword is such an effective and useful metaphor for truth. A Persian legend can help us better understand this metaphor. According to Persian mythology, Fulad-zereh was a massive horned demon who terrorized people as he flew over the countryside. Fulad-zereh means "[possessing] steel armor," and because he could not be harmed by spears or arrows, nobody could stop him from kidnapping women and killing innocent people. His mother was a witch who cast a spell on him, making him invulnerable to all weapons except a specific magic sword. The magic sword originally belonged to King Solomon, but Fulad-zereh now possessed it. Knowing it was the only weapon that could harm him, he carefully guarded the magic sword in his lair, where he kept it hidden.

The demon Fulad-zereh is a metaphor for state-sanctioned slavery, gender inequality, and other dominant systems of oppression. Just as Fulad-zereh is invulnerable to all weapons except a specific sword, the mightiest systems of oppression are also invulnerable to all weapons except a specific sword—the sword of truth. And just as Fulad-zereh protects himself by hiding the only weapon that can destroy him, systems of oppression also protect themselves by hiding the truth from people.

The Two Methods of Hiding the Truth

Systems of oppression hide the truth by using two methods. The first method is to restrict people's ability to express and hear new ideas, making it less likely they will learn the truth. The Roman Catholic Church did this when it banned Galileo's books and forced him to publically recant his views, because his evidence contradicted the church's worldview that the sun revolved around the earth. As another example, dictators often restrict freedom of speech, freedom of the press, and freedom of assembly. In addition, dictators often ban books because the written word is one of the most pow-erful things in the world. If you doubt the power of books, consider why it was illegal to teach slaves how to read. Also think about why the Nazis burned books and why throughout history dictators have banned books. One of the biggest threats to slavery, the Nazis, dictators, or any oppressive system is books. Slave owners knew this. The Nazis knew this. Dictators know this today. What makes books so dangerous is that they are filled with ideas, and once ideas are unleashed into the world they cannot be destroyed by violence.

When Frederick Douglass was around eight years old, he became deter-mined to learn how to read after hearing his master explain why slaves should be kept illiterate. Since it was illegal to teach slaves to read and write, he was largely self-taught. In the following excerpt from his first autobiography, Dou-glass explains how reading not only freed his mind, but convinced him that it would be better to risk his life escaping from slavery than accept being a slave:*

> Very soon after I went to live with Mr. and Mrs. Auld, she very kindly commenced to teach me the A, B, C. After I had learned this, she assisted me in learning to spell words of three or four letters. Just at this point of my progress, Mr. Auld found out what was going on, and at once forbade Mrs. Auld to instruct me further, telling her, among other things, that it was unlawful, as well as unsafe, to teach a slave to read. To use his own words, further, he said, "If you give a nigger an inch, he will take an ell. A nigger should know nothing but to obey his master—to do as he is told to do. Learning would *spoil* the best nigger in the world . . . If you teach that nigger (speaking of myself) how to read, there would be no keeping him. It would forever unfit him to be a slave. He would at once become unmanageable, and of no value to his master . . . It would make him discontented and unhappy."
>
> These words sank deep into my heart, stirred up sentiments within that lay slumbering, and called into

---

* This testimony from Frederick Douglass is a good illustration of the symbols and ideas expressed in the Plato's Cave allegory from my second book, *The End of War*. Frederick Douglass's experiences also parallel the themes in the first film of the *Matrix* trilogy.

existence an entirely new train of thought. It was a new and special revelation, explaining dark and mysterious things, with which my youthful understanding had struggled, but struggled in vain. I now understood what had been to me a most perplexing difficulty . . . the white man's power to enslave the black man [by keeping him in ignorance] . . . From that moment, I understood the pathway from slavery to freedom . . . I was gladdened by the invaluable instruction which, by the merest accident, I had gained from my master. Though conscious of the difficulty of learning without a teacher, I set out with high hope, and a fixed purpose, at whatever cost of trouble, to learn how to read. The very decided manner with which he spoke, and strove to impress his wife with the evil consequences of giving me instruction [in reading], served to convince me that he was deeply sensible of the truths he was uttering . . . What he most dreaded, that I most desired. What he most loved, that I most hated. That which to him was a great evil, to be carefully shunned, was to me a great good, to be diligently sought; and the argument which he so warmly urged, against my learning to read, only served to inspire me with a desire and determination to learn. In learning to read, I owe almost as much to the bitter opposition of my master, as to the kindly aid of [his wife]. I acknowledge the benefit of both . . .

[Around the age of twelve] I got hold of a book entitled "The Columbian Orator." Every opportunity I got, I used to read this book. Among much of other interesting matter, I found in it a dialogue between a master and his slave. The slave was represented as having run away from his master three times. The dialogue represented the conversation which took place between them, when the slave was retaken the third time. In this dialogue, the whole argument in behalf of slavery was brought forward by the master, all of which was disposed of by the slave. The slave was made to say some very smart as well as impressive things in reply to his master—things which had the desired though unexpected effect; for the conversation resulted in the voluntary emancipation of the slave on the part of the master.

In the same book, I met with one of [Richard] Sheridan's mighty speeches on and in behalf of Catholic emancipation. These were choice documents to me. I read them over and over again with unabated interest. They gave tongue to interesting thoughts of my own soul, which had frequently flashed through my mind, and died away for want of utterance. The moral which I gained from the dialogue [between the slave and slaveholder] was the power of truth over the conscience of even a slaveholder. What I got from Sheridan was a bold denunciation of slavery, and a powerful vindication of human rights. The reading of these documents enabled me to utter my thoughts, and to meet the arguments brought forward to sustain slavery; but while they relieved me of one difficulty, they brought on another even more painful than the one of which I was relieved. The more I read, the more I was led to abhor and detest my enslavers. I could regard them in no other light than a band of successful robbers, who had left their homes, and gone to Africa, and stolen us from our homes, and in a strange land reduced us to slavery. I loathed them as being the meanest as well as the most wicked of men. As I read and contemplated the subject, behold! that very discontentment which Master Hugh [Auld] had predicted would follow my learning to read had already come, to torment and sting my soul to unutterable anguish.

As I writhed under it, I would at times feel that learning to read had been a curse rather than a blessing. It had given me a view of my wretched condition, without the remedy. It opened my eyes to the horrible pit, but to no ladder upon which to get out. In moments of agony, I envied my fellow-slaves for their stupidity. I have often wished myself a beast. I preferred the condition of the meanest reptile to my own. Anything, no matter what, to get rid of thinking! It was this everlasting thinking of my condition that tormented me. There was no getting rid of it . . . The silver trump of freedom had roused my soul to eternal wakefulness. Freedom now appeared . . . It was heard in every sound, and seen in every thing. It was ever present to torment me with a sense of my wretched condition. I saw nothing without seeing it, I heard nothing without hearing it, and felt nothing without feeling it. It looked from every star, it smiled in every calm, breathed in every wind, and moved in every storm.

I often found myself regretting my own existence, and wishing myself dead; and but for the hope of being free, I have no doubt but that I should have killed myself, or done something for which I should have been killed. While in this state of mind, I was eager to hear any one speak of slavery. I was a ready listener. Every little while, I could hear something about the abolitionists. It was some time before I found what the word meant. It was always used in such connections as to make it an interesting word to me. If a slave ran away and succeeded in getting clear, or if a slave killed his master, set fire to a barn, or did anything very wrong in the mind of a slaveholder, it was spoken of as the fruit of *abolition*.[16]

When dictators ban books and outlaw freedom of speech, freedom of the press, and freedom of assembly, they are attempting to hide the sword of truth that can remove them from power, just as Fulad-zereh hides the only weapon that can destroy him. As philosopher John Locke realized in the eighteenth century, it is physically impossible for a single man or small group to control a large population without their consent. When we study oppressive systems throughout history, one thing becomes very clear: in order to keep people living under oppression, a ruler must first oppress their minds. This is why systems of oppression work so hard to hide the truth from the people they are oppressing.

In a "free society" like ours—where democratic ideals permit freedom of speech, freedom of the press, and freedom of assembly—an oppressive system has difficulty hiding the truth the way dictators do. For example, the government of Nazi Germany could arrest and kill any German citizen who expressed an idea it didn't like, but for the most part our government cannot do this to American citizens. As a result, free societies rely heavily on propaganda to hide the truth.

Propaganda is the second method of hiding the truth. Dictatorships also rely on propaganda to oppress people's minds, but a society that allows freedom of expression must rely far more heavily on propaganda. If Hitler's propaganda did not work, he could always arrest and kill his own citizens as a backup plan. But when propaganda does not work in a free society, the oppressive systems contained within it will collapse.

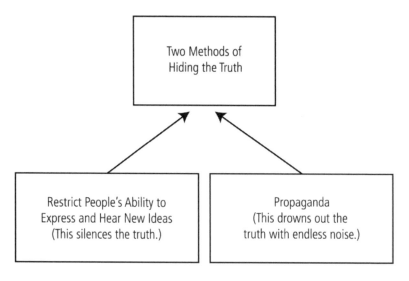

Figure 9.1 Two Methods of Hiding the Truth

Restricting people's ability to express and hear new ideas silences the truth, but propaganda drowns out the truth by creating endless noise. Propaganda generates so much noise that hearing the voice of truth can be as difficult as hearing the voice of a single person in a crowded football stadium. Liberty, justice, and peace are powerful ideals, but they cannot exist without the ideal of truth. Truth is the ideal that brings liberty, justice, and peace to life. It is the ideal that makes all of our other ideals possible.

As Americans who want to believe our country is based on liberty, justice, and truth, most of us don't like hearing that our politicians are using propaganda to hide the truth and oppress our minds. It might sound surprising to hear this at first, but when we look deeper we can see that every American already knows that propaganda plays a major role in our society. For example, every single conservative person I know thinks liberals use propaganda to hide the truth and oppress people's minds, and every single liberal person I know thinks conservatives use propaganda to hide the truth and oppress people's minds. In addition, every single conservative commentator in the media accuses liberals of using propaganda to distort the truth, and every single liberal commentator in the media accuses conservatives of using propaganda to distort the truth.

Politicians are often stereotyped as being dishonest, deceptive, two-faced, and self-interested. Of course, there are many honest politicians who work hard to maintain their integrity, but deception is a large part of the political game, and we all know it. So I think it is odd when Americans— who have no problem seeing politicians as dishonest, deceptive, two-faced, and self-interested—are surprised when their government lies to them. Who do they think is running our government? Politicians. Is it any surprise that our government sometimes lies to us? And is it so hard to believe that politicians in both political parties use deception and propaganda to advance their personal interests?

To believe that only liberal politicians use propaganda while conservative politicians always speak the truth, or to believe that only conservative politicians use propaganda while liberal politicians always speak the truth, is simply another illusion created by propaganda. This illusion divides us as human beings, and rulers have a much easier time controlling a population when they can divide people and turn them against each other. To quote the old adage from warfare, "Divide and conquer."

Why Waging Peace Is Mightier Than Violence

There is no reason to feel hopeless about the fate of our country, because we can overcome the harm caused by propaganda, deception, and illusion when we *practice democracy*. One of the most undemocratic things I have ever heard—which I hear often—is that the American president is the leader of the free world. If we understand what the ideal of democracy truly means, we realize that the people are supposed to lead, and the president is supposed to be the administrator of the people's will. When I was in elementary school my teachers told me that the president is supposed to be a "public servant" and the "employee of the American people." Although we live in a representative democracy instead of a direct democracy, we still have methods to pressure our politicians to do what we want. The evidence from American history shows that nothing will change for the better unless Americans tell the president what to do. American history also shows that ordinary citizens, not presidents, are the brightest visionaries and the true engine of progress.

For example, Lyndon Johnson was not a strong advocate for civil rights when he became president, but he later supported racial equality because Martin Luther King Jr. and other members of the civil rights movement pressured him to do so. Franklin Roosevelt was not a strong advocate for worker's rights, which included child labor laws and a five-day workweek, when he became president, but the workers' rights movement changed his viewpoint. Woodrow Wilson opposed women's equality when he became president, but he later supported the constitutional amendment that gave women the right to vote because Alice Paul and other members of the women's rights movement pressured him to do so. Abraham Lincoln was not a visionary who believed slavery should be completely abolished when he began his political career, but his views changed due to the influence of the abolitionist movement.

As a child I was taught that voting was the be-all and end-all of citizenship, and if I showed up at the polls to vote I was fulfilling my civic duty. But the women's and civil rights movements created dramatic change, even though many of their participants had little or no voting rights. Voting is just one tool in the democratic toolbox, and we cannot build a house with just a hammer. Susan B. Anthony and Martin Luther King Jr. used many democratic methods to wage peace—such as protests, petitions, boycotts, pressuring the legal system, and transforming how people think about controversial issues. Historian Howard Zinn said, "Democracy doesn't come from the top. It comes from the bottom. Democracy is not what governments do. It's what people do."[17]

Because democracy allows us to peacefully solve our problems without resorting to violence, "waging peace" is another way to say "practicing democracy." And because waging peace uses truth as a weapon to defeat injustice and heal the wounds of society, the "sword of truth" is another way to say "the sword that heals." As I mentioned earlier in this book, Martin Luther King Jr. said, "Nonviolence is a powerful and just weapon. It is a weapon unique in history, which cuts without wounding and ennobles the man who wields it. It is a sword that heals."[18] The sword of truth cuts propaganda, deception, and illusion without wounding justice, peace, and our humanity. Frederick Douglass said, "The truth can hurt nothing which ought not to be hurt, and it alone can make men and women free."[19] And Gandhi said, "Truth never damages a cause that is just."[20]

Martin Luther King Jr. realized that a dominant system of oppression is far more vulnerable to the nonviolent sword of truth than to violent weapons. To understand why oppressive systems tend to be vulnerable to the sword of truth but immune to violence, just as Fulad-zereh is vulnerable to a single magic sword but immune to all other weapons, I must explain one of the most important principles of military strategy.

Military strategy teaches us to not confront opponents where they are strongest, but to instead confront them where they are weakest. When Martin Luther King Jr. and the civil rights movement opposed segregation and other racist government policies, where was the U.S. government strongest? Its greatest strength then and now is the use of violence. Today the U.S. government controls the Army, Navy, Air Force, Marines, Special Forces, National Guard, FBI, CIA, and extensive police forces. If you fight the U.S. government with violence on its own soil—where it has "home-field advantage"—it will crush you.

When I discuss the progress achieved by the civil rights movement, people have responded to me by saying, "Martin Luther King Jr. would have made a lot more progress if he had started a violent uprising to end segregation in America rather than waging a peaceful campaign. Maybe if King had used violence, black people wouldn't still be discriminated against today. The slaves in Haiti won their freedom with a violent uprising, and that is what King should have done."

But there is a big difference between King's situation during the civil rights era and the conditions in Haiti during its violent uprising. During the civil rights era African Americans comprised less than 15 percent of the American population, and white people greatly outnumbered them. But in the French colony that later became known as Haiti, the proportions were reversed. White people and free blacks in Haiti comprised less than 15 percent of the population, and the black slaves greatly outnumbered their oppressors. At the start of the Haitian Revolution in 1791, the French colony consisted of an estimated 40,000 Europeans, 30,000 mulattos and free blacks, and 500,000 slaves.[21]

Even if the wealthy people who control an oppressive system are outnumbered, they are going to have significantly better access to weapons, supplies, equipment, and other resources necessary for winning a violent campaign. Due to the immense gap in wealth between the rich oppressor and the impoverished oppressed, the oppressor can acquire a much better armed, better trained, and better equipped army. Although the Haitian slaves succeeded in their violent uprising, the costs were high: around 100,000 slaves died during the Haitian Revolution.[22] If white and black people in Haiti had lived in the same racial proportions that existed in America in 1800, Haiti would have had 40,000 whites and less than 10,000 slaves. Obviously, black people in America would have had to at least outnumber white people to have a reasonable chance of winning a violent campaign.

Many peace activists discuss King's moral reasons for embracing nonviolence, but they ignore his strategic reasons. Like Gandhi, King would rather see oppressed people become disciplined soldiers trained to fight back violently than be helpless victims too afraid to resist. When King was asked during an interview whether he approved of Hungary's violent 1956 rebellion, he replied, "*I admire freedom fighters wherever they are* [emphasis added], but I still believe that nonviolence is the strongest approach."[23]

Today in our society, King has been portrayed as a naive pacifist who opposed violence strictly on moral grounds, rather than a brilliant strategist who saw nonviolence as a more powerful "weapon" than violence for fighting injustice. I have heard many people say that King used nonviolence instead of violence because he was a "wimp," when the truth is that King used nonviolence because he was a brave and brilliant strategist who saw the futility of fighting an oppressive system where it is strongest—in the use of violence. King, as a student of history, knew that when the Native Americans fought the American government, they were defeated by its much stronger military. King said:

> Our nation was born in genocide when it embraced the doctrine that the original American, the Indian, was an inferior race. Even before there were large numbers of Negroes on our shores, the scar of racial hatred had already disfigured colonial society. From the sixteenth century forward, blood flowed in battles over racial supremacy. We are perhaps the only nation which tried as a matter of national policy to wipe out its indigenous population. Moreover, we elevated that tragic experience into a noble crusade. Indeed, even today we have not permitted ourselves to reject or to feel remorse for this shameful episode. Our literature, our films, our drama, our folklore all exalt it . . .
>
> Our history teaches us that wielding the [violent] sword against racial superiority is not effective. The bravery of the [American] Indian, employing spears and arrows against the Winchester [rifle] and the Colt [pistol], had ultimately to eventuate in defeat. On the other hand, history also teaches that submission [to injustice] produces no acceptable result . . .
>
> The Negro's method of nonviolent direct action is not only suitable as a remedy for injustice; its very nature is such that it challenges the myth of [racial] inferiority. Even the most reluctant are forced to recognize that no inferior people could choose and successfully pursue a course involving such extensive sacrifice, bravery and skill . . .

Some [black people] called for a colossal blood bath to cleanse the nation's ills [of racial oppression]. To support their advocacy of violence and its incitement, they pointed to an historical tradition reaching back from the American Civil War to Spartacus in Rome. But the Negro in the South in 1955, assessing the power of the forces arrayed against him, could not perceive the slightest prospect of victory in this approach. He was unarmed, unorganized, untrained, disunited and, most important, psychologically and morally unprepared for the deliberate spilling of blood. Although his desperation had prepared him with the courage to die for freedom if necessary, he was not willing to commit himself to racial suicide with no prospect of victory . . .

I stand in the middle of two opposing forces in the Negro community. One is a force of complacency, made up in part of Negroes who, as a result of long years of oppression, are so drained of self-respect and a sense of "somebodiness" that they have adjusted to segregation . . . The other force is one of bitterness and hatred, and it comes perilously close to advocating violence. It is expressed in the various black nationalist groups that are springing up across the nation . . . I have tried to stand between these two forces, saying that we need emulate neither the "do-nothingism" of the complacent nor the hatred and despair of the black nationalist. For there is the most excellent way of love and nonviolent protest . . .

Today the Negro is *fighting* [emphasis added] for a finer America, and he will inevitably win the majority of the nation to his side because our hard-won [American] heritage of freedom is ultimately more powerful than our traditions of cruelty and injustice."[24]

It is very difficult to violently overcome an oppressor who has a far superior military, and this was as true in ancient history as it is in the modern era. What was the most militarized society in human history? What society was more militarized than the Romans, Americans, or even feudal Japan? The answer is Sparta. Spartan boys left home at age seven to begin military training, and they served in the military from ages twenty to sixty.[25] But why was Sparta such a militarized society? Why was it far more militarized than Athens, Thebes, and the other Greek city-states? Many people assume it was because the Spartans were trying to protect themselves from external invasions, but the Spartans actually became militarized in order to control a massive slave population. The Spartans had a much larger slave population than the other Greek city-states. In 400 BC, slaves comprised around 30 percent of the population in ancient Athens.[26] But in Sparta during the same time, the slaves (known as "Helots") outnumbered the Spartans around seven to one.[27]

The Greek historian Thucydides said, "Most Spartan institutions have always been designed with a view to security against the Helots.'"[28] And according to historian Paul Cartledge, "The name 'Helots' means 'captives' . . . The threat of Helot revolt, especially from the Messenians, was almost constant, and the Spartans responded by turning themselves into a sort of permanently armed camp, Fortress Sparta. Male Spartan citizens were forbidden any other trade, profession or business than war . . . Sparta had to be on a constant state of alert and readiness, for enemies within as well as without . . . The Helot system of the Spartans was the most controversial slave system in all Greece, presumably because the Helots were Greeks, not foreign barbarians like most of the unfree in the Greek world."[29]

Since the Helots outnumbered the Spartans so greatly, the Spartans managed most of the Helots in a manner closer to serfdom rather than "chattel" slavery. Nevertheless, the Spartans were known for their excessive cruelty toward the Helots. Paul Cartledge explains:

> As Aristotle observed, "the mere necessity of policing [the Helots] is a troublesome matter—the problem of how contact with them is to be managed. If allowed freedom, they grow insolent and think themselves as good as their masters; if made to live a hard life, they plot against and hate them . . ." Aristotle himself, influenced no doubt by

the fact that the Helots did not only plot [against their Spartan masters] but actually broke out in collective open revolt, believed that the Spartans had got it wrong, erring on the side of excessive brutality. "It is clear therefore," he added, "that those whose Helot-system works out like this have not discovered the best way of managing it."[30]

Myron of Priene, a Greek historian who lived around the third century BC, described how the Spartans treated the Helots: "[The Spartans] assign to the Helots every shameful task leading to disgrace. For they ordained that each one of them must wear a dogskin cap and wrap himself in skins and receive a stipulated number of beatings every year regardless of any wrongdoing, so that they would never forget they were slaves. Moreover, if any exceeded the vigour proper to a slave's condition, they made death the penalty."[31]

When oppressed people successfully use violence to resist an opponent with a stronger military, they often have the support of another powerful country. To mention a few examples, the Americans had the support of the French colonial empire during the American Revolution, the Vietnamese had the support of China and the Soviet Union during the Vietnam War, and the Afghans had the support of the United States when the Soviet Union invaded Afghanistan during the 1980s. A large group of Helots known as the Messenians tried to gain their freedom by fighting wars against the Spartans, but it was not until the Messenian Helots had the support of the powerful Greek city-state Thebes that they were freed.

The Theban politician and general Epaminondas (whom I discussed in chapter 7) freed the Messenian Helots when he invaded the Spartan homeland of Laconia. Although the Messenian Helots outnumbered their Spartan slave masters and tried to gain their freedom violently, they could not free themselves from their militarily superior oppressors without outside intervention. Historian Paul Cartledge tells us, "The Messenian Helots, with vital help from democratic Thebes led by the philosopher and general Epaminondas, revolted once more, but this time for good . . . *The final liberation of the Messenians could not have happened without outside intervention* [emphasis added], and intervention of the specific kind undertaken by the Greek world's most brilliant general who was also a man of a philosophic cast of mind. Epaminondas achieved fame chiefly on the battlefield, but Sir Walter Raleigh had good reason for rating him the greatest of the ancient Greeks, not just the greatest of ancient Greek generals."[32]

As I mentioned earlier, military strategy teaches us to attack our opponents at their weakest point, and Epaminondas knew that Sparta's weakest point was its heavy reliance on its slave population. The Helots were both the source of Sparta's imperial might and its Achilles heel.[33] When Epaminondas freed the Messenian slaves, Sparta forever ceased to be a great power. Paul Cartledge explains, "The brilliant Theban commander Epaminondas conducted a massive invasion of Laconia, the first-ever invasion of Laconia by land by a foreign power since the formation of the Spartan state some three to four centuries earlier. By freeing the Helots of Messenia, and so destroying the economic basis of the Spartan army's superiority, and by fortifying the Messenians' old stronghold on Mt. Ithome to ensure the independence of their new city of Messene, Epaminondas put an end to Sparta's 'Great Power' status for good."[34]

The Roman slave Spartacus was not as fortunate as the Messenians, because he did not have a brilliant general like Epaminondas or a powerful country like Thebes on his side. During the first century BC, Spartacus led a slave revolt against Rome. A slave and a gladiator, Spartacus helped plot an escape from the gladiator school where he was imprisoned. During the escape he and around seventy others fought for freedom using kitchen utensils as weapons. Within a few years after the successful prison break, Spartacus gathered enough slaves and people oppressed by the Romans to form an army of nearly 100,000 soldiers. His rebellion, known as the Third Servile War, ended when he was killed and his army was destroyed in a climactic battle with the Romans.

To deter future revolts, the Roman government crucified six thousand soldiers it had captured from Spartacus's army. They were crucified along the Appian Way, a major road leading to Rome. After the crucified soldiers died, the Roman government did not remove their bodies from the roadside for months, allowing the rotting corpses to serve as a warning. As is usually the case in history, a violent rebellion on behalf of the oppressed leads to increased cruelty from the oppressor. When the oppressed use violence against an unjust system, the oppressor seldom if ever has a change of heart, but instead feels more justified in using severe brutality to crush the oppressed.

All governments work hard to maintain a monopoly on the use of violence, and the most powerful monopolies on violence in history have been achieved by the United States government, British Empire, Roman Empire, Sparta, and other militarily strong nations. Throughout the second half of the twentieth century until today, the U.S. government has maintained the most powerful military in human history. The guerrilla leader Che Guevara used violence to overthrow a corrupt dictatorship in Cuba during the 1950s, but he succeeded partly because the Cuban government had a weak military. If he had attempted to use violence against the U.S. government on American soil—where it has home-field advantage—he and everyone in his violent rebellion would have been smashed and wiped out. In fact, the CIA helped capture Che Guevara in Bolivia (where he was subsequently executed), without him being on American soil.

Gandhi had a much better understanding of strategy than Che Guevara. During the Zulu rebellion against the British Empire in 1906, Gandhi witnessed British soldiers massacring the Zulus. He realized that using violence against the British would confront the British Empire where it is strongest, putting the Indians at a severe disadvantage. Gandhi wanted to win his struggle against the British, and he knew that waging peace gave him the best chance of achieving victory. Gandhi's grandson and biographer, Rajmohan Gandhi, explains:

> [During the Zulu rebellion against the British Empire in 1906] he was reminded of India's 1857 rebellion[against the British Empire], which too witnessed great brutality, including floggings and men blown from guns. That rising had only consolidated British power in India, even as the Zulu revolt seemed to be doing in South Africa . . . he also realized the folly of being excited into violence against the strong-in-arms . . .
>
> Within months of the Zulu rebellion, the Transvaal Indians launched their first non-violent defiance or, as it would eventually be called, satyagraha ("truth-force"), with

Gandhi saying on 11 September 1906, "I can boldly declare, and with certainty, that so long as there are even a handful of men true to their pledge [to fight with nonviolent resistance], there can be only one end to the struggle, *and that is victory* [emphasis added]."

In the Autobiography Gandhi says that his Zululand decisions were a necessary "preliminary . . . to satyagraha." Zululand had led to "the gift of the fight" that he would share with South Africa, India and the world. Every individual anywhere had the power to resist oppression, and non-violent resistance was legitimate.[35]

Gandhi is often misrepresented as someone who opposed war on strictly moral grounds. But his opposition to war had more to do with practical and strategic reasons rather than a strict moral objection to violence. After all, Gandhi was a war veteran and former military recruiter. Gandhi scholar Peter Brock tells us, "[Gandhi] admired the soldierly virtues, keenly resenting the fact that his countrymen as a whole had been deprived of the possibility of training in arms . . . Indeed he had never ceased to maintain that, while nonviolent resolution of conflict was preferable to the use of violence, himsa [violence] employed to right a wrong was preferable to tame submission to injustice or aggression. A follower of ahimsa [nonviolence], he believed, had to reckon with that fact."[36]

Why did Gandhi think that nonviolent struggle was a better way than violence to right the wrong of colonialism? From a practical and strategic perspective, he realized the British Empire had crushed violent uprisings such as the Indian Rebellion of 1857 and Zulu Rebellion of 1906, allowing the British to gain more control over its colonies. Gandhi said we must always resist oppression and injustice by any means necessary, but he saw how waging peace was more effective than violence at resisting tyranny. He later explained, "You cannot successfully fight them [powerful countries] with their own weapons. After all, you cannot go beyond the atom bomb. Unless we have a new way of fighting imperialism of all brands in place of the outworn one of violent rising, there is no hope for the oppressed races of the earth."[37]

Waging peace is a new way of fighting oppression, injustice, deception, and hatred that attacks the root causes of problems rather than the symptoms. Martin Luther King Jr. called waging peace "the sword that heals" and I call it "the sword of truth," but Gandhi called waging peace "the sword of love." Gandhi realized that truth and love are two features of the same face. He said, "The sword of the satyagrahi [one who uses truth-force] is love, and the unshakable firmness that comes from it."[38]

For Gandhi, victory did not mean crushing the British Empire, but creating a new peaceful relationship with them where they respected the dignity of the Indians. He said, "A non-violent revolution is not a program of seizure of power. It is a program of transformation of relationships, ending in a peaceful transfer of power . . . In satyagraha [truth-force] the cause has to be just and clear as well as the means . . . Satyagraha can never be used to defend a wrong cause."[39]

For years I have studied jiu-jitsu, which taught me that a skilled boxer is like a lion. Just as a lion is called the "king of the jungle," a skilled boxer usually reigns supreme in a fistfight. But when a jiu-jitsu fighter wrestles a boxer to the ground and applies a submission hold, it is like pulling a lion into a shark tank. A boxer on the ground, like a lion in the water, is out of his element. In a similar way, Gandhi wanted to confront the British Empire at its weakest rather than strongest point. He wanted to pull the lion that was the British Empire into the shark tank of waging peace.

When we use violence against an oppressive system that possesses a strong military, we are attacking its strongest point where it is best prepared to smash us. But when we wage peace, we are taking an oppressive system out of its element and dragging it into deep water. When we fight an opponent at his weakest rather than strongest point, the military refers to this as *asymmetric warfare*. Examples of asymmetric warfare include terrorism and guerrilla warfare. Terrorism attacks unarmed civilians—very vulnerable and weak targets. And guerrilla warfare attacks military targets, but uses ambushes to strike their weakest points. During the Vietnam War, the Vietnamese relied on guerrilla warfare because the U.S. military would have annihilated them in a traditional battle.

Gandhi was a strategic genius who realized that waging peace, rather than terrorism or guerrilla warfare, is the most effective way to asymmetrically defeat a militarily stronger opponent. He said, "No doubt the non-violent way is always the best, but where that does not come naturally the violent way is both necessary and honorable. Inaction here is rank cowardice and unmanly. It must be shunned at all cost."[40] Although Gandhi preferred violence to inaction and cowardice, he knew that the nonviolent action of waging peace is more effective than violence. He said, "People listened to me because I showed them how to give fight to the British without arms when they had no arms and the British Government was fully equipped and organized for an armed fight . . . [Nonviolence is] more effective than any other weapon, in fact, the mightiest force in the world."[41]

Since Gandhi's death, numerous studies have shown that waging peace is more likely than violence to defeat a militarily superior adversary. According to the Metta Center on Nonviolence:

> Maria Stephan of the International Center on Non-violent Conflict (ICNC) and Erica Chenoweth of the University of Colorado Boulder have discovered remarkable findings in their study of the relative strategic effectiveness of violent and nonviolent asymmetric conflict. Their study of terrorist groups, guerrilla movements, and nonviolent resistance movements found that nonviolent resistance movements have achieved partial or full success nearly 90% of the time, compared to 50% for guerilla warfare. It is based on the newly-created Nonviolent and Violent Conflicts and Outcomes ("NAVCO") dataset, which compiles data on the characteristics of various violent and nonviolent insurgency campaigns and attempts to systematically explain their outcomes.
>
> Another recent study conducted by terrorism expert Max Abrahms found that terrorist groups have achieved their stated objectives a mere 7% of the times. These findings suggest that when it comes to fighting an adversary of superior military might, nonviolent civilian-based resistance is more effective than terrorism or guerrilla warfare.[42]

Even if a country wins a guerrilla war against a much stronger opponent, most of the people in that country may not be any better off. As I discussed at the beginning of this book, America's Founding Fathers rebelled against the British Empire because they felt unfairly treated. They believed it was unjust to be taxed or controlled without the opportunity to participate in the political process. They also believed that those who govern must gain the consent of the governed. The motto "No taxation without representation" echoed their outrage and became a call to arms, leading to the American Revolution (1775–1783). Yet decades after the war ended, less than 10 percent of the American population could vote in national elections. Women could not vote. African Americans could not vote. And most white people could not vote unless they owned land. During the early nineteenth century "No taxation without representation" only seemed to apply to the rich.

How did so many Americans increase their liberties during the past two hundred years? Did nonlandowners fight a war to obtain the right to vote? Did women fight a war to get the right to vote? Did African Americans fight a war to attain their civil rights? Did American workers fight a war to gain their rights? Was a war fought for child labor laws? These victories for liberty and justice were achieved because people waged peace, but this is a part of our history many people do not remember. Our society also teaches us that "war freed the slaves," but not a single European country had a war to free the slaves. Instead, the slaves in Europe were freed through nonviolent struggle. And although the American Civil War was a vital struggle that kept the country together, African Americans did not gain their human rights until they waged peace during the civil rights movement in the 1950s and 1960s.*

When the oppressed violently overthrow their oppressor, they often become as tyrannical as their oppressor. This happened during the violent Russian Revolution, when the Bolsheviks became similar to the oppressive monarchs they had overthrown. This also happened during the violent French Revolution, when the dead aristocrats were replaced by a series of

---

* Was the American Civil War necessary to free the slaves? This question is still open to debate, but in Frederick Douglass's third autobiography he makes a very convincing argument that slavery was so deeply-entrenched in the Southern states that a war was needed to abolish it. Although a strong argument can be made that the Civil War was necessary to keep the country together and abolish slavery, it is important to remember that war never fully solves a problem. It took a campaign of waging peace—the civil rights movement—to gain human rights for African Americans and transform how people saw the issue of race.

repressive regimes, culminating in Napoleon's dictatorship. And after the violent Haitian Revolution, Haiti was ruled by several brutal dictators.

George Orwell's book *Animal Farm* is an allegory about how the oppressed, after winning a violent revolution, often become as tyrannical as their oppressor. In *Animal Farm* the pigs lead the other farm animals in a violent uprising that overthrows the human farmer who is oppressing them. Prior to overthrowing the farmer, the farm animals created a motto: "All animals are equal." But after the pigs violently overthrow the farmer they begin to exploit the other animals. The pigs not only act like their former oppressor, the tyrannical farmer, they even begin wearing his clothes, walking on two legs, and carrying whips. The pigs then change the original motto "All animals are equal" to a new motto: "All animals are equal but some animals are more equal than others."

Nonviolent revolutions are less likely to replace an oppressive regime with another equally oppressive regime, because waging peace often creates a *spiritual change* in the people waging the nonviolent campaign, making it less likely they will become like their oppressor after they achieve victory. When a person wields the sword of truth and love, some of that truth and love leaves a positive imprint on their innermost being. An obvious example of spiritual change is Nelson Mandela, who became much more compassionate and understanding toward his opponents after embracing waging peace as a strategy, philosophy, and way of life. After Mandela was elected president, he did not treat his former white oppressors with the same cruelty they had inflicted on him.

Erica Chenoweth, co-author of *Why Civil Resistance Works: The Strategic Logic of Nonviolent Conflict*, explains how nonviolence has been effective since the beginning of the twentieth century through to the "Arab Spring" protests in 2011:

> Oppressive regimes need the loyalty of their personnel to carry out their orders. Violent resistance tends to reinforce that loyalty, while civil resistance undermines it. When security forces refuse orders to, say, fire on peaceful protesters, regimes must accommodate the opposition or give up power—precisely what happened in Egypt [in

2011]. This is why the Egyptian president, Hosni Mubarak, took such great pains to use armed thugs to try to provoke the Egyptian demonstrators into using violence, after which he could have rallied the military behind him.

But where Mr. Mubarak failed, Col. Muammar el-Qaddafi succeeded: what began as a peaceful movement became, after a few days of brutal crackdown by his corps of foreign militiamen, an armed but disorganized rebel fighting force. A widely supported popular revolution has been reduced to a smaller group of armed rebels attempting to overthrow a brutal dictator. These rebels are at a major disadvantage, and are unlikely to succeed without direct foreign intervention . . .

Although the change is not immediate, our data show that from 1900 to 2006, 35 percent to 40 percent of authoritarian regimes that faced major nonviolent uprisings had become democracies five years after the campaign ended, even if the campaigns failed to cause immediate regime change. For the nonviolent campaigns that succeeded, the figure increases to well over 50 percent. The good guys don't always win, but their chances increase greatly when they play their cards well. Nonviolent resistance is about finding and exploiting points of leverage in one's own society. Every dictatorship has vulnerabilities, and every society can find them.[43]

The strongest point of a powerful empire is its military, but where is its weakest point? *Moral authority* refers to the influence we have over others when our behavior embodies justice and goodness. Gandhi realized the weakest point of the British Empire was its moral authority, because it was supporting the injustice of colonialism. And Martin Luther King Jr. realized the weakest point of the federal and state governments in America was also their moral authority, because they were supporting the injustice of segregation. Gandhi and King taught us to confront an oppressive system not violently where it is strongest, but in the realm of moral authority where it is weakest. By exposing the moral injustice of these oppressive systems, Gandhi and King were able to weaken and eventually remove popular support for these unjust policies.

When we wage peace and those in power use violence against us, it not only weakens their moral authority, but it can also increase *our* moral authority. This is what King meant when he said the sword that heals "ennobles the man who wields it." When peaceful civil rights protestors were shown on television being blasted with fire hoses and attacked by police dogs, public support for the civil rights movement increased. When the U.S. government attacked the Bonus Marchers—World War I veterans protesting for the wages they had been promised while serving overseas—it increased the moral authority of their movement and public opinion shifted in their favor.

In the film *Star Wars*, the death of the Jedi knight Obi-Wan Kenobi symbolizes how a righteous cause can grow stronger when violence is used against it. Right before Darth Vader kills him, Obi-Wan Kenobi says, "You can't win, Darth. If you strike me down I shall become more powerful than you can possibly imagine." This is a metaphor for those who died in the struggle for justice, because when the Athenians killed Socrates he also became more powerful. After executing him the Athenians later regretted it and created a statue to honor him. Socrates, like many others who died for justice, became a symbol that has inspired countless people around the world.

When the Romans killed Jesus he also became more powerful as a symbol, and when Gandhi and King were assassinated they too became symbols that will never go away. The *Chicago Sun Times* published a political cartoon in 1968 shortly after the assassination of Martin Luther King Jr. It depicted Gandhi, who was assassinated in 1948, speaking with King. Extending a peaceful hand toward King, Gandhi said, "The odd thing about assassins, Dr. King, is that they think they've killed you."

This is one reason why the apartheid government in South Africa kept Nelson Mandela in prison instead of killing him, and the dictatorship in Burma held democratic leader Aung San Suu Kyi under house arrest rather than executing her. However, unjust imprisonment can still create public outrage and shift national and global consensus. When oppressive systems deal with nonviolent activists today, it is better to imprison than to kill them, but it is far better to slander someone's reputation than be perceived as holding an innocent person in jail. Nevertheless, although an oppressive system can lock our bodies behind bars, it cannot fully imprison the truth once a new idea has begun to spread. As I mentioned earlier, Frederick Douglass said, "When a great truth once gets abroad in the world, no power on earth can imprison it, or prescribe its limits, or suppress it."[44]

Truth is eternal, but the lies that sustain oppression and injustice have a lifespan. Since the birth of humanity it has always been true that women are not less than human and no race was designed for slavery, but lies suppress these truths. Unlike truth, which can be concealed but never destroyed, the lifespan of a lie can be cut short by the sword of truth. According to Persian mythology, Fulad-zereh was eventually defeated by a warrior named Amir Arsalan,[45] who slayed him with the legendary magic sword. Just as Amir Arsalan used the magic sword to defeat the demon Fulad-zereh, we can use the sword of truth to defeat demons such as war, environmental destruction, injustice, and oppression. Now that I have explained what the sword of truth is and why it is the most powerful weapon in the world, I must now explain how to wield it with maximum force.

CHAPTER 10

The Power of Persuasion and Strategic Thinking

Transforming How People Think

Why is it so difficult to have a political discussion with those who disagree with us? Why do discussions about controversial issues so often devolve into angry shouting matches? As I mentioned earlier, all societal problems—such as racism, sexism, injustice, war, and environmental destruction—come from how people think. And all progress comes from transforming how people think. But how are we supposed to transform how people think when we cannot have a productive conversation with those who disagree with us? How are we supposed to change attitudes about a controversial issue when so many people's minds seem resistant to change? How are we supposed to end war when so many Americans perceive peace activists as unpatriotic hippies who are a threat to national security?

To understand the answers to these questions, we must first understand how the human mind works. Have you ever wondered why you cannot discuss politics and religion in a civilized way with most people? Have you ever wondered why people can become so aggressive and hostile when discussing controversial issues? I wondered these same things at West Point when one of my friends told me, "Never discuss politics, religion, or any controversial issue with people. It's a waste of time, because people never listen and get very angry when their viewpoints are questioned." Ever since he told me that, I was determined to find a way to dialogue about important and controversial issues. I thought, "Since the most serious problems in our world are also controversial, how will anything ever change for the better if we cannot discuss controversial issues in a productive and civilized way?"

My determination to understand the art of dialogue led me to a deeper understanding of the human condition. Just as the human body requires physical necessities such as food and water to survive, the human mind requires psychological necessities such as a worldview and sense of identity to remain sane. In his book *The Anatomy of Human Destructiveness*, psychologist Erich Fromm says that when others assault our worldview and sense of identity, we will often react with aggression as if they were threatening our physical body. This is because new ideas that attack our worldview and sense of identity can endanger our "psychic equilibrium," which is another way of saying our "mental stability." Erich Fromm explains:

> Man, like the animal, defends himself against threat to his vital interests. *But the range of man's vital interests is much wider than that of the animal.* Man must survive not only physically but also psychically. He needs to maintain a certain psychic equilibrium lest he lose the capacity to function; for man everything necessary for the maintenance of his psychic equilibrium is of the same vital interest as that which serves his physical equilibrium. First of all, man has a vital interest in retaining his frame of orientation. His capacity to act depends on it, and in the last analysis, his sense of identity. If others threaten him with ideas that question his own frame of orientation, he will react to these ideas as to a vital threat. He may rationalize this reaction in many ways. He will say that the new ideas are inherently "immoral," "uncivilized," "crazy," or whatever else he can think of to express his repugnance, but this antagonism is in fact aroused because "he" feels threatened.[1]

A frame of orientation, also known as a worldview, is just as important to our mind as oxygen is to our body. We need a worldview, a way of orienting ourselves to our surroundings, in order to remain sane. When we threaten people's worldview with new ideas, they will often respond with the same aggression as if we were threatening their physical body. When

Galileo proposed a new view of the universe, where the planets revolve around the sun, the leaders of the Roman Catholic Church reacted with aggression as if Galileo had held a knife to their throats. Galileo had threatened their worldview, and throughout history a common punishment for challenging the predominant worldview was ridicule, imprisonment, or even execution.

The human condition requires us to have a worldview, but the human condition does not require us to always be afraid of new ideas. Throughout history all progress has resulted from new ideas that change how people think. Democracy, the right to vote, freedom of speech, freedom of religion, freedom of the press, freedom of assembly, and women's and civil rights became widespread, for example, because new ideas changed how people thought and perceived their humanity.

When someone promotes a new idea, such as ending racial segregation in America, a minority of people will react with fear and aggression no matter what. But the majority of people are capable of accepting a new idea without fear if we use the right approach. We can use a simple yet effective technique to make a new and controversial idea sound more persuasive and less threatening. To do this, connect a new idea to a familiar idea. This can be accomplished by framing a new idea within their current worldview, rather than using a new idea to directly assault their worldview. In his book *Strategy*, military historian Liddell Hart explains:

> In all such cases, the direct assault of new ideas provokes a stubborn resistance, thus intensifying the difficulty of producing a change of outlook . . . Opposition to the truth is inevitable, especially if it takes the form of a new idea, but the degree of resistance can be diminished—by giving thought not only to the aim but to the method of approach. Avoid a frontal attack on a long established position; instead, seek to turn it by flank movement, so that a more penetrable side is exposed to the thrust of truth. But, in any such indirect approach, take care not to diverge from the truth—for nothing is more fatal to its real advancement than to lapse into untruth.

The meaning of these reflections may be made clearer by illustration from one's own experience. Looking back on the stages by which various fresh ideas gained acceptance, it can be seen that the process was eased when they could be presented, not as something radically new, but as the revival in modern terms of a time-honored principle or practice that had been forgotten. This required not deception, but care to trace the connection . . . A notable example was the way that the opposition to mechanization was diminished by showing that the mobile armored vehicle—the fast-moving tank—was fundamentally the heir of the armored horseman, and thus the natural means of reviving the decisive role which cavalry had played in past ages."[2]

For example, ending racial segregation in America was a new and controversial idea that threatened the worldview of many people, challenging everything they had ever been taught. But Martin Luther King Jr. used a very intelligent approach. He connected the new idea of racial equality to the Declaration of Independence, the American dream, and our most cherished American ideals such as justice, opportunity, freedom, and democracy. In his famous "I Have a Dream" speech, King did not directly assault the worldview of white Americans. Instead, he brilliantly delivered a speech that framed the new idea of racial equality within their current worldview. In the following excerpt from the "I Have a Dream" speech, I have italicized the instances where King connected the new idea of racial equality to concepts familiar to most Americans.

In a sense we've come to our nation's capital to cash a check. *When the architects of our republic wrote the magnificent words of the Constitution and the Declaration of Independence, they were signing a promissory note to which every American was to fall heir. This note was a promise that all men, yes, black men as well as white men, would be guaranteed the "unalienable Rights of Life, Liberty, and the pursuit of Happiness."* It is obvious today that America has defaulted on this promissory note insofar as her citizens of color are concerned. Instead of honoring this sacred obligation, America has given the Negro people a bad check, a check which has come back marked "insufficient funds."

[In the following paragraph King ties the new idea of racial equality to cherished American ideals such as justice, opportunity, freedom, and democracy.] But we refuse to believe that the bank of *justice* is bankrupt. We refuse to believe that there are insufficient funds in the great vaults of *opportunity* of this nation. And so we've come to cash this check, a check that will give us upon demand the riches of *freedom* and the security of *justice* . . . Now is the time to make real the promises of *democracy* . . .

I say to you today, my friends, so even though we face the difficulties of today and tomorrow, I still have a dream. It is a dream deeply rooted in the *American dream.* [Here King is tying his dream of racial equality to the American dream.] I have a dream that one day this nation will rise up and live out the true meaning of its creed: "*We hold these truths to be self-evident, that all men are created equal.*" I have a dream that one day on the red hills of Georgia, the sons of former slaves and the sons of former slave owners will be able to sit down together at the table of brotherhood . . .

This will be the day when all of God's children will be able to sing with new meaning:

My country, 'tis of thee, sweet land of liberty,
   of thee I sing.
Land where my fathers died, land of the pilgrim's
   pride,
From every mountainside, let freedom ring![3]

Figure 10.1 shows how Martin Luther King Jr. strategically connected the new and controversial idea of racial equality to the powerful ideals contained within the predominant American worldview. As I explained in chapter 5, it is impossible to convince every single person. But for progress to happen, we don't have to convince every single person; we just have to convince *enough* people. King's strategic approach made the new idea of racial equality much more persuasive to the majority of Americans.

The "I Have a Dream" speech is one of the most moving, inspiring, and *patriotic* speeches I have ever read. The word "patriotism" makes many peace activists cringe, because that word has been misused and abused by American politicians and the media, especially after the 9/11 terrorist attacks. For example, peace activists were called unpatriotic for questioning whether our country should go to war. As a result, many people today associate patriotism with blind obedience and aggressive nationalism, but that is not what patriotism truly means.

What It Truly Means to Love Our Country

The simplest and least controversial definition of patriotism is "love of country." But what does it mean to truly love our country? As I explain in *Will War Ever End?*, we can better understand love of country by realizing what it means to love a child. Parents who love their children will try to correct a child caught stealing, abusing people, or being dishonest. For parents who do not truly love their children, apathy will cause them not to care, enabling their children to get away with anything. In this same way, if we love our country we will do our best to improve it. We will try to make America a better place for everyone, as courageous citizens have always done.

Since our country's founding, brave patriots have worked to give us the many freedoms we enjoy today. Two hundred years ago in America, anyone who was not a white, male landowner suffered oppression. During this era, the majority of people lacked the right to vote, and many Americans lived as slaves. Our country is much more humane today than it was then. This happened because courageous citizens such as Martin Luther King Jr., Mark

The Predominant American Worldview in the 1960s

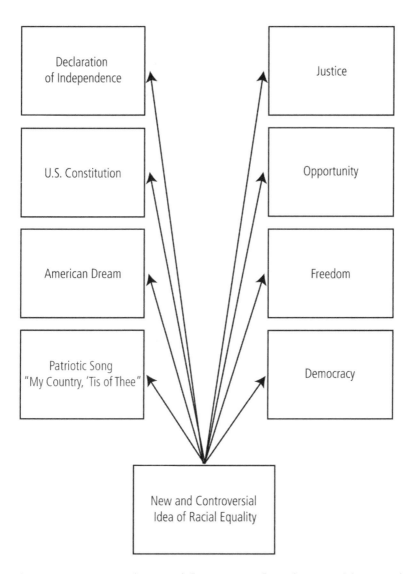

Figure 10.1 How Martin Luther King Jr.'s "I Have a Dream" speech connected the new and controversial idea of racial equality to the powerful ideals contained within the predominant American worldview

Twain, Helen Keller, Susan B. Anthony, Frederick Douglass, Elizabeth Cady Stanton, Woody Guthrie, Smedley Butler, Henry David Thoreau, and many others struggled to make our country a better place for all people.

Because of the patriotic Americans who loved and were therefore willing to question, constructively criticize, and improve their country, America has made a lot of progress. When my father was drafted into the army in 1949, the military was segregated because the government upheld an official policy that viewed African Americans as inferior and subhuman. Fifty years before then, the government would not allow women to vote, and only fifty years prior to that, the government supported and protected slavery.

I have met peace activists who refuse to use phrases such as "patriotism" and "love of country" to describe their work for peace, because they feel that the advocates of war have monopolized and corrupted those terms. But if we refuse to use a word because someone else uses it in a way we don't like, then eventually we will run out of words to use.[4] Phrases such as "patriotism" and "love of country" are so powerful that we can no longer afford to let the advocates of war monopolize and corrupt them.

In ancient battles an army gained an advantage when it occupied "high ground" such as a hilltop. On the battlefield of ideas, patriotism and love of country are high ground that give us an enormous strategic and persuasive advantage, and we must take back the high ground. When a social movement's message can authentically stand atop the high ground of patriotism and love of country, the movement will appeal more broadly to the masses. Mark Twain also said we must take back the meaning of words such as patriotism. In 1905 he explained, "Remember this, take it to heart, live by it, die for it if necessary: that our patriotism is medieval, outworn, obsolete; that the modern patriotism, the *true patriotism* [emphasis added], the only rational patriotism, is loyalty to the Nation all the time, loyalty to the Government when it deserves it."[5]

In 1967 Martin Luther King Jr. said, "We believe the *highest patriotism* [emphasis added] demands the ending of the [Vietnam] war and the opening of a bloodless war to final victory over racism and poverty."[6] In 1882 women's rights activist Olympia Brown said, "Now was the time for every *true patriot* [emphasis added] to demand that no new State should be admitted except on the basis of suffrage to women as well as negroes."[7]

During the American Revolution, "patriots" such as Founding Father Thomas Paine rebelled against tyranny and challenged the status quo. Those are the same kind of patriots we need today. General Dwight Eisenhower believed all worthwhile progress requires dissent and that opposing injustice is the highest form of patriotism. He said, "Here in America we are descended in blood and in spirit from revolutionaries and rebels—men and women who dared to dissent from accepted doctrine. As their heirs, may we never confuse honest dissent with disloyal subversion."[8]

In the army I learned that being loyal to your leaders requires you to question them. If your commander's plan is flawed, the highest form of loyalty is disagreeing with the plan whether your superior officer wants to hear it or not. On the other hand, letting your commander march toward disaster without properly expressing your disagreement is an act of disloyalty.

Telling the truth can put us at personal risk, because people may not be kind to those who bear bad news, hence the saying "Don't shoot the messenger." But to truly be loyal we must be willing to take that risk. As I mentioned in chapter 5, the *Code of the Samurai* tells us, "Once you have become someone's confidant, it shows a certain degree of dependability to pursue the truth and speak your mind freely even if the other person doesn't like what you say. If, however, you are fainthearted and fear to speak the truth, lest you cause offense or upset, and thus say whatever is convenient instead of what is right, thereby inducing other people to say things they shouldn't, or causing them to blunder to their own disadvantage, then you are useless as an advisor."[9]

As American citizens, we have a sacred duty to love and be loyal to our country. This means correcting the politicians who run our government when they stray from the path of justice. This means taking the harder path of love and loyalty over the convenient path of apathy and disloyalty. When King spoke against the Vietnam War in his speech "Beyond Vietnam," he said, "I speak as one who loves America."[10] If we truly love our country, we will work hard to help it achieve its full potential by correcting its mistakes, and we will do what is necessary to serve and sacrifice for our nation, even if it means taking a stance that makes us unpopular. The same can be said of parents who truly love their children.

Just as parents who do not let their children eat a lot of junk food may be less popular than parents who let their children get away with anything, doing what is right for our country can also make us less popular than those who enable harmful behavior. In the Bible, the prophets who flattered the king were much more popular within the royal court than the prophets who challenged the king's injustice. The flatterers were later called "false prophets," while those who challenged the king's injustice were recognized by later generations as the true prophets. During their lives, however, the false prophets were often rewarded by the king, while the true prophets were usually punished.

When Martin Luther King Jr. spoke against the Vietnam War, many of his friends and allies turned against him. The NAACP and many black churches disowned him, and his own organization, the Southern Christian Leadership Conference, issued a public statement criticizing his stance on the war. But during a 1967 television interview on *The Mike Douglas Show*, King said:

> I think the things that I'm saying and the things that I'm trying to do and all of the people in the peace movement are trying to do are really geared toward bringing the boys [U.S. soldiers] back home. In other words, we are trying to prove to be their best friends by doing something to bring about the climate that will bring an end to this war . . . When I first spoke out against the war, only twenty-one percent of the American people were against it. Both the Gallup and the Harris polls reveal now that the majority of Americans are against the war in Vietnam . . .
>
> A man of conscience can never be a consensus leader. He doesn't take a stand in order to search for consensus. He is ultimately a *molder* of consensus. And I've always said that the ultimate measure of a man is not where he stands in moments of comfort and moments of convenience, but where he stands in moments of challenge and moments of controversy. And I would take this position [against the Vietnam War] even if I didn't have the majority of people agreeing with me now.[11]

The U.S. Army has a saying, "We need leadership, not likership." What does this mean? The army taught me that "leadership" means doing what is right, while "likership" means doing what is popular in order to be liked—with no concern for whether your actions are right or wrong. In a democracy, "what is right" usually becomes a majority position only after overcoming the long and difficult path of being a minority position. To offer an example, most Americans today support women's right to vote and oppose slavery and segregation. But these viewpoints used to be extremely unpopular, and the advocates of racial and gender equality were ridiculed and attacked for challenging popular support for slavery, segregation, and the oppression of women.

Just as the advocates of racial and gender equality transformed attitudes in America, Martin Luther King Jr. realized that our democracy cannot function correctly unless conscientious citizens become "molders of consensus" who also transform attitudes. But to transform attitudes, especially toward controversial issues, we must have a persuasive message that resonates with many people who do not already agree with us. In other words, we must do more than preach to the choir.

How to Effectively Frame a New Idea

When we connect a new and controversial idea to powerful ideals such as patriotism (love of country), justice, opportunity, freedom, and democracy, our new idea becomes much more persuasive. Martin Luther King Jr. was not the only pioneer who connected new ideas to powerful ideals within people's existing worldviews. Although new ideas such as women's rights and ending slavery sounded controversial and radical in the nineteenth century, the ingenious women's rights activists of that era framed these new ideas in a way that did not directly assault the worldview of most Americans.

In 1866, Lucretia Mott, Elizabeth Cady Stanton, Susan B. Anthony, Theodore Tilton, and Frederick Douglass made a statement on behalf of the American Equal Rights Association. They connected the new idea of racial and gender equality to the powerful ideals of the American Revolution: "Woman and the colored man are loyal, patriotic, property-holding, tax-paying, liberty-loving citizens; and we cannot believe that sex or complexion should be any ground for civil or political degradation . . . And is not our protest pre-eminently as just against the tyranny of 'taxation without representation' as was that thundered from Bunker Hill, when our revolutionary fathers fired the shot that shook the world?"[12]

During the first convention for women's rights in 1848, Elizabeth Cady Stanton wrote a declaration affirming the rights of women. Known as the "Declaration of Rights and Sentiments," it became the founding document of the women's rights movement. In an act of strategic brilliance, she connected the new and controversial idea of women's rights to the greatly admired founding document of America: the Declaration of Independence. In the Declaration of Rights and Sentiments, she even borrowed many popular phrases from the Declaration of Independence. Elizabeth Cady Stanton wrote: "We hold these truths to be self-evident: that all men *and women* [emphasis added] are created equal; that they are endowed by their Creator with certain inalienable rights; that among these are life, liberty, and the pursuit of happiness; that to secure these rights governments are instituted, deriving their just powers from the consent of the governed."[13]

Frederick Douglass also connected the new and controversial idea of women's rights to the Declaration of Independence. In 1853 he said, "Whereas, according to the Declaration of our National Independence, Governments derive their just powers from the consent of the governed, we earnestly request the Legislature of New York to propose to the people of the State such amendments of the Constitution of the State as will secure to Females an equal right to the Elective Franchise with Males."[14]

By connecting the new and controversial idea of women's rights to our highest American ideals, Frederick Douglass framed the women's rights movement within the same revolutionary spirit that America was founded upon. He said:

> The American doctrine of Liberty, is that governments derive their right to govern from the just consent of the governed, and declares that taxation without representation is tyranny, and the founders of the Republic went so far as to say that resistance to tyrants is obedience to God. On these principles woman no less than man has

a right to vote. She has all the attributes that fit her for citizenship and a voter. Equally with man she is a subject of the law. Equally with man she is bound to know the law. Equally with man she is bound to obey the law. There is no more escape from its penalties for her than for him. When she commits crimes or violates the Law in any way, she is arrested, arraigned, tried, condemned, imprisoned like any other felon. Her womanhood does not excuse her from condign punishments. The Law takes no thought of her sex when she is accused of crime. Why should it take thought of her sex when bestowing its privileges? Plainly enough woman has a positive grievance. She is taxed without representation, tried without a jury of her Peers, governed without her consent, punished for violating laws she has had no hand in making. She may well enough ask as she does ask: *Is this right?*[15]

Frederick Douglass saw the women's rights activists as patriotic Americans who were helping their country achieve its full potential. To him, the American flag, "Old Glory," represented what America *should* be, and he connected the new and controversial idea of women's rights to the American flag—a powerful symbol. He said, "Ever since George Washington and Betsy Ross put their heads together to evolve old glory, woman has been doing her part in lifting the nation up towards all Old Glory ought to signify."[16]

Although Frederick Douglass, Elizabeth Cady Stanton, and Martin Luther King Jr. strategically connected new and controversial ideas to familiar and beloved American ideals and symbols, they were not being disingenuous. Their life's work shows they truly believed in the American ideals of liberty and justice, and they really wanted the American flag to represent a nation of liberty and justice *for all.* Because oppression and injustice poisoned so many aspects of American society, they dedicated their lives to curing this poison and making the democratic ideals a reality for all people.

The Declaration of Independence is actually a visionary human rights charter. Inspired by the eighteenth-century European Enlightenment philosophers, the United States of America became the first country to ever be founded on such a bold declaration of human rights. But it was a document ahead of its time, because when our country was founded only wealthy landowners fully enjoyed the ideal of liberty. Fortunately for us, patriotic Americans such as Frederick Douglass, Susan B. Anthony, Elizabeth Cady Stanton, Martin Luther King Jr., and countless others worked hard to bring America closer to its highest potential. To fulfill my responsibilities as an American citizen, I have a duty to continue this patriotic legacy by helping our country, to the best of my ability, make further progress. America has journeyed a long way toward the ideals of liberty, justice, and opportunity, but we still have a long way to go before these ideals truly become a reality for all Americans.

My existence is proof that progress is possible, because if a descendant of slaves can write these words today, why can't our country keep moving in a positive direction? If we want to keep moving in a positive direction, however, we must be strategic and persuasive, just like the patriotic activists who came before us. But how can we promote the new and controversial idea of waging peace when the "worldview of waging war" has become the predominant worldview in America today? This worldview associates waging war with national security, freedom, safety, and even peace.

Because we live in a society where violence has become synonymous with strength, many Americans have the misconception that nonviolence means passivity and weakness. Many Americans also have the misconception that peace activists are unpatriotic hippies who are a threat to national security. With these misconceptions in the way, how can we show Americans that waging peace is a more effective way to solve our domestic and international problems than violence?

Waging peace is already a proud part of our American heritage, even though most of us don't realize it. As I explained earlier, because democracy allows us to peacefully solve our problems without resorting to violence, "waging peace" is another way to say "practicing democracy." Frederick Douglass, Susan B. Anthony, Elizabeth Cady Stanton, and Martin Luther King Jr. are just a few examples of the many patriotic Americans who waged peace through democratic struggle. In school I was taught that as American citizens we owe all of our freedom to war. But decades after the American Revolutionary War ended, the majority of Americans were still not free because most people in our country lacked the freedom to vote and other basic rights, and many Americans lived as slaves. When Americans used democratic struggle to gain their basic rights, they were in fact waging peace. But why was I not taught about the art of waging peace in school?

There are many other ways to connect the new and controversial idea of waging peace to the predominant worldview in America today. When discussing waging peace in my books and lectures, I often say I was inspired to wage peace by the warrior ideals and the education I received at West Point. I also reference democratic ideals such as liberty and justice, along with highly respected military veterans such as Douglas MacArthur, Dwight Eisenhower, Omar Bradley, and Smedley Butler, among many others.

Eisenhower and MacArthur were not only West Point graduates, war veterans, and generals, but they were also Republicans. It is difficult to call them naive, unpatriotic, or hippies. General MacArthur said, "If the historian of the future should deem my service worthy of some slight reference, it would be my hope that he mention me not as a Commander engaged in campaigns and battles . . . Could I have but a line a century hence crediting a contribution to the advance of peace, I would gladly yield every honor which has been accorded by war."[17]

Martin Luther King Jr. and military veterans are among the most admired people in America today. Not only can we connect the new and controversial idea of waging peace to them, but we can also connect waging peace to the person many Americans see as the greatest genius who ever lived: Albert Einstein. A committed and lifelong peace activist, Einstein said, "It is my belief that the problem of bringing peace to the world on a supranational basis will be solved only by employing Gandhi's method on a larger scale."[18]

Even more importantly, we can also connect the new and controversial idea of waging peace to the person more Americans admire than anyone else: Jesus Christ, who is referred to in the Bible as the "Prince of Peace." It is difficult to find a person in history who was a stronger advocate for peace than Jesus. I once saw a bumper sticker that asked WHO WOULD JESUS BOMB? Gandhi said, "Jesus was the most active resister known perhaps to history. This was non-violence par excellence."[19]

When the issue of peace is concerned, Jesus told us to love our enemies, not judge others, and be peacemakers. In the Sermon on the Mount, he said,

"Blessed are the peacemakers, for they will be called children of God . . . You have heard that it was said, 'Eye for eye, and tooth for tooth . . .' [But] if anyone slaps you on the right cheek, turn to them the other cheek also . . . You have heard that it was said, 'Love your neighbor and hate your enemy.' But I tell you, love your enemies and pray for those who persecute you . . . Do not judge, or you too will be judged."[20]

General Omar Bradley admired the peaceful ideals expressed by Jesus in the Sermon on the Mount. After the devastation of World War II and rise of the nuclear arms race, he realized that Jesus's peaceful ideals were more important than ever before. In a 1948 speech, General Bradley said, "We have grasped the mystery of the atom and rejected the Sermon on the Mount . . . The world has achieved brilliance without wisdom, power without conscience. Ours is a world of nuclear giants and ethical infants."[21]

General MacArthur, who was in charge of rebuilding Japan after World War II, also admired Jesus's Sermon on the Mount. During the occupation of Japan, MacArthur's priorities included giving Japanese women the right to vote, promoting religious freedom, and spreading the ideals expressed in the Sermon on the Mount. He said:

> I am a Christian and an Episcopalian, but I believe in all religions. They may differ in form and ritual, but all recognize a divine Creator, a superior power, that transcends all that is mortal . . . Should I, with my full military power, arbitrarily decree the adoption of the Christian faith as a national religion [in Japan]? . . . The solution I adopted . . . was to befriend all religions; to permit complete freedom of religious worship as individuals might choose; to free all creeds—Shinto, Buddhist, and Christian—from any Government . . . The concept of Christ that man should do what is right, even if it entailed personal sacrifice, that the urge of conscience was greater than any material reward, was something new and novel . . . If the lessons of the Scriptures of the Sermon on the Mount could be integrated and welded into their own religious cultures, if basic spirituality could be common to all, it

would mean little whether a Japanese were a Buddhist, a Shintoist, or a Christian.[22]

Although Christianity is a complex religion that is interpreted in many different ways, the abolition of war can certainly be connected to the Christian worldview, because peace is a central part of Jesus's teachings. Christianity was originally a peace-loving religion. When people tell me the majority of Americans will never reject war as a method of conflict resolution, I often say, "If Jesus—who is admired by more Americans than any other person—was a peace activist, isn't it possible that a large number of Americans might someday support the abolition of war?" Of course this will not be easy, because we must first achieve spiritual change before we can become less judgmental and love our enemies as Jesus, Martin Luther King Jr., Gandhi, and other great peacemakers did. Spiritual change requires us to heal our inner wounds and increase our empathy through personal growth and transformation. When we achieve spiritual change, we become more effective warriors in the struggle for peace, justice, and the abolition of war.

Connecting a new and controversial idea to powerful ideals within someone's worldview means nothing if the truth is not on our side. For example, connecting the new and controversial idea of racial and gender equality to the Declaration of Independence would have meant nothing if African Americans and women were in fact intellectually and morally inferior to white men. Most Americans used to believe this myth of inferiority, but the truth was on the side of the advocates for racial and gender equality, because it is a scientific fact that African Americans and women are not intellectually and morally subhuman. In a similar way, oppressors throughout history have misused the Bible to justify many unjust policies such as slavery, the oppression of women, and even the persecution of Galileo. But Galileo, along with the advocates for racial and gender equality, had the truth on their side. When we question and think critically, the sword of truth allows us to cut through layers of deception and heal the wounds of oppression and injustice.

It is important to question and think critically. I don't agree with every opinion expressed by MacArthur or Gandhi. When anyone walks the path of truth, it is common to stumble and even make wrong turns. To reference a quote I used in chapter 2, after Malcolm X learned the truth of human brotherhood, he said, "Well, I guess a man's entitled to make a fool of himself if he's ready to pay the cost. It cost me twelve years. That was a bad scene, brother. The sickness and madness of those days—I'm glad to be free of them . . . The cause of brotherhood [is] the only thing that can save this country. I've learned it the hard way—but I've learned it."[23] I quote many people who searched for truth and understanding just as we are. We should be grateful to them, because learning from their victories and failings can help us better navigate the path of truth.

How Today's Activists Can Benefit from Strategic and Tactical Thinking

I have learned a great deal from others who walked the path of truth, and in this book I focus less on opinions and more on evidence, logic, and facts. My ideas about waging peace and the abolition of war have less to do with religious beliefs and a lot more to do with scientific evidence showing that human beings are not naturally violent and war is not inevitable. By offering abundant evidence from military history, psychology, and many other subjects, my books show the numerous ways human beings can be *conditioned* to be extremely violent. But my books also show that we are not born with a natural urge to maim and kill our own species.

Gandhi lacked much of the evidence we have today, but he said that if human beings are in fact naturally violent, his entire philosophy of nonviolence falls to pieces. Gandhi said, "If love or non-violence be not the law of our being, the whole of my argument falls to pieces . . . It is the law of love that rules mankind. Had violence, i.e., hate, ruled us, we should have become extinct long ago."[24] Gandhi called love the "law of our being," and earlier in this book I showed that even armies must create love between soldiers to make them fight most effectively, and every aggressive empire in history claims it is fighting for self-defense and peace.

Thomas Merton said, "Gandhi firmly believes that non-violence is actually more natural to man than violence. His doctrine is built on this confidence in man's natural disposition to love. However, [when] man finds himself deeply wounded . . . his inmost dispositions are no longer fully true to themselves."[25]

By understanding how Gandhi, Frederick Douglass, Elizabeth Cady Stanton, Martin Luther King Jr., and many others successfully waged peace, we can improve on their techniques. This allows us to apply the strategic principles of persuasion to a wide variety of new and controversial ideas. To offer a recent example, the new and controversial Occupy Wall Street movement began in 2011. Although it was initially framed by its opponents and many within the movement as a struggle against corporations and the rich, it is more persuasive to frame the Occupy movement as a struggle for fairness, justice, and democracy. In a similar way, Martin Luther King Jr. did not frame the civil rights movement as a struggle against white people, but as a struggle for fairness, justice, and democracy. Our message becomes more effective when we are *for* something rather than against something.

Although some in the Occupy movement are still framing it as a struggle against corporations and the rich, there are many reasons why it is more effective and *accurate* to frame the movement as a struggle for fairness, justice, and democracy. Here is one way I would frame the Occupy movement: *The problem isn't that corporations are making a profit, but that so many of them are focused on maximizing profit with no regard for the well-being of our country and health of our planet. I think corporations should be allowed to make computers and other useful products, but I don't think they should be allowed to buy politicians with massive campaign contributions. Democracy is supposed to be a system where one person equals one vote, not one dollar equals one vote.*

I have heard opponents of the Occupy movement say, "Those protestors are hypocrites, because they want to destroy corporations, yet they use cell phones, laptops, Google, and Facebook." But by framing the Occupy movement around ideals such as fairness, justice, and democracy, a person can respond by saying, "This is not about corporations making things. It's about fairness, justice, and democracy. It's about reducing the influence of money in politics, because the influence of money in our political system damages fairness, justice, and democracy." As long as corporate money has so much control over our democratic system, it becomes more difficult for American citizens to make meaningful progress on issues such as peace, environmental sustainability, and worker's rights, because these issues often threaten the maximization of corporate profits.

The Occupy movement can also be connected to Martin Luther King Jr., who is widely admired in America today. If King had not been assassinated, he would have begun the Occupy movement decades ago. King had a vision called the Poor People's Campaign, which was a plan to occupy Washington, DC, and pressure the U.S. government to create fairness and justice in our political and economic system. Samuel Kyles, a minister who worked closely with King and was with him during the last hour before his assassination, said: "With the Poor People's Campaign, Martin is talking about taking these poor people to Washington, build tents, and live on the [Washington] mall until this country did something about poverty . . . Can you imagine what would happen if all these black and white and brown people go to Washington and build tents and live in tents in Washington?"[26]

King's plan to occupy Washington, DC, differed from the Occupy movement in several ways. Many members of the Occupy movement originally resisted the idea of making demands, but King saw demands as a necessary means of applying political pressure. King also emphasized the importance of detailed strategic planning and thorough training. In fact, King wanted the activists involved in a nonviolent occupation movement to undergo three months of training, since this challenging struggle would strain their patience, compassion, hope, and willpower.

Nonviolence strategist Gene Sharp has criticized the Occupy movement for its lack of planning. A *New York Times* article stated: "Sharp emphasizes in all his work the need for preparation and care, and he says that not all nonviolent movements work. Occupy Wall Street did not have a plan, he says, which was its downfall. 'It's well intentioned,' he says, 'but occupying a small park in downtown New York is pure symbolism. It doesn't change the distribution of wealth.'"[27]

Gene Sharp did not critique the Occupy movement to be mean, but because he wants activists to learn, adapt, and succeed. Unlike Sharp, I am not ready to say the Occupy movement has failed, and I think it has had some impact. I have been impressed with many people in the movement, and I don't see any reason why they cannot adapt and succeed. Humanity needs people willing to struggle for peace and justice, and those within the Occupy movement still have a lot of potential to help solve our national and global problems. By critiquing their own actions, they can adapt by taking their strategy and training to a new level, as King did.

King put a great deal of thought into the steps necessary for a successful nonviolent occupation, and if he had not been assassinated in 1968 at the age of thirty-nine, he and many other Americans would have camped in Washington, DC, while creatively, strategically, and persistently waging peace. In the following excerpt from a 1967 speech, King explained the detailed strategic planning and thorough training that are necessary to make a nonviolent occupation movement succeed:

> For the 35 million poor people in America—not even to mention, just yet, the poor in the other nations—there is a kind of strangulation in the air. In our society it is murder, psychologically, to deprive a man of a job or an [adequate] income. You are in substance saying to that man that he has no right to exist. You are in a real way depriving him of life, liberty, and the pursuit of happiness, denying in his case the very creed of his society. Now, millions of people are being strangled that way. The problem is international in scope. *And it is getting worse, as the gap between the poor and the "affluent society" increases* [emphasis added] . . .
>
> Beginning in the New Year, we will be recruiting three thousand of the poorest citizens from ten different urban and rural areas to initiate and lead a sustained, massive, direct-action movement in Washington. Those who choose to join this initial three thousand, this nonviolent army, this "freedom church" of the poor, will work with us for three months to develop nonviolent action skills. Then we will move on Washington, determined to stay there until the legislative and executive branches of the government take serious and adequate action on jobs and income. A delegation of poor people can walk into a high official's office with a carefully, collectively prepared list of

demands. (If you're poor, if you're unemployed anyway, you can choose to stay in Washington as long as the struggle needs you.) And if that official says, "But Congress would have to approve this," or, "But the President would have to be consulted on that," you can say, "All right, we'll wait." And you can settle down in his office for as long a stay as necessary.

If you are, let's say, from rural Mississippi, and have never had medical attention, and your children are undernourished and unhealthy, you can take those little children into the Washington hospitals and stay with them there until the medical workers cope with their needs, and in showing [Washington] your children you will have shown this country a sight that will make it stop in its busy tracks and think hard about what it has done. The many people who will come and join this three thousand, from all groups in the country's life, will play a supportive role, deciding to be poor for a time along with the dispossessed who are asking for their right to jobs or income . . . Why camp in Washington to demand these things? Because only the federal Congress and administration can decide to use the billions of dollars we need for a real war on poverty.[28]

Without strategy and training, nonviolent movements can easily descend into rioting. This occurred in Occupy Oakland, a spin-off of the Occupy Wall Street movement. King said the following about riots: "There is something painfully sad about a riot. One sees screaming youngsters and angry adults fighting hopelessly and aimlessly against impossible odds. Deep down within them you perceive a desire for self-destruction, a suicidal longing . . . [During the civil rights movement] nowhere have the riots won any concrete improvement such as have the organized protest demonstrations."[29]

The Poor People's Campaign did in fact occupy Washington, DC, after King's death, but the encampment was problematic and had strayed from his plan of a massive and organized civil disobedience campaign. The failure of the encampment during the Poor People's Campaign has caused people to question the very tactic of nonviolent occupation, but the Bonus Marchers (whom I discuss in *Will War Ever End?*) were able to successfully implement this tactic during the 1930s. The Bonus Marchers were World War I veterans who protested during the Great Depression for the wages the U.S. government owed to them, and King based his plan on their successful nonviolent occupation campaign. Why were the Bonus Marchers successful? Because they had lived in encampments while serving in the military, were they better prepared to live and work together in the difficult circumstances of an encampment?

King recognized the inherent difficulty of nonviolent occupation by saying, "This is not an easy program to implement. Riots are easier just because they need no organization. To have effect we will have to develop mass disciplined forces that can remain excited and determined without dramatic conflagrations."[30] Activists should discuss which tactics are most likely to be effective in the twenty-first century, while remembering that these tactics must strategically apply pressure and persuasively promote a "true revolution of values." King described how a true revolution of values would cause us to question many of America's domestic and foreign policies:

> A true revolution of values will soon cause us to question the fairness and justice of many of our past and present policies. On the one hand we are called to play the Good Samaritan on life's roadside, but that will be only an initial act. One day we must come to see that the whole Jericho Road must be transformed so that men and women will not be constantly beaten and robbed as they make their journey on life's highway. True compassion is more than flinging a coin to a beggar. It comes to see that an edifice which produces beggars needs restructuring.
>
> A true revolution of values will soon look uneasily on the glaring contrast of poverty and wealth. With righteous indignation, it will look across the seas and see individual capitalists of the West investing huge sums of money in Asia, Africa, and South America, only to take the profits

out with no concern for the social betterment of the countries, and say, "This is not just." . . . A true revolution of
values will lay hand on the world order and say of war,
"This way of settling differences is not just." . . . A nation
that continues year after year to spend more money on
military defense than on programs of social uplift is
approaching spiritual death. America, the richest and most
powerful nation in the world, can well lead the way in this
revolution of values.[31]

I currently teach many kinds of workshops, including a workshop on
persuasion and strategic thinking. One method I teach in this workshop is
"connecting a new and controversial idea to powerful ideals within someone's
worldview," which can strengthen the message of any just cause. When my
own work is concerned, waging peace and the abolition of war are new and
controversial ideas—at least in the minds of most Americans. But in my
books and lectures I make dozens of connections between these new ideas
and the predominant worldview in America. The following diagram shows
how the Occupy movement in its beginning could have made its message
more persuasive to the majority of Americans. I have only scratched the surface in terms of the many connections that could have been made, and many
more boxes could be added to the diagram:

The Predominant American Worldview in 2011

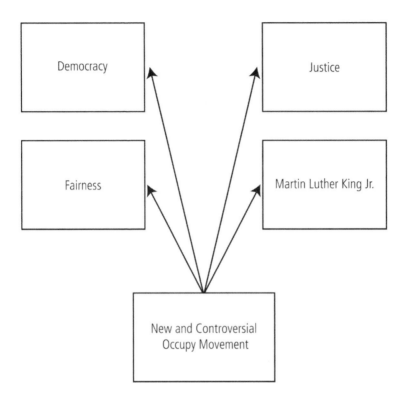

Figure 10.2. How the Occupy movement could have been connected to the powerful ideals contained in the predominant American worldview in 2011

There are strategically minded people in the Occupy movement who are framing the movement around ideals such as fairness, justice, and democracy rather than an "us versus them" mentality; just as King said it's not about black versus white, it's about our highest ideals. But as I am writing this there has not yet been a strategic consensus within the Occupy movement to ensure it has the most persuasive message possible. The people who were drawn to the Occupy movement in 2011 were mostly those who already agreed with it, but a movement's success is actually determined by its ability to reach beyond the choir and persuade those who do not agree with it.

How can we do more than preach to the choir? By thinking strategically, we can optimize our message in a way that will magnify its impact. Whether the issue is women's rights, racial equality, peace, protecting the environment, the humane treatment of animals, or creating fairness and justice in our political system, every movement must interact with four kinds of people.

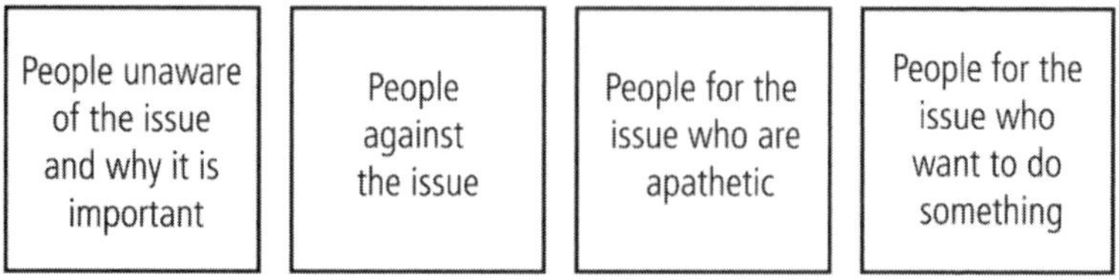

People unaware of the issue and why it is important	People against the issue	People for the issue who are apathetic	People for the issue who want to do something

Figure 10.3 The Four Kinds of People Every Movement Must Interact With

To promote any issue that has truth and justice on its side, we must influence these four kinds of people. But how can we do this? We can influence these people and move them toward action by using four strategies: raise awareness, persuade, motivate, and empower. The following diagram shows how these four strategies allow us to influence the four kinds of people every movement must interact with.

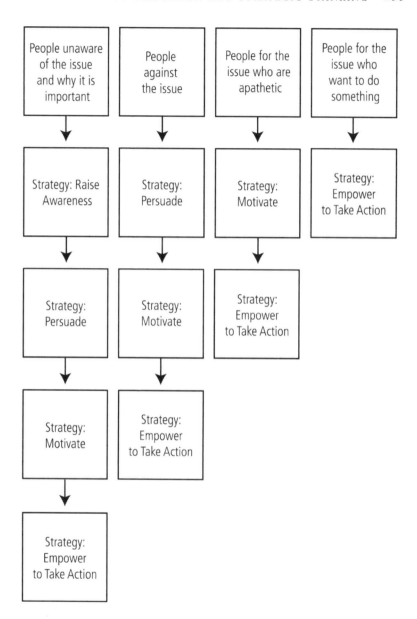

Figure 10.4 The Four Strategies for Moving People Toward Action

If your movement is trying to promote justice but the majority of people do not realize injustice is occurring, they must first be made aware before they can be persuaded, motivated, and empowered to take action. And if people disagree with your point of view, they cannot be motivated or empowered to take action in support of your cause unless they are first persuaded. Likewise, people cannot be empowered to take action unless they are first motivated to do something.

Lack of motivation is a major reason why progress does not happen. Henry David Thoreau said, "There are thousands who are *in opinion* opposed to slavery and war who yet do nothing to put an end to them. There are nine hundred and ninety-nine patrons of virtue to every virtuous person."[32] According to Thoreau, for every thousand people who think something is a good idea, only one person has the motivation to actually do something about it. This is not just Thoreau's viewpoint. It is also a fact of history. Less than one percent of Americans were actively involved in the women's rights movement or the civil rights movement.

How do we motivate people to take action? The most effective way to motivate people to wage peace is not by appealing to their hatred and fear (which lead to war), but by appealing to their compassion, conscience, hope, and reason. I discuss how we can motivate people to wage peace in the "moral fury" chapter of *The End of War* and the hope, empathy, appreciation, conscience, and reason chapters of *Peaceful Revolution*. When we motivate people to wage peace, it is also very important to empower them. During my lectures a common question people ask me is, "I am motivated to do something and I want to take action, but I don't know what I can do to make a difference." To help these people transform their motivation into action, we must empower them with waging peace strategies and tactics.

When waging peace is concerned, what is the difference between strategy and tactics? Strategy is the *intention*, while tactics are the *actions*. When people wage peace together, they are like an orchestra playing beautiful music together. Strategy is a tune you hum in your head. It is a melody written on paper. It is a song waiting to be heard. Tactics bring the music of strategy to life.

Examples of tactics (actions) include protests, petitions, boycotts, and spreading new ideas that transform how people think. When we perform any tactic (action), we should ask what our strategy (intention) is. Are we trying to raise awareness, persuade, motivate, empower, or all of the above? Nonviolence strategist Gene Sharp lists 198 tactics people have used in nonviolent movements around the world, but I encourage you to question the tactics on his list. Although most of them are useful and effective, some will actually hurt your cause. For example, number 30 on his list is "rude gestures," but these disrespectful actions are more likely to hurt rather than help your movement. If someone had taken a picture of Martin Luther King Jr. flipping off a group of white people with his middle finger, it would have greatly harmed the civil rights movement by reducing the moral authority not only of King, but the entire movement.

Just as a few instruments playing out of tune can turn the beautiful music of an orchestra into noise, a thoughtless tactic not based on effective strategy can hurt an entire movement. If someone bombs a corporate building in the name of "peace" or "protecting the environment," it can damage the work of everyone associated with the movement. It also gives government officials an excuse to use violence against the protestors in the name of "self-defense," "national security," and "fighting terrorism." Activist Blase Bonpane says, "If anyone in your movement advocates violence, always assume they are an undercover government agent."[33] Governments have been known to plant undercover agents who advocate violence in social movements, because when a movement becomes violent it loses its moral authority and its members can be labeled as "terrorists." Now the government can take the gloves off and fight you where *it* is strongest: the realm of violence. Journalist Seth Rosenfeld, from the Center for Investigative Reporting, tells us:

> The man who gave the Black Panther Party some of its first firearms and weapons training—which preceded fatal shootouts with Oakland police in the turbulent 1960s—was an undercover FBI informer, according to a former bureau agent and an FBI report. One of the Bay Area's most prominent radical activists of the era, Richard Masato Aoki was known as a fierce militant who touted his street-fighting abilities. He was a member of several radical groups before joining and arming the Panthers, whose members received international notoriety for

brandishing weapons during patrols of the Oakland police and a protest at the state Capitol. Aoki went on to work for 25 years as a teacher, counselor and administrator at the Peralta Community College District, and after his suicide in 2009, he was revered as a fearless radical.

But unbeknownst to his fellow activists, Aoki had served as an FBI intelligence informant, covertly filing reports on a wide range of Bay Area political groups, according to the bureau agent who recruited him. That agent, Burney Threadgill Jr., recalled that he approached Aoki in the late 1950s, about the time Aoki was graduating from Berkeley High School. He asked Aoki if he would join left-wing groups and report to the FBI. "He was my informant. I developed him," Threadgill said in an interview. "He was one of the best sources we had . . ." The FBI later released records about Aoki in response to a federal Freedom of Information Act request made by this reporter. A Nov. 16, 1967, intelligence report on the Black Panthers lists Aoki as an "informant" with the code number "T-2."[34]

In his book *Subversives*, Seth Rosenfeld provides more information about the harm caused by Aoki: "He had given the Black Panthers some of their first guns and weapons training, *encouraging them on a course that would contribute to shootouts with police and the organization's demise* [emphasis added]. And during the Third World Strike, *he encouraged physical confrontations that prompted Governor Reagan to take the most severe law-enforcement measures against the Berkeley campus yet* [emphasis added]—ones that ultimately would have fatal consequences."[35]

When people in a social movement use violent tactics they severely damage their own cause. But even peaceful tactics, if they are not strategic, can be counterproductive and damaging to a cause. An example is an Occupy movement protestor who was photographed defecating on a police car. The photograph was widely circulated to discredit the Occupy movement, and I cannot count the number of times I have heard opponents of the Occupy movement refer to the protestors as "dirty hippies" or "filthy bums who need to occupy a shower."

During the civil rights movement, the activists used strategic thinking to anticipate how they would be criticized. They knew that their opponents would call them "dirty," so they took proactive steps to protect themselves from this criticism. Diane Nash, an African American student at Fisk University who participated in the Nashville sit-ins, said, "We spent many, many hours anticipating some of the opposition, and we knew . . . they would say, 'We don't want to sit next to dirty people while we have lunch.' And so one of the ways we combated that was by having a dress code."[36]

When the Occupy movement began, the criticisms against it were easy to predict. The protestors would be called "dirty hippies," "lazy bums who don't want to get a job," and "spoiled kids with a sense of entitlement who want government handouts." I have met many people in the Occupy movement who are hard-working Americans from all walks of life, but it is difficult for the American people to know this when the protestors are being stereotyped as dirty, lazy, and entitled. Whenever we wage peace, we should *expect* to be criticized, but we should make ourselves as difficult a target as possible. We should not make it easy for our critics by dressing and acting exactly as they have negatively stereotyped us, giving them abundant ammunition to attack us with.

During peace protests, some activists dress and behave in a way that reinforces the unfair stereotype of the "dirty hippie." But Martin Luther King Jr. discussed the importance of not dressing in a "comic display of odd clothes" that reinforces negative stereotypes, because it distracts from the core message and makes it easier for opponents of the movement to dismiss the activists' important message. Regarding the march on Washington in 1963, King said, "The stereotype of the Negro suffered a heavy blow. This was evident in some of the comment, which reflected surprise at the dignity, the organization and even the wearing apparel and friendly spirit of the participants. If the press had expected something akin to a minstrel show, or a brawl, or a comic display of odd clothes and bad manners, they were disappointed."[37]

When King used the phrase "comic display of odd clothes," he was aware of the fact that the media will photograph and publish pictures of the most outrageously dressed activists they can find, which serves to discredit their movement. But when civil rights protestors wearing church clothes were shown on national television being assaulted by mobs, blasted with fire hoses, and attacked by police dogs, it had a much stronger impact on the American people than if the protestors had been wearing outlandish outfits or very casual clothing. If I want to wear shorts and flip-flops during my spare time that is fine, but I would not wear such casual clothing when lecturing at a university or participating in a public protest. People can wear whatever they want in their daily lives, but I encourage all activists to consider how adopting a dress code during a protest can make their message more persuasive to those who disagree with them.

A dress code does not have to be overly complicated, because even a simple act such as not wearing sunglasses can make a big difference. I advise activists to never conceal their eyes or any other part of their face during a protest, because when people cannot see our face they also cannot see our humanity. As I mentioned in chapter 3, the army taught me to take off my sunglasses when speaking with people in the Middle East, because so much of our humanity and trustworthiness is expressed through our eyes. As I discuss in *Peaceful Revolution*, it is also much easier to dehumanize and kill people when we cannot see their faces.

In his groundbreaking book *On Killing*, Lieutenant Colonel Dave Grossman explains that when people's faces are concealed, it is much easier to hurt them and justify our hostile actions:

> Looking in a man's face, seeing his eyes and his fear, eliminate denial [of his humanity] . . . Instead of shooting at a uniform and killing a generalized enemy, now the killer must shoot at a person and kill a specific individual. Most [human beings] simply cannot or will not do it . . .
>
> It seems that soldiers intuitively understand that when they turn their backs, they are more apt to be killed by the enemy . . . This same enabling process explains why Nazi, Communist, and gangland executions are traditionally conducted with a bullet in the back of the head, and why individuals being executed by hanging or firing squad are

blindfolded or hooded. And we know from Miron and Goldstein's 1979 research that the risk of death for a kidnap victim is much greater if the victim is hooded. In each of these instances the presence of the hood or blindfold ensures that the execution is completed and serves to protect the mental health of the executioners. Not having to look at the face of the victim provides a form of psychological distance that enables the execution party and assists in their subsequent denial and the rationalization and acceptance of having killed a fellow human being.

The eyes are the window of the soul, and if one does not have to look into the eyes when killing, it is much easier to deny the humanity of the victim. The eyes bulging out "like prawns" and blood shooting out of the mouth are not seen. The victim remains faceless, and one never needs to know one's victim as a person.[38]

James Lawson, a civil rights leader whom Martin Luther King Jr. called "the leading theorist and strategist of nonviolence in the world," said we must allow people to see our eyes and face when we wage peace. Lawson explains, "It had much more meaning to the attacker if, as he strikes you on the cheek you are looking him in the eyes."[39] Covering our face makes us appear less peaceful and more intimidating, which is one reason why members of the Ku Klux Klan often cover their faces with hooded masks. Also, covering our face gives us a sense of anonymity, making us more likely to engage in mob violence.

Many protestors feel the need to wear gas masks during protests, but this makes them look like aliens from another planet. If government officials unjustly use tear gas against peaceful protestors, the protestors should capture it on camera so the American people can witness this injustice. The image of pain on a woman's face as she chokes on tear gas is much more disturbing to the American public than the image of someone being attacked whose face (and humanity) is concealed by a gas mask, which creates a non-human and alien appearance. In the army we had to be tear-gassed during basic training. It is uncomfortable, but Gandhi said nonviolent activists must be willing to suffer and die for their cause. To many peace activists I know, being tear-gassed is a small price to pay when they are willing to die for a cause.

If we conduct a protest while wearing a gas mask or outlandish costume, it is easier for those who disagree with us to dehumanize us or dismiss us as "crazy." The dress code of the civil rights protestors minimized barriers between them and the American public, making it easier for many Americans to see them as human beings with dignity. When the black sanitation workers in Memphis—who lived in extreme poverty—protested during the civil rights movement for fair wages and equal treatment, they had a dress code. They also wore a sign that read I AM A MAN.

When the diverse instruments in an orchestra are on the same sheet of music, they can create beautiful music. Strategy puts the diverse people in a movement on the same sheet of music, allowing them to create beautiful and effective actions. If we want to play the melody of waging peace so that the whole world can hear it, we must be strategic, organized, and disciplined. James Lawson explains, "You cannot go on a demonstration with twenty-five people doing whatever they want to do. They have to have a common discipline, and that's a key word for me . . . The difficulty with nonviolent people and efforts is that they don't recognize the necessity of fierce discipline, and training, and strategizing, and planning, and recruiting, and doing the kinds of things to have a movement."[40]

James Lawson, Gandhi, and King all understood that *disciplined teamwork* is essential when waging peace. Disciplined teamwork is necessary to accomplish any challenging goal, whether it is waging peace as a nonviolent movement, performing Beethoven's Ninth Symphony as a large orchestra, making a film involving hundreds of people, winning the Super Bowl as a team of athletes, or putting a man on the moon. In *Peaceful Revolution* I discuss how discipline can greatly improve our quality of life and ability to wage peace.

When we are outnumbered by a much larger opponent—as nonviolent movements always are when challenging injustice—disciplined teamwork becomes even more important. Naganuma Muneyoshi, a seventeenth-century Japanese military scientist, explained: "A disciplined army can beat an undisciplined army even three to five times its size. Suppose there is a huge boulder that dozens of men cannot roll. Now, if one man gives a call so that the group responds in unison, pushing at once, even a few men can move it. There is no technique to this but coordinating efforts as one . . . Disciplined order is a means of coordinating energetic force and momentum . . . If you gain victory without discipline, this should be called being lucky you didn't lose."[41]

Although discipline and strategy are crucial, there is also a concept in the military called *grand strategy*. When waging peace is concerned, I define grand strategy as *the overarching spiritual vision that guides a movement.* The most effective social movements are also spiritual movements. The word "spiritual" does not have to mean "religious." When I use the word "spiritual," I am referring to a movement's ability to give people a sense of hope, meaning, purpose, and belonging. I am also referring to a movement's ability to help people *transcend* their personal desires in order to identify with high ideals, all of humanity, and even all life.

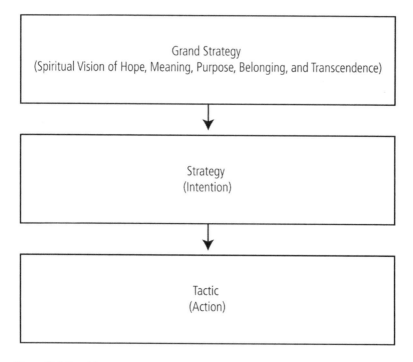

Figure 10.5 Grand Strategy

Why is a spiritual vision that gives people a solid foundation of hope, meaning, purpose, belonging, and transcendence so important to a movement? This foundation nurtures spiritual change within us, giving us the inner strength to overcome the most significant obstacles. In the army I heard a saying: "A human being can survive for a few weeks without food, a few days without water, but only a few moments without hope." A person with absolutely no hope at all would be depressed and suicidal. If we do not have at least a little hope, it is difficult to get out of bed in the morning.

Hope is as vital for human survival as food and water. People are drawn to a message of hope, and this is one reason why Martin Luther King Jr. was so effective. King had the amazing ability to talk about something bad like racism and make people feel good, but many activists today tend to talk about something good like peace and make people feel bad. As one of my friends in the peace movement told me half jokingly, "Whenever I go to a lecture on peace, the speaker usually makes me feel so depressed about the state of our country and the world that I want to go home and shoot myself." King's "I Have a Dream" speech, even though it is about racism and segregation, is one of the most hopeful and inspiring speeches I have ever read. King could give a speech about tragic subject matter, but frame it in a way that made people feel more hopeful afterward.

King's hope is even more remarkable when we consider the terrible conditions that surrounded him. He had many reasons to be hopeless and hateful, because black people were being murdered by the supporters of segregation and he was receiving daily death threats—where people threatened to not only kill him but also his wife and children. The death threats became real when his house was bombed in 1956. His wife and children, who were in the house when the bombing occurred, were fortunate to survive the attack. These bombings were directed not only at him and his family, but at civil rights advocates throughout the South. In 1963 King said, "Local racists [in Birmingham] have intimidated, mobbed, and even killed Negroes with impunity . . . From the year 1957 through January of 1963, while Birmingham was still claiming its Negroes were 'satisfied,' seventeen unsolved bombings of Negro churches and homes of civil-rights leaders had occurred."[42]

Today we would call these bombings terrorism, but King did not allow terrorism to transform him into a hateful human being. Whether he was discussing racism and segregation, or war and American foreign policy, King always found a way to give people realistic hope. Speaking truthfully without hatred or cynicism, he ended his 1967 speech "Beyond Vietnam" by saying:

> Now let us begin. Now let us rededicate ourselves to the long and bitter, but beautiful, struggle for a new world . . . And if we will only make the right choice, we will be able to transform this pending cosmic elegy into a creative psalm of peace. If we will make the right choice, we will be able to transform the jangling discords of our world into a beautiful symphony of brotherhood. If we will but make the right choice, we will be able to speed up the day, all over America and all over the world, when justice will roll down like waters, and righteousness like a mighty stream.[43]

King's hope was not based on naive and wishful thinking, but realistic reasons to be hopeful and not surrender to despair. In *Peaceful Revolution* I describe how we can base our hope on realism. It is important for activists to understand the power of hope, because just as a military unit must feed its soldiers with food and water, we must feed a movement with hope, meaning, purpose, belonging, and transcendence. And just as a military unit must train its soldiers to wield the weapons of war, we must train activists to wield a far more powerful weapon. Gandhi called it "the sword of love," I call it "the sword of truth," and King called it "the sword that heals."

CHAPTER 11

How We Can Protect
Our Country and Planet
in the Twenty-first Century

What Conservatives and Liberals Have in Common

Governments control people by dividing them. One of the greatest dangers to the war system is for conservatives and liberals to realize how much they have in common. In October 2010 I gave a lecture at the University of Kentucky to a class studying diplomacy and U.S. foreign policy. The students had a diverse range of political views. Many were liberals, many were conservatives, and some were members of the Tea Party. To demonstrate how much the students had in common despite their different political views, I said, "Raise your hand if you want America to be less safe and less secure. Raise your hand if you want terrorism to increase. Raise your hand if you want the American economy to collapse. Raise your hand if you want government waste [in spending]. Raise your hand if you want unnecessarily high taxes. Raise your hand if you want innocent people to die. Raise your hand if you want a worse future for you and your children." None raised their hands.

Whether we are conservative or liberal, we all want a better future for ourselves and our families, and we all want a meaningful and fulfilling life. Most people inaccurately perceive the conservative and liberal worldviews as two *separate* circles, but a more accurate representation of these worldviews are two *overlapping* circles.

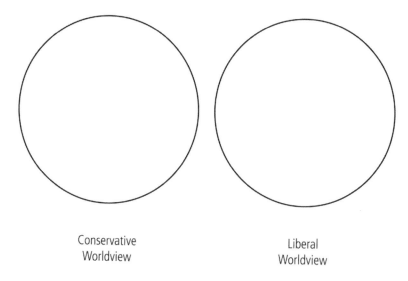

Conservative
Worldview

Liberal
Worldview

Figure 11.1 Most people inaccurately perceive the conservative and liberal worldviews as two separate circles.

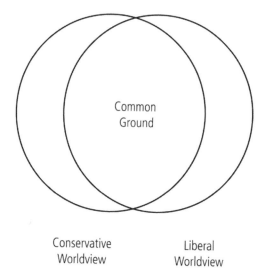

Common
Ground

Conservative
Worldview

Liberal
Worldview

Figure 11.2 The conservative and liberal worldviews actually *overlap*.

What common ground do most conservatives and liberals share? Most conservatives and liberals want America to be safe from terrorism and war. Most conservatives and liberals want a healthy economy. Most conservatives and liberals do not want innocent people to be hurt or killed. Two hundred years ago, few people supported basic rights of African Americans and women, but today most conservatives and liberals oppose state-sanctioned slavery and support women's right to vote.*

Not all conservatives and liberals share these views, but most do. If they did not share this common ground, why would so many conservative *and* liberal politicians tell us that war promotes peace and keeps us safe from terrorism? Why would so many conservative *and* liberal politicians tell us that their political party's agenda improves the health of our economy? Why would so many conservative *and* liberal politicians tell us that war protects innocent people by killing the "bad guy"?

Because of President George W. Bush's wars in Afghanistan and Iraq, I have met many people who assume that Republicans are warmongers while Democrats are peacemakers, but this is historically inaccurate. One of my friends in the peace movement grew up in the 1950s. When she was a little girl she asked her mother, "If the Republicans favor the rich and we are poor, why are we Republicans?" Her mother replied, "Because the Democrats get us into all the wars."

General MacArthur was a committed Republican. Toward the end of his life, one reason he claimed to dislike the Democratic Party was because it waged too much war.† He said he saw too many Democratic politicians putting our country in the middle of international conflicts where American soldiers had to pay with their lives. MacArthur said the following during his keynote speech at the 1952 Republican National Convention:

---

* I hear many liberals accuse the Tea Party of being racist and sexist, but I think it's interesting that the Tea Party's two favorite candidates during the 2012 Republican Party presidential primaries were Herman Cain (a black man) and Michele Bachmann (a woman). And the two biggest Tea Party "rock stars" through 2012 were Allen West (a black man) and Sarah Palin (a woman).

† Prior to the 1950s, some Republicans also supported war, but over the years more Republicans have supported the war system. When speaking with President John F. Kennedy, General MacArthur blamed Republican President Eisenhower for starting the intervention in Vietnam.

[President Truman and the Democratic Party] have divided the world into armed camps and rendered us dependent, not alone upon the wisdom of our own foreign policy to keep us out of war, but upon the foreign policies and diplomatic moves of other nations as well. We must fully understand that, once we commit ourselves to the defense of others, the issue of war or peace is no longer in our exclusive hands, *for we become but another pawn in the game of international power politics* [emphasis added]—a dangerous game—in which the present administration has demonstrated no peculiar adeptness. It has talked and pledged peace while moving toward war. Indeed, none can deny what history so clearly records—that the Democratic Party has well earned the doubtful distinction of being the war party of modern American politics. The dead of World War I, of World War II, and of the Korean War render mute testimony.[1]

In addition, the Vietnam War was escalated by Presidents Kennedy and Johnson—both Democrats. Since the Vietnam War, the war system has gained more control over both political parties. Republican presidents Ronald Reagan and George H. W. Bush authorized war, but so did President Bill Clinton—a Democrat. As I will discuss later in this chapter, President Obama during his first term escalated drone warfare to a new and dangerous level.

This is one among many reasons why we should never stereotype. When we see people only as narrow political labels such as "conservative" or "liberal" rather than as complex human beings, we see the world not as it really is, but as an oversimplification of reality. Propaganda oversimplifies reality by turning our colorful world into a black-and-white war of "us versus them." Most human beings are too complex to fit within a stereotypical label, and people on both sides of the political spectrum can have virtues and vices. I know conservatives and liberals who are compassionate human beings, and I know conservatives and liberals who lack compassion. If we see people as human beings first,* Americans second, and conservatives or liberals further down the list, we will become better at finding the common ground that unites us.

Life experience has taught me it is unwise to even stereotype groups such as the military and peace movement. Some of the most peaceful people I have ever met are in the military, and some of the most aggressive people I have ever met are in the peace movement. Some of the most disciplined people I have ever met are in the peace movement, and some of the most undisciplined people I have ever met are in the military.

Our allegiance to America, the Constitution, and American ideals should always outrank our allegiance to a political party, because political parties are inconsistent organizations, and their views change over time. When Republican Abraham Lincoln was president, the Republican Party was the anti-slavery party that supported the rights of African Americans, and when Democrat Lyndon B. Johnson was president, the Democratic Party became the anti-segregation party that supported the rights of African Americans. Although President Johnson was known as a civil rights advocate, Republicans such as President Eisenhower supported civil rights legislation during a time when Johnson opposed it. Historian David Nichols explains:

> President Dwight D. Eisenhower signed a law providing voting protections for blacks known as the Civil Rights Act of 1957. While that act is hardly as well remembered as the landmark laws of the 1960s, it's not because it wasn't important: at the time, it had been 82 years since any federal civil rights legislation had been passed because a coalition of Southern Democrats and conservative Republicans had consistently blocked progress . . .
>
> Eisenhower complained in 1967 that if his critics felt "there was anything good done" in his presidency, "they mostly want to prove that it was somebody else that did it and that I went along as a passenger." That has been especially true of his championship of civil rights. The

---

* We can broaden our view of people even further by seeing our similarities with mammals and other living creatures on the planet.

"somebody else" in this instance was Lyndon B. Johnson, who in 1957 was the Senate's Democratic majority leader. Historians have consistently credited Johnson for the bill's passage. Yes, Johnson played a role, but hardly the one his advocates might imagine: Eisenhower and his attorney general, Herbert Brownell Jr., first proposed strong legislation, and it was Johnson and his Southern cronies who weakened it beyond recognition.

Johnson wanted a cosmetic bill that would enhance his presidential ambitions without alienating his white Southern base . . . If Eisenhower's original proposals had passed, the cause of civil rights would have been significantly advanced . . . Eisenhower's bravery on the act went largely unrecognized by the civil rights leadership [such as Martin Luther King Jr. who believed Eisenhower was not truly committed to civil rights].[2]

Because both political parties have changed so much, there is no reason to believe that one or both parties could not become anti-war parties if the American people exert enough pressure on their politicians. Who would have imagined in the 1850s that both parties would someday become anti-slavery parties that support women's right to vote? As more people learn the truth and begin to actively wage peace, we can transform attitudes toward war across America and throughout the political spectrum. The first step on this transformational journey requires us to debunk the myths of war and reveal the power of waging peace.

Falling into Osama bin Laden's Trap

There is no instance of a country having benefited from prolonged warfare.

—Sun Tzu, *The Art of War*[3]

In chapter 8 I explained that all countries wage war in the name of self-defense, peace, and noble ideals. Most of the Americans who support war are not immoral people. Instead, they are told over and over again that war is necessary to protect their families, freedom, and way of life. Peace studies professor and activist Tom Hastings says, "The efforts to build any nonviolent movement are hampered by those who favor violence. However, the numbers of people who favor violence because they are pathologically drawn to it are very small; most favor violence because they have no logic that tells them that nonviolence can actually work. The logic is there, but not taught and not held as a primary value . . . In short, for most humans, nonviolence is a nice idea that they don't equate with effective liberation or national defense."[4]

The war system is a master of deception, and one of its biggest illusions is that war is needed to make us safe. But if we explore military strategy, we will see a much different story. From a strategic, economic, and security perspective, our response to the terrorist attacks on September 11 has created many more problems than it has solved. For example, invading the Greater Middle East violated the most basic principles of military strategy. According to Sun Tzu, who wrote *The Art of War* over two thousand years ago, one of the worst things someone can do in war is become angry. Sun Tzu knew that when people are enraged, they cannot think clearly and will make self-destructive decisions. Consequently, one of the best things someone can do in war is make an opponent angry. When people become angry they behave recklessly and carelessly, losing concern for consequences. An angry and reckless opponent is much easier to lure into a trap than a calm and rational opponent.

In *The Art of War*, Sun Tzu says two of the most dangerous flaws a general can have are "a hasty temper, which can be provoked by insults" and "recklessness, which leads to destruction."[5] Sun Tzu also says, "A government should not mobilize an army out of anger, military leaders should not provoke war out of wrath . . . A nation destroyed cannot be restored to existence, and the dead cannot be restored to life. Therefore an enlightened government is careful about this, a good military leadership is alert to this. This is the way to secure a nation and keep the armed forces whole."[6]

By invading the Greater Middle East, we fell right into Osama bin Laden's trap. Although he was never put on trial and convicted for planning the September 11 attacks, he stated on numerous occasions that he wanted to provoke us into a war on "Muslim soil." He wanted to make us so angry that we would make a catastrophic strategic error. The attacks on September 11 did just that, generating so much rage that many Americans could not think clearly. During the months and years following the September 11 attacks, I have a difficult time imagining any American saying, "Let's do exactly what Osama bin Laden wants us to do." Yet by invading Afghanistan and Iraq, we did exactly what he wanted us to do. We fell right into his trap.

Abdul Bari Atawan, a Western journalist who interviewed Osama bin Laden in 1996, said:

> It seems Osama bin Laden had a long-term strategy. He told me personally that he can't go and fight the Americans and their country. But if he manages to provoke them and bring them to the Middle East and to their Muslim worlds, where he can find them or fight them on his own turf, he will actually teach them a lesson . . . He told me, again, that [while President Clinton was in office] he expected the Americans to send troops to Somalia and he sent his people to that country to wait for them in order to fight them. They managed actually to shoot down an American helicopter where 19 soldiers were killed [in the battle that followed] and he regretted that the Clinton Administration decided to pull out their troops from Somalia and run away.* He was so saddened by this. He

---

* During the Battle of Mogadishu, eighteen U.S. soldiers were killed and one was captured. When Osama bin Laden talked about "his people" killing the American soldiers, he may have been speaking less specifically about Al Qaeda and more broadly about all Muslim militants who fight against the United States. He may also have been claiming credit for an attack conducted by militants not associated with Al Qaeda.

thought they would stay there so he could fight them there. But for his bad luck, according to his definition, they left, and he was planning another provocation in order to drag them to Muslim soil.[7]

Why did Osama bin Laden want us to invade Muslim soil? Prior to the United States invading Afghanistan and Iraq after the September 11 attacks, many Muslims saw Osama bin Laden as a dangerous extremist. But he knew that provoking us to invade the Greater Middle East would allow him to mobilize more people in the region against us and increase recruitment for his terrorist ideology. Imagine if a foreign army invaded the United States tomorrow. Many Americans would rise up to defend their homeland, because most people don't like armed foreign soldiers on their land. Because of our increased military presence in the Greater Middle East, Osama bin Laden gained a larger number of sympathizers and supporters. Today he is seen by many marginalized Muslims as a martyr who died for his cause, and the amount of Al Qaeda, Al Qaeda imitators, Al Qaeda sympathizers, and insurgents throughout the Greater Middle East and Africa who want to kill Americans is significantly higher today than it was prior to 2001.

Another principle of military strategy is that it is extremely dangerous to underestimate your opponent. Osama bin Laden had a track record of beating superpowers in the Greater Middle East. He was part of the military campaign that defeated the Soviets when they invaded and attempted to occupy Afghanistan. Of course, the Soviet Union collapsed due to many reasons, but in front of the twenty-seventh congress of the Soviet Union's Communist Party in February 1986, Mikhail Gorbachev referred to the war in Afghanistan as "our bleeding wound."[8] The war in Afghanistan accelerated the collapse of the Soviet Union by wasting large amounts of money the Soviets desperately needed, and the war also used up a great deal of time, energy, resources, and brainpower that the Soviets could have invested toward solving their other problems.

Osama bin Laden could never have won a decisive battle against the United States, but he could defeat us in Afghanistan the same way he beat the Soviets, by bankrupting our country. By making us chase his mujahedin

(Muslim soldiers) on foreign soil, he wanted to impoverish the American people by causing our government to waste enormous amounts of money on overseas wars. In 2004 the Arabic news network Al Jazeera aired a video-taped speech given by Osama bin Laden. A translated transcript of the speech was published online by the *Washington Post*. Even though the intended audience for his speech was the American people, most Americans do not know what he said. Here is an excerpt:

> All that we have to do is to send two Mujahedin to the farthest point East to raise a piece of cloth on which is written al-Qa'ida in order to make the [American] generals race there to cause America to suffer human, economic, and political losses without their achieving for it anything of note other than some benefits to their private companies . . . We alongside the Mujahedin bled Russia for 10 years until it went bankrupt and was forced to withdraw in defeat . . . So we are continuing this policy in bleeding America to the point of bankruptcy . . .
>
> The policy of the White House that demands the opening of war fronts to keep busy their various corporations—whether they be working in the field of arms or oil or reconstruction—has helped al-Qa'ida to achieve those enormous results. And so it has appeared to some analysts and diplomats that the White House and us are playing as one team towards the economic goals of the United States even if the intentions differ. And it was to these sorts of notions and their like that the British diplomat and others were referring in their lectures at the Royal Institute of International Affairs [when they pointed out that] for example, al-Qa'ida spent $500,000 on the event [September 11 attacks], while America in the incident and its aftermath lost—according to the lowest estimates—more than 500 billion dollars, meaning that every dollar of al-Qa'ida defeated a million dollars [of America] . . . As for the size

of the [American] economic deficit, it has reached record, astronomical numbers estimated to total more than a trillion dollars. And even more dangerous and bitter for America is that the Mujahedin recently forced Bush to resort to emergency funds to continue the fight in Afghanistan and Iraq which is evidence of the success of the bleed-until-bankruptcy plan . . .

It is true that this shows that al-Qa'ida has gained, but on the other hand it shows that the Bush administration has also gained something of which anyone who looks at the size of the contracts acquired by the shady Bush administration-linked mega-corporations, like Halliburton and its kind will be convinced. And it all shows that the real loser is . . . you. It's the American people and their economy.[9]

When Osama bin Laden made these statements in 2004, many Americans probably could not imagine our country ever going bankrupt. But when we look at how our country today is being strangled by massive national debt, high unemployment, and the recent recession, we can see the effects of Osama bin Laden's plan. By increasing our war spending beyond what our country can afford, his plan has worked. Many Americans are concerned about the soaring national debt and festering economic crisis, but few are discussing the trillions of dollars we are spending on war, which could be better used to help the American people.

On September 8, 2011, seven years after Osama bin Laden made his 2004 statement, the *New York Times* published a report estimating how much money the September 11 attacks and our "war on terrorism" will cost the American people. This estimate included the damage caused by the September 11 attacks, the money spent on homeland security and the wars in Afghanistan and Iraq, and future expenses such as medical care for wounded veterans. The *New York Times* said: "Al Qaeda spent roughly half a million dollars to destroy the World Trade Center and cripple the Pentagon. What has been the cost to the United States? In a survey of estimates by the *New York Times*, the answer is 3.3 trillion, or about $7 million for every dollar Al Qaeda spent planning and executing the attacks. While not all of the costs have been borne by the government—and some are still to come—this total equals one-fifth of the current national debt."[10] The *New York Times* estimated the costs as follows: homeland security and related expenses are $589 billion, war funding and related expenses are $1.649 trillion, future war and future veterans' care are $867 billion, economic impact from the September 11 attacks is $123 billion, and the toll and physical damage from the September 11 attacks amount to $55 billion. I expect the total war costs will be even higher.

When I began my senior year at West Point in August 2001, I took a class on national security that had a big impact on me. It was the first time I had seriously questioned the size of the military budget. My professor was a West Point graduate, Rhodes scholar, and major in the army. One day he walked into the classroom and wrote the names of eighteen countries on the board. Then he looked at us and said, "The U.S. military budget is higher than the military budgets of the next eighteen countries in the world combined. Why do we need that much military spending? Isn't that insane?" None of the students in the class said anything. I was shocked by what he told us and did not know what to say. Aggravated by our silence, he said, "I'm surprised you all aren't more outraged by this. Why do we need that much military spending?"

Today we spend more on war and our military than most of the countries in the world combined, because military spending has more than doubled since September 11, 2001.[11] In 1953 President Dwight Eisenhower, also a West Point graduate, gave a speech that mirrored my professor's outrage about the massive military budget. Eisenhower described how the money spent on weapons could instead be used to help the American people:

> Every gun that is made, every warship launched, every rocket fired signifies, in the final sense, a theft from those who hunger and are not fed, those who are cold and are not clothed. This world in arms is not spending money alone. It is spending the sweat of its laborers, the genius of its scientists, the hopes of its children. The cost of one modern heavy bomber is this: a modern brick school in more than thirty cities. It is two electric power plants, each

serving a town of 60,000 population. It is two fine, fully equipped hospitals. It is some fifty miles of concrete highway. We pay for a single fighter plane with a half million bushels of wheat. We pay for a single destroyer with new homes that could have housed more than 8,000 people. This, I repeat, is the best way of life to be found on the road the world has been taking. This is not a way of life at all, in any true sense. Under the cloud of threatening war, it is humanity hanging from a cross of iron.[12]

General MacArthur, like Eisenhower, also realized that a massive military budget creates a kind of economic crucifixion that slowly bleeds our country into bankruptcy. MacArthur said, "We must understand that in final analysis the mounting cost of preparation for war is in many ways as materially destructive as war itself."[13] Eisenhower and MacArthur wanted us to consider what we lose when the U.S. government spends our tax dollars on weapons. The money countries spend on war preparation and war itself could be used to improve the lives of their citizens and end poverty on a global scale. At the beginning of *Peaceful Revolution*, I share the following excerpt from a speech General MacArthur gave in 1961:

> The great question is: Can global war now be outlawed from the world? If so, it would mark the greatest advance in civilization since the Sermon on the Mount. It would lift at one stroke the darkest shadow which has engulfed mankind from the beginning. It would not only remove fear and bring security—it would not only create new moral and spiritual values—it would produce an economic wave of prosperity that would raise the world's standard of living beyond anything ever dreamed of by man. The hundreds of billions of dollars now spent in mutual preparedness [for war] could conceivably abolish poverty from the face of the earth.[14]

Eisenhower and MacArthur both talked about the money wasted on war being used in more productive ways, such as improving the American people's quality of life. Today enormous amounts of money are spent on war, nuclear weapons, and homeland defense. According to the National Priorities Project, "Discretionary spending refers to the part of the federal budget that Congress debates and decides every year . . . In FY 2011, approximately 58% of the discretionary budget is allocated to national defense. This is consistent with previous budgets in which national defense has accounted for at least 50%, and sometimes close to 60% of discretionary spending."[15]

In *The Art of War*, Sun Tzu explains how military spending impoverishes a country: "When a country is impoverished by military operations, it is because of transporting supplies to a distant place. Transport supplies to a distant place, and the populace will be impoverished. Those who are near the army sell at high prices. Because of high prices, the wealth of the common people is exhausted. When resources are exhausted, then levies are made under pressure. When power and resources are exhausted, then the homeland is drained. The common people are deprived of seventy percent of their budget, while the government's expenses for equipment amount to sixty percent of its budget."[16]

I, along with most Americans, would understand the need for a massive military budget if it were truly making our country safer, but it is actually doing the opposite. It is threatening our security along with our economy, and it is causing us to become more entangled in Osama bin Laden's trap. During this critical time in American history we have an amazing opportunity to implement a *more effective security paradigm* that would not only reduce the military budget, but truly promote peace and freedom around the world.

Osama bin Laden wanted us to waste money on war so that America would slowly bleed to death economically, but we must not give him what he wanted. His trap is not the sole cause of our economic problems, but it is more difficult to fix the other causes of our economic problems when our country is being bled into bankruptcy by vast war spending.

I am against doing what Osama bin Laden wanted us to do. I am against letting his trap impoverish the American people, bankrupt our country, and endanger our security. I think we certainly have to fight terrorism, but there is a more effective way to combat terrorism that is not only better for our economy, but better for American and global security, along with peace and freedom around the world.

Hypocrisy Threatens National Security

Before I can describe the more effective security paradigm, I must first explain why the greatest threat to American security are not Muslims. Instead, the greatest threat to American security is the hypocrisy of many American politicians. Jesus described a hypocrite as someone who does not practice what he or she preaches. A modern example of a hypocrite is someone who preaches freedom and democracy while supporting dictatorships around the world. A timeless example is someone who criticizes the vices of others while ignoring his or her own vices. Jesus said, "Why do you look at the speck of sawdust in your brother's eye and pay no attention to the plank in your own eye? How can you say to your brother, 'Let me take the speck out of your eye,' when all the time there is a plank in your own eye? You hypocrite, first take the plank out of your own eye, and then you will see clearly to remove the speck from your brother's eye."[17]

President Eisenhower witnessed how hypocrisy endangers national security. He was the first American president to identify Middle Eastern hatred for the United States. In 1958 he asked the National Security Council why so many Middle Eastern people hated us. He called Middle Eastern animosity toward the United States the "campaign of hatred against us, not by the governments but by the people."[18] Although American politicians say they hate us because we're free, the National Security Council revealed that they hate us because we *block* freedom, democracy, and development in the Middle East.

If you doubt this, just look at the governments we have supported in the Middle East and surrounding regions. Most of them have been dictatorships that help us control natural resources such as oil. American politicians supported Saddam Hussein, the Shah of Iran, and dictatorships in Tunisia, Egypt, Yemen, and Pakistan. In addition to supporting corrupt governments in countries such as Afghanistan, our politicians still support dictatorships in Bahrain and many other countries. Our politicians also support the most fundamentalist Islamic government in the world: the dictatorship in Saudi Arabia.

America has some of the most noble ideals in the world, such as freedom, democracy, justice, and opportunity. But the world for the most part isn't angry at our ideals. The world for the most part is angry that we don't live up to our ideals. The world for the most part is angry at hypocritical American policies. In 2011 the nonviolent movement in the Greater Middle East that demanded democracy became known as the "Arab Spring." Wael Ghonim helped lead the peaceful protests in Egypt that overthrew Hosni Mubarak, the Egyptian dictator. During an interview on *60 Minutes*, Ghonim was asked how he felt when President Obama spoke in support of the Egyptian protestors. Ghonim replied, "It was good that he supports the revolution. That's a good stand, but we don't really need him. I wrote a Tweet. I wrote 'Dear western governments, you have been supporting the regime that was oppressing us for 30 years. Please don't get involved now. We don't need you.'"[19]

After the September 11 attacks, American politicians said, "They hate us because we're free." But during the Arab Spring, people all over the Greater Middle East protested because they wanted their freedom. Arab Spring protestors in Tunisia, Egypt, Yemen, and Bahrain struggled for freedom and democracy against dictatorships our politicians support. American politicians have actually supported dictatorships in the Greater Middle East for decades. In 1953 the Eisenhower administration overthrew a democratically elected government in Iran. The democratic government in Iran wanted to control its own oil, instead of letting Western countries have control. After overthrowing Iran's democratic government, the Eisenhower administration reinstated Mohammed Reza Pahlavi, the dictator known as the "Shah," who restored to Western countries their access to Iranian oil. In return, we gave the Shah support and military aid.

Andrew Bacevich is a West Point graduate, Vietnam veteran, and retired army colonel who has written extensively about American foreign policy. During a television interview with Bill Moyers on PBS, Bacevich explained that most Americans do not know about the hypocrisy and injustice of American foreign policy: "Let's walk outside the studio and ask a hundred of our fellow citizens, 'Tell me about what happened between the United States and Iran in 1953,' and none will know. Let's go to Tehran and ask them, and a hundred out of a hundred Iranians will say, 'That's when the [American] C.I.A. and British MI-6 collaborated to overthrow a democratically elected government and to reinstall the Shah on his throne.' An action undertaken with absolutely no concern about the well-being of the Iranian people, but in pursuit of near-term strategic interest."[20]

In his book *All the Shah's Men*, Stephen Kinzer explains how Iranian prime minister Mohammad Mossadegh—who admired America, embraced democratic ideals, and opposed Islamic extremism—was overthrown by the U.S. government:

> In 1953 the United States was still new to Iran. Many Iranians thought of Americans as friends, supporters of the fragile democracy they had spent half a century trying to build. It was Britain, not the United States, that they demonized as the colonialist oppressor that exploited them.
>
> Since the early years of the twentieth century a British company, owned mainly by the British government, had enjoyed a fantastically lucrative monopoly on the production and sale of Iranian oil. The wealth that flowed from beneath Iran's soil played a decisive role in maintaining Britain at the pinnacle of world power while most Iranians lived in poverty. Iranians chafed bitterly under this injustice. Finally, in 1951, they turned to Mossadegh, who more than any other political leader personified their anger at the Anglo-Iranian Oil Company (AIOC). He pledged to throw the company out of Iran, reclaim the country's vast petroleum reserves, and free Iran from subjection to foreign power . . .
>
> British agents began conspiring to overthrow Mossadegh soon after he nationalized the oil company . . . Immediately, the British asked President Truman for help. Truman, however, sympathized viscerally with nationalist

movements like the one Mossadegh led. He had nothing but contempt for old-style imperialists like those who ran Anglo-Iranian. Besides, the CIA had never overthrown a government, and Truman did not wish to set the precedent.

The American attitude toward a possible coup in Iran changed radically after Dwight Eisenhower was elected president in November 1952. Within days of the election, a senior agent of the [British] Secret Intelligence Service, Christopher Montague Woodhouse, came to Washington for meetings with top CIA and State Department officials. Woodhouse shrewdly decided not to make the traditional British argument, which was that Mossadegh must go because he had nationalized British property. That argument did not arouse much passion in Washington. Woodhouse knew what would.

"Not wishing to be accused of trying to use the Americans to pull British chestnuts out of the fire," he wrote later, "I decided to emphasize the Communist threat to Iran rather than the need to recover control of the oil industry . . ."

Britain had risen to world power largely because of its success in exploiting the natural resources of subject nations . . . The *New York Times* said that many Middle East specialists considered Mossadegh a liberator comparable to Thomas Jefferson or Thomas Paine . . . Mossadegh had already proven himself adept at reaching the American public. He appeared several times on television, and the seeming logic of his case, which he always compared to the struggle for American independence, won him considerable sympathy . . . [When Mossadegh travelled to the United States in 1951] he visited Independence Hall, which he said symbolized the aspirations that united Americans and Iranians. Hundreds of onlookers cheered as he was photographed beside the Liberty Bell . . . He supported women's rights, defended religious freedom, and allowed courts and universities to function freely. Above all, he was known even by his enemies as scrupulously honest and impervious to the corruption that pervaded Iranian politics . . .

Roger Goiran, the chief of the CIA station in Tehran . . . believed that [overthrowing Mossadegh] would be a great mistake and warned that if the coup was carried out, Iranians would forever view the United States as a supporter of what he called "Anglo-French colonialism." His opposition was so resolute that [CIA director] Allen Dulles had to remove him from his post . . . The Anglo-Iranian Oil Company, which later changed its name to British Petroleum, tried [unsuccessfully] to return to its old position in Iran . . . The logic of power dictated that since the United States had done the dirty work of overthrowing Mossadegh, American companies should share the spoils.[21]

What do America's Founding Fathers, Gandhi, and Mossadegh all have in common? They all rebelled against British occupation and risked their lives to oppose the tyranny of the British Empire. America's Founding Fathers, Gandhi, and Mossadegh all lived according to the revolutionary motto "Live free or die." Despite American idealism and its fierce opposition to tyranny, Martin Luther King Jr. noticed in the 1960s that many American politicians had increasingly adopted an un-American foreign policy of supporting dictatorships and overthrowing democracies in order to pursue economic interests. During the Vietnam War, King realized many American politicians were preaching freedom and democracy while hypocritically supporting a dictatorship in Vietnam. In his 1967 speech "Beyond Vietnam," King said:

[The Vietnamese] must see Americans as strange liberators. The Vietnamese people proclaimed their own independence in 1954—in 1945 rather—after a combined French and Japanese occupation and before the communist revolution in China. They were led by Ho Chi Minh. Even though they quoted the American Declaration of Independence in their own document of freedom, we refused to recognize them. Instead, we decided to support France in its reconquest of her former colony. Our government felt then that the Vietnamese people were not ready for independence, and we again fell victim to the deadly Western arrogance that has poisoned the international atmosphere for so long. With that tragic decision we rejected a revolutionary government [in Vietnam] seeking self-determination and a government that had been established not by China—for whom the Vietnamese have no great love—but by clearly indigenous forces that included some communists. For the peasants this new government meant real land reform, one of the most important needs in their lives.

For nine years following 1945 we denied the people of Vietnam the right of independence. For nine years we vigorously supported the French in their abortive effort to recolonize Vietnam. Before the end of the war we were meeting 80 percent of the French war costs. Even before the French were defeated at Dien Bien Phu, they began to despair of their reckless action, but we did not. We encouraged them with our huge financial and military supplies to continue the war even after they had lost the will. Soon we would be paying almost the full costs of this tragic attempt at recolonization.

After the French were defeated, it looked as if independence and land reform would come again through the Geneva Agreement. But instead there came the United States, determined that Ho should not unify the temporarily divided nation, and the peasants watched again as we supported one of the most vicious modern dictators, our chosen man, Premier Diem. The peasants watched and cringed as Diem ruthlessly rooted out all opposition, supported their extortionist landlords, and refused even to discuss reunification with the North. The peasants watched as all of this was presided over by United States influence and then by increasing numbers of United States troops who came to help quell the insurgency that Diem's methods had aroused. When Diem was overthrown they may have been happy, but the long line of military dictators seemed to offer no real change, especially in terms of their need for land and peace. The only change came from America as we increased our troop commitments in support of governments which were singularly corrupt, inept, and without popular support.[22]

Martin Luther King Jr. realized that American economic interests were causing the U.S. government to suppress freedom in other regions of the world, such as South America. In his 1967 speech "Beyond Vietnam," he also added:

In 1957 a sensitive American official overseas said that it seemed to him that our nation was on the wrong side of a world revolution. During the past ten years we have seen emerge a pattern of suppression which has now justified the presence of U.S. military advisors in Venezuela. This need to maintain social stability for our investments accounts for the counterrevolutionary action of American forces in Guatemala. It tells why American helicopters are being used against guerrillas in Cambodia and why American napalm and Green Beret forces have already been active against rebels in Peru. It is with such activity in mind that the words of the late John F. Kennedy come back to haunt us. Five years ago he said, "Those who make peaceful revolution impossible will make violent revolution inevitable."

Increasingly, by choice or by accident, this is the role our nation has taken, the role of those who make peaceful revolution impossible by refusing to give up the privileges and the pleasures that come from the immense profits of overseas investments. I am convinced that if we are to get on the right side of the world revolution, we as a nation must undergo a radical revolution of values. We must rapidly begin the shift from a thing-oriented society to a person-oriented society. When machines and computers, profit motives and property rights, are considered more important than people, the giant triplets of racism, extreme materialism, and militarism are incapable of being conquered.[23]

After I gave a talk in Bellingham, Washington, a student from Pakistan told me, "There is something I never understood until I heard your talk. I always saw Americans as being the friendliest people in the world. Americans are so kind, generous, and optimistic, but their government does so many horrible things around the world. I never understood this contradiction. I never understood how the American people could be so wonderful, yet their government could support dictatorships, overthrow democracies, and do so many violent things in other countries. But after hearing your talk I finally understand this contradiction. I finally understand how the American people can be so wonderful, while at the same time their government can be so terrible. *Most Americans don't know what their government is doing around the world.*"

The bottom line is that many people in the Greater Middle East are fed up with living under oppression and tyranny, just as our Founding Fathers were fed up with British colonialism, the women's rights activists were fed up with gender inequality, and the civil rights activists were fed up with segregation. It is a myth that the majority of people in the Greater Middle East are a bunch of freedom-hating terrorists who want to kill us because they despise democracy. If this were true, the Arab Spring movement that demanded freedom and democracy would never have happened.

Throughout the Greater Middle East, there are dangerous people with extremist religious views (similar to Osama bin Laden) who want to control the region with their own oppressive ideology. They manipulate the resentment many Middle Eastern people feel toward American foreign policy to further their personal ambitions. Because we have supported brutal dictatorships in the Greater Middle East for so long, we should not be surprised if a reactionary anti-American government rises from the aftermath of the Arab Spring. America is certainly not the cause of all the problems in the Greater Middle East. But we must recognize that when American politicians betray American ideals by promoting a hypocritical foreign policy, this generates poverty and resentment in foreign countries, creating fertile soil for extremism and terrorism to grow.

The hypocritical behavior of many American politicians should not surprise us. As I mentioned earlier, politicians are often stereotyped as being dishonest, deceptive, two-faced, and self-interested. Of course, there are certainly honest politicians who work hard to maintain their integrity, but deception is a large part of the political game, and we all know it. So I think it is odd when Americans—who have no problem seeing politicians as dishonest, deceptive, two-faced, and self-interested—are surprised when their government lies to them. Who do they think is running our government? Politicians. Is it any surprise that our government lies to us? Furthermore, honest politicians can also be manipulated and lied to, just as Christopher Montague Woodhouse (the senior British Secret Intelligence Service agent quoted in the *All the Shah's Men* excerpt) lied to the Eisenhower administration about Iran.

When American politicians preach about freedom and democracy while supporting dictatorships, this hypocrisy causes people around the world to question our true intentions. Did we really invade Iraq to spread democracy, protect ourselves from "weapons of mass destruction," and liberate the Iraqi people, or were we more concerned with oil? In 2006 West Point invited Noam Chomsky to give a lecture on "just war theory" to the sophomore class. During his West Point lecture, a cadet asked him if the invasion of Iraq in 2003 was a "just war" due to Saddam Hussein's human rights violations. Chomsky replied:

> As for [Saddam Hussein's] human rights violations,
> they were horrendous. And here is one of the cases where
> it really is important to look at facts before you make

decisions. We know the facts. They're not secret. So yes, Saddam Hussein carried out horrendous human rights violations. In fact, he's on trial for them right now. But have a look at the trial. Saddam Hussein is on trial for crimes that he committed in 1982 . . . signing the death warrant for a hundred and fifty or so Shiites who were involved in an uprising. Yeah that's a crime. 1982 happens to be an important year in U.S.–Iraqi relations . . . 1982 was the year in which Ronald Reagan dropped Iraq from the list of states supporting terrorism so the U.S. could start providing him with extensive aid, including military aid, including means to develop biological and chemical weapons . . . And Donald Rumsfeld shortly after went to firm up the agreement.

The next charge against Saddam Hussein, the one that's going to come along . . . It's a much more serious crime, the atrocities against the Kurds in 1987, 1988, the Anfal Massacres, Halabja [poison gas attack] . . . They were terrible, probably killed 100,000 people. The U.S. didn't object. In fact, the Reagan administration blocked efforts in Congress even to protest against it. Furthermore, the support for Saddam increased and continued. In fact, Saddam was given an extraordinary privilege . . . He got away with attacking a U.S. naval vessel and killing thirty-seven seamen in 1987. That's pretty astonishing. Nobody can get away with that. But the Reagan administration was so strongly in support of Saddam right through the worst atrocities, they even let him get away with that. This continued, after the end of [Iraq's] war with Iran, after the worst atrocities. In 1989, Iraqi nuclear engineers were invited to the United States to take part in a conference in Portland, Oregon in which they were trained in how to develop weapons of mass destruction . . . Yeah, the human rights violations were horrendous. Does that have anything to do with the invasion [of Iraq in 2003]? No. Nothing.[24]

If we believe the U.S. government is spreading democracy and freedom around the world, then American foreign policy is filled with contradictions and does not make any sense. But if we realize our government is more concerned with economic interests that often benefit a few corporations at the expense of the American people, then we can see a pattern in American foreign policy. Our government tends to support dictators who do exactly what it wants. But when a dictator no longer does exactly what our government wants, he is labeled as an enemy. This is what happened to Saddam Hussein. Although we supported his aggressive war against Iran during the 1980s (which killed over half a million people), his invasion of Kuwait went against the wishes of the U.S. government.

I often hear peace activists say, "The problem with the U.S. government is that it acts like the policeman of the world." But I disagree with that statement, because I don't think the U.S. government's behavior remotely resembles the behavior we expect from police officers. When a police officer comes to your house to stop a crime, does he spend the next fifty years camped out in your living room? That is what the U.S. government does when it defends a country in a war and maintains military bases in that country decades after the war has ended. When a police officer claims to be keeping your neighborhood safe, does he let his friends take your belongings? That is what the U.S. government does when it claims to be protecting freedom while allowing American corporations to plunder the natural resources of foreign countries. When a police officer preaches about the importance of stopping crime, does he arm and fund brutal criminal organizations? That is what the U.S. government does when it preaches about the importance of democracy while arming and funding brutal dictatorships. Some police officers do in fact behave like this. What do we call them? *Corrupt cops.* As an American citizen who embraces American ideals, I think it is un-American and unacceptable for our politicians to run our government in a way that resembles a corrupt cop.

Just look at the facts. How can a government that preaches democracy and freedom support dictatorships in Saudi Arabia and so many other countries? During one of my lectures, a person who supports American foreign policy told me, "Look, spreading democracy is not the main objective of American foreign policy. The main objective is oil. We just tell the American people it's about democracy because it sounds nice. If our politicians instead told the American people, 'We are going to war for oil,' it would bother a lot of Americans. But these oil companies are just securing Middle Eastern oil because they want to provide cheap energy to the American people. Isn't cheap gas worth the price of war?"

During my lectures, I have heard comments similar to this more than once. When I reply, I remind the audience of a few key points. First of all, shouldn't politicians at least be honest with the American people? Some Americans might not have a problem with our country going to war for oil, but many Americans would be deeply disturbed by it. When I was in the army one of the most offensive things a peace activist could say to an American soldier was, "You are fighting for oil." In a democracy, shouldn't we tell the American people the truth and let them make up their own minds? When we consider our highest American ideals of liberty and justice, is cheaper gas worth the cost of thousands of dead American soldiers, tens of thousands of wounded soldiers, and hundreds of thousands of innocent civilians killed in war?

Second, when we consider the trillions of taxpayer dollars being used to pay for war and how that money could instead be used to help the American people, it is obvious that most Americans are not benefitting economically from war. Nor is there any convincing evidence that the primary objective or final outcome of American foreign policy is to simply lower gas prices for Americans. If the economic and overall well-being of the American people were really the top priority of oil companies, why would their lobby efforts stifle the development of alternatives to oil? Wouldn't alternative forms of energy and less reliance on oil benefit the American people? When people say the top priority of oil companies is to lower gas prices for the American people, they are talking as if oil companies are charities. Let's be realistic here. Although there are many different opinions about oil companies, I think we can all agree upon one basic fact. *Oil companies are not charities.*

American foreign policy has less to do with providing cheap oil for the American people (gas prices have risen over the past twenty years while oil companies have been making record profits), and more to do with giving powerful corporations control of Middle Eastern oil in order to maximize their profits. For the U.S. government to control access to oil in Muslim countries, all the countries in the Greater Middle East—even those that don't have oil—have strategic value. In his book *Rogue States*, written in 2000, Noam Chomsky predicted that the United States government would soon target oil-rich countries such as Iraq and Iran for attack: "And US energy corporations will not be happy to see foreign rivals—now including China and Russia—gain privileged access to Iraqi oil reserves, second only to Saudi Arabia's in scale, or to Iran's natural gas, oil, and other resources."[25]

The Four Steps Necessary to Create a More Effective Security Paradigm

Many peace activists criticize the size of the military budget, but this has no meaningful impact if we do not first show people that war, in the twenty-first century, does not make them safe. If you truly believe that war protects your family and freedom, how much are you willing to pay? If you truly believe that war is synonymous with national security, then you will probably pay almost anything, because most people cannot put a price on their family and freedom.

If we do not show people the true dangers that war poses to our national security, they may perceive a discussion about cutting the military budget as a threat to their loved ones and liberty. In addition, it is not enough to just be anti-war, because we must also offer a better solution than war. In other words, we must offer a more effective security paradigm that is more proactive and versatile at keeping us safe than the war system.

To replace the old paradigm of war with a more effective security paradigm, we must implement four necessary steps. The first step is to *develop a foreign policy based on respect.* Our country will be much safer if we, the American people, force our politicians to end their hypocrisy and fully embrace American ideals such as democracy, freedom, and justice. Toward the end of his life, General MacArthur noticed how the condescending and paternalistic way American politicians deal with other countries creates resentment. In 1952 he said, "Through the paternalistic attitude which has dominated our material assistance abroad, we have promoted as much weakness as strength, as much resentment as friendship."[26]

To achieve a foreign policy based on respect, we must lead by example as a nation. This involves no longer supporting dictatorships, ending the hypocrisy of American politicians, and truly promoting democratic ideals such as liberty and justice. A foreign policy based on respect applies the infinite shield to an international scale. The less resentment people around the world feel toward the United States because of unjust foreign policies, the less effective Al Qaeda and other terrorist groups will be at recruiting people to kill us.

During one of my lectures, someone said, "But when Iran's dictator the Shah was overthrown, an extremist anti-American government rose to power. So perhaps it is best to keep supporting dictatorships in the Middle East." I replied, "Why does this surprise us? After we overthrew the democratically elected government in Iran in 1953 and supported the oppressive Shah for a couple of decades, is it really so surprising to see anti-American anger in Iran? Imagine if the French or Chinese government overthrew our democracy and installed a dictatorship in America. If we managed to remove the dictatorship and win back our country, don't you think an anti-French or anti-Chinese government would probably rise to power in America? The longer we support these dictatorships, the more extreme the anti-American anger is likely to be." During many of my talks people have also told me, "But people in the Middle East don't want democracy and freedom." My response has been, "But what about the Arab Spring?"

Although the nonviolent and violent uprisings in the Greater Middle East demonstrated a yearning for democracy and freedom, the Arab Spring has a long and difficult road ahead. As I said in *The End of War*, peaceful campaigns are waged over longer periods of time than violent campaigns. After a nonviolent or violent movement overthrows a dictatorship, it often takes decades of waging peace before democracy can truly flourish. America's Founding Fathers defeated the British Empire in the 1780s, yet it wasn't until the 1960s—nearly two hundred years later—that democracy started to become a reality for African Americans. Even today, the struggle for democracy in America continues.

The second step to create a more effective security paradigm is for America to *wage peace, not war*. Waging peace rather than war allows us to heal the underlying problems that cause conflicts. Problems such as poverty, hopelessness, and lack of opportunity create conditions that make people more likely to resort to violence. The purpose of the American military is to protect the American people, and one of the best ways to protect the American people in the twenty-first century is to help people around the world. The cover of the July 2011 issue of *Military Officer* magazine featured an article titled "Waging Peace: America's fighting forces are working to build peace and stability through assistance and relief." According to the article, in 2009 U.S. military units conducted 154 humanitarian projects in sixty-one countries. These efforts focused on medical, dental, and veterinary needs as well as construction projects.

The U.S. military performs "waging peace" missions, because it understands how mass media has changed warfare in the twenty-first century. The Roman Empire did not have freedom of speech or freedom of the press. Nor were there any reporters, photographers, or video cameras in ancient Rome. As a result, when the Roman Empire committed an atrocity, it was easy for them to hide it or even "spin" it as a propaganda tool. But when American soldiers go berserk and kill innocent civilians in the Greater Middle East, pictures of the atrocity can be shown on television, the Internet, or newspapers around the world. This increases resentment against the United States. Brian Fishman, who teaches at the Combating Terrorism Center at West Point, says that a photograph of even a seemingly harmless act can have disastrous consequences:

> With the cadets in class, we walk through some of the jihadi chat rooms that are used to spread propaganda against their fellow soldiers. And they need to understand—there's a photo out there, a very famous photo that's on all of these chat rooms. It's a picture of a bunch of American soldiers taking a rest in a mosque with their boots on. And it's everywhere. And because it's just a symbol of sort of insult to Islam. And the cadets need to understand that even if they are doing something that they think is completely benign, that they don't mean any sort of insult, it can be used against them. And it's that kind of awareness that they need to get to the point where they understand that they could accidentally do something

extraordinarily insulting. That photograph is more of the strategic defeat than any sort of tactical engagement on the battlefield. And we need to understand it and the cadets need to understand that . . . And so what we tell these cadets is, look, this war against Al Qaeda cannot be won or lost in Iraq. Ultimately, this is a fight for hearts and minds around the Middle East. And that's a cliché, but it's true. And that's why these cadets, they can't win that fight with an M-4 [carbine]."[27]

Just as negative photos and stories can damage our national security, positive photos and stories can strengthen our national security. There is a saying around the world that "America gives with one hand and takes with both hands." But imagine if around the world the United States instead had the following reputation: when a humanitarian crisis or natural disaster happens, the Americans arrive, genuinely help others without expecting anything in return, improve the local infrastructure, and *leave*. This would not only help us win hearts and minds around the world, but it would also combat the poverty, hopelessness, and rage that provide fertile soil for terrorism to grow. If a group of people in a foreign country then tried to recruit their countrymen to attack us, many of their own people would say, "Are you crazy? The Americans selflessly came and helped us. Why would you want to hurt them?"

Waging peace as a country allows us to apply the sword that heals to an international scale. If we increase the number of humanitarian aid and natural disaster relief missions, instead of relying on expensive military bases around the world and the use of high-tech weapons, the military budget could also be greatly reduced. We currently have hundreds of military bases in other countries. Most Americans do not realize we have so many bases around the world. Our global military presence is not only economically unsustainable, but it makes people suspicious when we provide humanitarian aid and natural disaster relief. They wonder if we are really there to help them, or if our true intentions are to put a military base in their country.

To understand why having military bases all over the world endangers our national security, we must remember that the U.S. government supported Osama bin Laden during the 1980s, but he turned against the U.S. government when it put military bases in Saudi Arabia—where Islamic holy land is located. How would Americans feel if a foreign country put a military base on our soil? How would we react? As I mentioned earlier, we would fight back. In 2007, Brian Fishman said, "It's not good enough to leave 20 or 30 thousand troops in Iraq . . . those 20 or 30 thousand Americans are going to remain a sticking point and a propaganda tool for Al Qaeda around the world."[28]

The third step to create a more effective security paradigm is to *strengthen international laws against dictatorships and corrupt governments.* Laws are a form of deflection I discussed in chapter 5, and the third step applies them to an international scale.

The third step is important, because many of the dictatorships around the world are supported by influential countries such as the United States. If the most powerful country on the planet, the United States, no longer supported brutal dictatorships, it would be an important step toward strengthening international laws against oppression, especially when we consider the effectiveness of *leading by example.* Other countries such as Russia, China, and England also support dictatorships, but since America was founded on the ideal of resisting tyranny, what could possibly be more un-American than supporting dictatorships? Because supporting dictatorships is so un-American, our politicians have to gain public support for their agendas by telling us they are spreading democracy and freedom around the world. Because supporting dictatorships is so un-American, I have met Americans who are offended by the mere mention that our government supports tyranny rather than democracy, but the facts of American foreign policy tell a much different story than the propaganda spread by the war system.

When dictatorships do arise, how can we stop them? According to nonviolence strategist Gene Sharp, waging peace is a more effective and less expensive way to overthrow a dictatorship than waging war. For a long time I was skeptical of Sharp's claim. Gandhi and King successfully waged peace because their respective opponents, the British Empire and United States, allowed freedom of speech. But I do not think waging peace would have worked against more oppressive governments that outlawed freedom of speech, such as the Roman Empire.

Because waging peace uses freedom of speech to spread new ideas that transform how people think, Gandhi's nonviolent methods would have been far less effective against the Roman Empire. Gandhi leveraged reporters and newspapers to document the injustices of British colonialism, and Martin Luther King Jr. also leveraged television coverage to spread his message. Freedom of speech creates a sky where new ideas can soar. But in the Roman Empire, where rebels were often executed and there was no freedom of speech, reporters, mass media, or modern camera technology to capture images of injustice, Gandhi and King would have had much more difficulty getting their new and controversial ideas off the ground.

I still think it is unlikely that waging peace would have been effective against the Roman Empire, but Gene Sharp's writings have convinced me that waging peace can be very effective against modern dictatorships. He has studied numerous examples where waging peace overthrew dictatorships in the twentieth and twenty-first century, most recently during the Arab Spring. Unlike the ancient era of the Roman Empire, the modern era has a more interconnected international system, greater global consensus about "human rights," and more sophisticated technological tools that enable waging peace to work even against a dictatorship. If people doubt the potential of waging peace to overthrow a modern dictatorship, Gene Sharp offers facts that can change their mind. Waging peace does not always succeed against tyranny, but as people become better trained in the art of waging peace, they will unlock the full potential of this powerful weapon.

To develop a respect-based foreign policy that wages peace and opposes all dictatorships, we must use the sword of truth to cut through the immense propaganda that deceives and confuses us. Only then can we show the American people what national security truly means in the twenty-first century. West Point graduate and retired army colonel Andrew Bacevich explains why we cannot understand national security unless we first recognize the dangers created by our addiction to Middle Eastern oil:

> The contest in which we are engaged is one to determine the fate of the Greater Middle East, with particular attention to the oil-rich Persian Gulf. That contest began during World War I when Great Britain and France

collaborated to dismantle the Ottoman Empire and to replace it with a New Middle East organized to serve the needs of London and Paris. During World War II, the United States became party to this effort when Franklin Roosevelt committed the United States to guaranteeing the safety and well-being of the Saudi royal family, which owned but needed help in exploiting a veritable El Dorado of oil.

By the 1960s, with European power in decline, the United States became the principal Western guarantor of Middle Eastern stability (and therefore of Western access to its riches) . . . Jimmy Carter's promulgation of the Carter Doctrine committed the United States to using all necessary means—diplomatic code for threatening to employ force—to prevent any hostile power from controlling the Gulf. What followed was an ever-escalating penchant for US military interventionism, to which Ronald Reagan, George H.W. Bush, and Bill Clinton each contributed in turn. Rather than simply preventing others from dominating the Gulf, we sought willy-nilly to dominate it ourselves. This escalation of US military presence and activities elicited a hostile response . . .

Fatefully, George W. Bush chose to play Bin Laden's game. He responded to 9/11 by escalating even further the US attempt to impose order on the Greater Middle East, confident that the United States possessed the necessary military power to do so. Instead of quasi-war, there was now all-out war, with no holds barred. Instead of periodic hostilities, there was now open-ended fighting . . . Although Mr. Obama can rightly cite the killing of Bin Laden as a notable victory, it will not prove decisive, if only because *the essential issues giving rise to war in the first place remain unresolved* [emphasis added].[29]

Our addiction to Middle Eastern oil harms our national security in other ways. In August 2012, General Martin Dempsey, the eighteenth

Chairman of the Joint Chiefs of Staff, said: "I attended the groundbreaking ceremony for the solar wind farm at the Tooele Army Depot's Renewable Energy Farm yesterday. With this energy farm, Tooele brings DOD [the Department of Defense] closer to achieving its goal of operating 16 'net-zero' bases by 2020. *Improving our energy security improves our national security* [emphasis added]."[30]

In an article titled "The Real Reason the Military Is Going Green," published in *Yes! Magazine*, Natalie Pompilio further explains:

> Retired [Brigadier General] Steven Anderson calls himself "an accidental environmentalist . . ." Anderson, like many military leaders, has realized that guzzling oil makes the United States vulnerable in other ways. "I'm a soldier," Anderson said. "Why should I be concerned about climate change? Climate change brings about global instability. That makes the world more vulnerable and it's more likely that soldiers like myself will have to fight and die somewhere . . ."
>
> The Department of Defense isn't denying that climate change is a major national security threat. "The change is happening. It's just a reality," said retired Marine Col. Mark Mykleby, a former strategy assistant to the Joint Chiefs of Staff. "Science tells us it's coming our way."
>
> The Defense Department first acknowledged climate change as a factor in its operations in its 2010 Quadrennial Defense Review. "[Climate change] may act as an accelerant of instability or conflict, placing a burden to respond on civilian institutions and militaries around the world," read the report. Now the military is going green. Taking fuel trucks off the road. Developing solar energy. Their reasons are strategic, not altruistic.[31]

The 2009 U.S. Army Sustainability Report lists several threats to national security, which include severe income disparity, poverty, and climate change. The U.S. Army Sustainability Report states: "The Army is facing several global challenges to sustainability that create a volatile security environment with an increased potential for conflict . . . *Globalization's* increased interdependence and connectivity has led to greater disparities in wealth, which foster conditions that can lead to conflict . . . *Population growth and poverty*; the poor in fast-growing urban areas are especially vulnerable to antigovernment and radical ideologies . . . *Climate change and natural disasters* strain already limited resources, increasing the potential for humanitarian crises and population migrations."[32]

When the U.S. Army says that "greater disparities in wealth . . . poverty . . . and climate change" are dangerous, these are among the same concerns expressed by the Occupy movement. When the U.S. Army and Occupy movement agree on something, I think we should pay attention. However, even if we confront these threats by implementing the first three steps (develop a foreign policy based on respect, wage peace rather than war to heal the underlying problems that cause conflicts, and strengthen international law) there may still be people around the world who want to kill us. That is why we must also have a fourth step, which involves *international police work.*

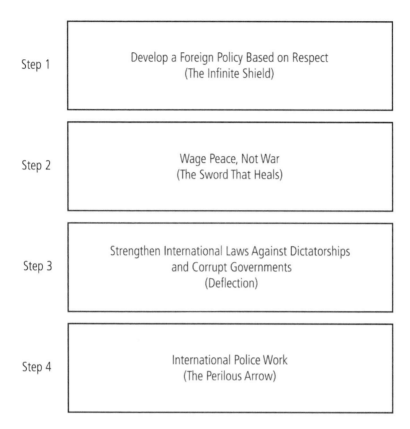

Step 1	Develop a Foreign Policy Based on Respect (The Infinite Shield)
Step 2	Wage Peace, Not War (The Sword That Heals)
Step 3	Strengthen International Laws Against Dictatorships and Corrupt Governments (Deflection)
Step 4	International Police Work (The Perilous Arrow)

Figure 11.3 The Four Steps to Create a More Effective Security Paradigm

To understand why this fourth step is needed, we must first understand that Al Qaeda has more in common with a criminal organization like the Mafia than with a monolithic government like the Soviet Union or Nazi Germany. Al Qaeda is a transnational criminal network, and you cannot defeat a transnational criminal network by invading and occupying a country. The September 11 hijackers planned their attack from Hamburg, Germany, and a person can plan a terrorist attack from San Francisco. Since a person can plan a terrorist attack from any country or within the United States, waging war in a Muslim country does not truly combat terrorism, but instead creates a high number of civilian casualties that exacerbates terrorism.

In a *60 Minutes* interview, Marine lieutenant colonel Christian Cabaniss said, "Killing a thousand Taliban [fighters] is great, but if I kill two civilians in the process, it's a loss."[33] Killing civilians turns the local population against you, and this is why the U.S. military is trying to minimize civilian casualties. But since World War II, the majority of people killed in wars have been civilians, and no matter how hard we try to not kill civilians in war, many will die. This is due to many factors, including the chaotic and confusing nature of war.

The organizations best trained to combat criminal networks are the FBI and police. The FBI helped capture terrorists such as Ted Kaczynski (the "Unabomber") and Timothy McVeigh, along with numerous serial killers. In the past, international police work was used to arrest people on foreign soil, including some of the Nazis who escaped from Germany following World War II. After September 11, much of the world's sympathy went out to us, and we had an opportunity to treat the September 11 attacks as a horrible criminal act. We could have worked with other countries to go after Al Qaeda the way we went after Timothy McVeigh, the Nazis who fled from Germany after World War II, and other people who commit crimes.

Treating the September 11 attacks as a criminal act—rather than an act of war that requires the invasion and occupation of a foreign country— would have freed up the U.S. military to do more humanitarian aid and natural disaster relief missions. Many people don't think the military is capable of adapting its tactics in order to meet the challenges of a new era, but we should never underestimate the military's ability to adapt and overcome. Militaries around the world used to fight with spears and ride horses into battle, but they adapted as technology and the world changed. During World War I, trench warfare was common, but again the military adapted and fought much differently during World War II. Today the military is already adapting and evolving in ways many people don't realize. For example, due to the urban terrain where modern wars are often fought, many U.S. Special Forces soldiers spend more time fighting like a sophisticated SWAT team than the World War II veterans who invaded the beaches of Normandy. Today the U.S. military has embraced tactics used by law enforcement officers and even humanitarian aid organizations.

Currently, the U.S. military is the only organization in the world that can deploy tens of thousands of physically fit, mentally tough, well-trained people to any spot on the globe in a matter of days. Shifting its mission further in the direction of humanitarian aid and natural disaster relief would better protect America by winning hearts and minds around the world. It would also reduce the military budget, because much of the military budget is spent on high tech weapons incapable of winning hearts and minds. A waging peace mission would also give many soldiers what they truly want. Military recruitment commercials appeal largely to young people's idealism, yearning for self-improvement, and desire to do good around the world. The new navy motto is "A Global Force for Good," and have you ever seen a military recruitment commercial that makes any reference to killing? General Douglas MacArthur said, "The Soldier above all other people prays for peace, for he must suffer and bear the deepest wounds and scars of war."[34]

Although soldiers are stereotyped as brainwashed robots who all think alike, there are a variety of ideologies within the military, and soldiers disagree on many issues. According to a 2011 Pew research study:

> Just half of all post-9/11 veterans say that, given the costs and benefits to the U.S., the war in Afghanistan has been worth fighting. A smaller share (44%) says the war in Iraq has been worth it. Only one-third (34%) say both wars have been worth fighting, and a nearly identical share (33%) say neither has been worth the costs. About half of post-9/11 veterans (51%) say relying too much on military force creates hatred that leads to more terrorism, while four-in-ten endorse the opposite view: that overwhelming force is the best way to defeat terrorism . . . About six-in-ten post-9/11 veterans (59%) support the noncombat "nation-building" role the military has taken on in Iraq and Afghanistan. The public and pre-9/11 veterans are less enthused. Just 45% of both groups say they think this is an appropriate role for the military.[35]

By educating people about the effectiveness of waging peace, we can increase popular support for a national security strategy no longer based on the outdated and ineffective method of waging war, but based on the four steps of a more effective security paradigm (develop a foreign policy based on respect, wage peace rather than war to heal the underlying problems that cause conflicts, strengthen international law, and use international police work). If we apply these four steps toward combating terrorism and improving our national and global security, we will certainly not put the United States at risk of being occupied by a foreign country. If you think our country is at any risk of being occupied, please consider this. The United States has the most powerful military in human history and the support of NATO allies. Yet it cannot successfully occupy Afghanistan, which is a small and impoverished country.

If the most powerful military in human history and our NATO allies cannot successfully occupy a country as small and poor as Afghanistan, what country on earth could possibly occupy the United States? We have a large population, a vast amount of territory, a lot of mountains, and almost as many guns as people. Since we would have "home-field advantage," a foreign invading army that landed on the Pacific Coast would suffer a humiliating military defeat if it attempted to occupy even a single state such as California, especially if we maintained a strong national guard. And a foreign army wouldn't even get to our shore in the first place if we maintained a competent navy and air force, which would also be performing important missions in our new humanitarian aid and natural disaster relief role.

The greatest threat to our country is actually from within. Our current approach to fighting terrorism not only threatens to bankrupt our country, but it is also causing many of our politicians to betray American ideals. When America sanctions torture and takes away the civil liberties of its citizens, it ceases to be the America that can be a beacon of hope, freedom, and justice around the world.

Betraying American ideals is not the only internal threat to our national security. The U.S. government's escalation of drone warfare also makes our country less safe. While I was in the army I worked at DARPA for several months. DARPA is the Defense Advanced Research Projects Agency, which is responsible for the military's high-tech research. DARPA helped create the Internet, GPS, Stealth Fighter, M-16, and Predator drone. The Predator drone is a pilotless airplane that can operate anywhere in the world via remote control from the United States. It has the ability to perform surveillance missions and kill people with Hellfire missiles. It is often criticized for its lethal role in the Greater Middle East, but I learned something interesting about the drone's origin while I was at DARPA.

Throughout human history, the bulk of military research has focused on making weapons deadlier and more destructive. For thousands of years, many of humanity's most brilliant scientific minds were devoted to making sharper swords, deadlier guns, and bigger bombs. But for the first time in history, a large amount of military research is devoted to making weapons *less* destructive and more *precise*. At DARPA I learned that a dream of many military researchers is to develop a precision-guided "smart bomb" that can accurately kill an enemy combatant while not harming innocent people standing only a few meters away.

Due to mass media's immense growth during and after World War II, people all over the world could see pictures and videos that revealed the horror of war and the suffering of innocent civilians. In World War II the U.S. government targeted civilian populations when it bombed cities such as Dresden, Tokyo, Hiroshima, and Nagasaki. The intention of the bombing campaigns was to kill as many civilians as possible, and this had become a common method of waging war. Great Britain and Germany also bombed civilian populations, and the Japanese massacred hundreds of thousands of civilians in Nanking and other cities.

But during the late twentieth century, targeting civilians during bombing campaigns was no longer acceptable within the international community, so the United States had to develop precision-guided smart bombs that minimize civilian casualties. Based on my conversations with the military researchers at DARPA, the Predator drone sounds like a great idea, at least in theory. It has high-tech targeting systems and precision-guided missiles that are supposed to kill enemy combatants without hurting innocent civilians. And because it does not have a pilot, an American will not be killed or captured if it is shot down. I got the impression at DARPA that many of the military researchers had good intentions, but the Predator drone is an example of good intentions gone terribly wrong.

The Predator drone has been used in countries such as Iraq, Afghanistan, Yemen, Somalia, and Pakistan. Wherever it is being used, it is killing civilians. This is because military researchers have been unable to create a precision-guided missile capable of overcoming two major obstacles: human fallibility and technological problems. An example of human fallibility is a flawed intelligence report claiming that an Al Qaeda operative is alone in a house in Pakistan, when in reality the house also contains women and children, or perhaps the Al Qaeda operative is not even there. The Predator drone launches a missile based on this flawed intelligence report, and innocent people are killed. Another example of human fallibility is the person operating the Predator drone making a mistake.

Another reason the Predator drone can kill civilians is because of technological problems. Think of all the problems people have every day with their computers. When technological problems happen with the Predator drone, innocent people can die. There are other reasons why the escalation of drone warfare endangers our national security. In a June 2012 article in the *Guardian*, journalist Paul Harris wrote:

> A former top terrorism official at the CIA has warned that President Barack Obama's controversial drone programme is far too indiscriminate in hitting targets and could lead to such political instability that it creates terrorist safe havens. Obama's increased use of drones to attack suspected Islamic militants in Pakistan, Afghanistan, Somalia and Yemen has become one of the most controversial aspects of his national security policy. He has launched at least 275 strikes in Pakistan alone; a rate of attack that is far higher than his predecessor George W. Bush.
>
> Defenders of the policy say it provides a way of hitting high-profile targets, such as al-Qaida number two, Abu Yahya al-Libi. But critics say the definition of militant is used far too broadly and there are too many civilian casualties. The London-based Bureau of Investigative Journalism estimates up to 830 civilians, including many women and children, might have been killed by drone attacks in Pakistan, 138 in Yemen and 57 in Somalia. Hundreds more have been injured.

Now Robert Grenier, who headed the CIA's counter-terrorism center from 2004 to 2006 and was previously a CIA station chief in Pakistan, has told the Guardian that the drone programme is targeted too broadly. "It [the drone program] needs to be targeted much more finely. We have been seduced by them and the unintended consequences of our actions are going to outweigh the intended consequences . . . We have gone a long way down the road of creating a situation where we are creating more enemies than we are removing from the battlefield. We are already there with regards to Pakistan and Afghanistan . . . Young men, who are typically armed, are in the same area and may hold these militants in a certain form of high regard. If you strike them indiscriminately you are running the risk of creating a terrific amount of popular anger. They have tribes and clans and large families. Now all of a sudden you have a big problem . . . I am very concerned about the creation of a larger terrorist safe haven in Yemen."[36]

Should the drones be used much more specifically, or should they not be used at all? Instead of assassinating people with drones, what if we explored more practical ways to solve our problems? Colonel Bacevich said the following about drone warfare:

But I also have this question to ask. And that is, what is the political objective of a strategy of targeted assassination? How many people do we think we're going to kill [with drones]? How long are we going to kill people in Yemen or in Somalia or in Pakistan before we get to some point where we can say, "Yes, now our political purposes have been achieved, and therefore the war can end . . ." And my fear is that we'll never, we'll never run out of targets. And that describes where we are . . . Permanent, open-ended war cannot be good for the country. Permanent, open-ended war, in essence, is an abdication of strategic thought. Are we so unimaginative, are we so wedded to the reliance on military means, that we cannot conceive of any way to reconcile our differences with groups, nations, in the Islamic world, and therefore bring this conflict to an end? . . . And it seems to me that the strategic imperative is to . . . understand the grievances that ultimately gave rise to this animosity expressing itself in terrorist activity . . . It seems to me that there are indications that we can engage or have some hope in positive change. And here I'm alluding to the Arab Spring.[37]

What I am offering is a very hopeful message, because if we believe that people in the Greater Middle East hate us simply because we're free, then we will be at war forever. But if we understand that many people in the Greater Middle East want freedom just like we do, and we as the American people have the power to change our hypocritical foreign policy, then peace becomes a realistic possibility.

The Arab Spring demonstrated that many people in the Greater Middle East want freedom, justice, and democracy just like we do. Some American politicians want to end our hypocritical foreign policy, but if they promote a foreign policy of waging peace, their political opponents will attack them as being unpatriotic, un-American, and endangering our national security. We must back up our politicians by showing the American people that patriotism means working to improve our country, being American means not supporting dictatorships, and our national security depends on waging peace.

Most American politicians are not bad people who want to cause harm; they too have been deceived by the war system's propaganda. This chapter counters war propaganda by beginning a discussion based on facts. It is impossible for me to cover the entire history of American foreign policy in a single chapter, but I have included many crucial facts that propaganda leaves out. When we are armed with facts and the methods of waging peace, we can begin a productive dialogue about how to overcome the threats to our country and planet.

Just as Frederick Douglass, Susan B. Anthony, Elizabeth Cady Stanton, Martin Luther King Jr., and many others exposed the truth of racial and gender equality, we must expose truths such as the power of waging peace and the harm caused by American foreign policy. Like Douglass, our intention of exposing the truth is not to harm our country, but to transform America into a great nation that fully embodies its own ideals. Regarding the oppression of women, in 1888 Douglass said, "There is still a great nation to be brought to a knowledge of the truth [about women's equality]. We are not to be appalled by the magnitude of the work, or discouraged by this or any other form of opposition."[38] As committed American citizens, we must be dedicated to learning and sharing the truth, and we must demand that our politicians tell us the truth.

Ultimately, we must overcome deception, ignorance, misunderstanding, hatred, and greed. When we wage peace, those are our real enemies, and we have the power to defeat them. People often ask me, "But how can we possibly defeat greed?" War is very profitable for some corporations, causing them to pressure our politicians to support unjust policies that ultimately hurt the American people. But unjust policies—even the ones that are extremely profitable—have been defeated before. State-sanctioned slavery and the trans-Atlantic slave trade were extremely profitable, but they were abolished. In addition, for much of human history women had virtually no political or economic rights and were treated as property. This allowed men to have a monopoly on wealth, but that has changed in the United States and many other countries.

Although a small percentage of people profit from war, if more Americans knew how economically destructive war is to our country, they would better understand why Eisenhower compared war spending to crucifixion. In 1870, five years after the American Civil War ended, Frederick Douglass said, "War is among the greatest calamities incident to the lives of nations. They arrest the progress of civilization, corrupt the sources of morality, destroy all proper sense of the sacredness of human life, perpetuate the national hate, and *weigh down the necks of after coming generations with the burdens of debt* [emphasis added]."[39]

In the end, Americans want decent jobs. According to a study conducted by Robert Pollin and Heidi Garrett-Peltier at the University of Massachusetts,

Amherst, an economy that wages peace would employ many more Americans than an economy that wages war. In their study they said:

> This study focuses on the employment effects of military spending versus alternative domestic spending priorities, in particular investments in clean energy, health care and education. We first present some simple alternative spending scenarios, namely devoting $1 billion to the military versus the same amount of money spent on clean energy, health care, and education, as well as for tax cuts which produce increased levels of personal consumption. Our conclusion in assessing such relative employment impacts is straightforward: $1 billion spent on each of the domestic spending priorities will create substantially more jobs within the U.S. economy than would the same $1 billion spent on the military. We then examine the pay level of jobs created through these alternative spending priorities and assess the overall welfare impacts of the alternative employment outcomes. We show that investments in clean energy, health care and education create a much larger number of jobs across all pay ranges, including mid-range jobs and high-paying jobs. Channeling funds into clean energy, health care and education in an effective way will therefore create significantly greater opportunities for decent employment throughout the U.S. economy than spending the same amount of funds with the military.[40]

By transforming our war economy into a peace economy, American workers will benefit. For example, if the military focuses on humanitarian aid and natural disaster relief, millions of people will keep their jobs, and the money previously spent on high-tech weapons can be diverted to numerous industries. If we transfer a fraction of the bloated military budget to NASA, the corporations making missiles and drones for war can instead make rockets and robotic vehicles that explore other planets. If we improve our national security by ending our addiction to Middle Eastern oil, the engineers in the military-industrial complex can instead develop clean forms of energy and other technological innovations that human beings need.

These changes will not happen easily, and we will face challenges, obstacles, and setbacks as we confront the war system. But no matter how difficult the struggle may be, there is a way to win. When we wield the infinite shield and the sword that heals, we become soldiers of peace with the strength to defeat the master of deception.

CHAPTER 12

The Underdog Journey

Captain Ahab and the White Whale

In our struggle to defeat the war system, we are the underdogs. The war system is a mighty and challenging adversary, but so was the giant Goliath when the young shepherd David, another underdog, defeated him. During my journey to free my mind from the war system's illusions, I have had to fight another opponent just as mighty, and in some ways more challenging than the war system. This other opponent destroys countless lives, yet it remains a secret rarely discussed in our society. To uncover this secret, Herman Melville's novel *Moby-Dick* offers us a useful metaphor.

In Melville's novel, a white whale called Moby Dick bit off the leg of the whale hunter Captain Ahab. Consumed by rage and madness, Ahab became obsessed with killing the white whale in revenge. Ahab said his purpose in life was "to chase that white whale on both sides of land, and over all sides of earth, till he spouts black blood."[1] After years of searching, Ahab and his ship's crew hunted down Moby Dick. In the battle that followed, the white whale severely damaged the ship, but Ahab wounded his nemesis with a harpoon. The crew watched in horror as the rope of the harpoon wrapped around Ahab's neck, pulling him from the boat and dragging him beneath the ocean's roaring waves. The ship sank, and all the crew members drowned except Ishmael, the narrator of the novel. Ahab's lifeless body descended to the dark depths of the ocean, and the white whale was not seen again.[2]

To me, this tragic novel symbolizes the *self-destructive cycle of trauma.* When the white whale bites off his leg in a traumatic incident, Ahab is filled with rage and madness. The white whale did not directly kill Ahab. Instead, he is killed by his insatiable rage, which fueled his obsession for revenge and led him down a self-destructive path. When we are deeply wounded by betrayal, abuse, and other forms of trauma, we not only become Ahab; we also become the white whale he is hunting. Trauma puts us at war with ourselves.

Trauma creates an internal war in our mind, heart, and innermost being. This internal war takes the form of self-destructive behaviors, which can kill us quickly or slowly. The five self-destructive behaviors that result from trauma are rage, meaninglessness, addiction, mistrust, and shame. As we descend into the downward spiral of self-destruction, trauma transforms us into both Ahab and the white whale. Just as Ahab and the white whale wound each other, trauma causes us to continually wound ourselves and become our own worst enemy.

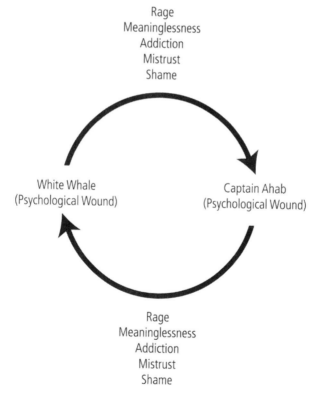

Figure 12.1 The Self-Destructive Cycle of Trauma

Suicide has a variety of causes, and people commit suicide for different reasons. Trauma is one reason, and it leads to many forms of suicide. Because of my self-loathing, much of my rage is directed inward. When the siren song of rage seduces me, the temptation to kill myself in a quick and violent berserker rampage can be almost overwhelming. When people are overcome with a chronic sense of meaninglessness, another common product of trauma, this can also cause them to commit suicide quickly and violently.

When we are imprisoned by problems such as addiction, mistrust, and shame, our suicide does not have to happen quickly. It can unfold in slow motion over years and even decades. When people suffer from trauma, they can develop an addiction to things such as drugs, alcohol, overeating, danger, and uncommitted sex. They can even become addicted to an artistic pursuit, just as I am addicted to writing. If we are not careful, our addiction can lead to a slow motion suicide that gradually destroys our physical health, mental well-being, and relationships with other human beings.

Just as blood and chunks of flesh erupt from a traumatic gunshot wound, feelings such as mistrust and shame can erupt from a traumatic psychological wound. Mistrust can cause us to hate others, and shame can cause us to hate ourselves. Mistrust and shame can turn everyone around us, including ourselves, into an enemy. The result is a slow-motion suicide that causes our joy and compassion to die long before our body perishes.

But it does not have to be this way. We can stop the self-destructive cycle of trauma that multiplies and magnifies our psychological wounds. We can end the metaphorical war in our psyche between Ahab and the white whale. Waging peace not only gives us the power to end the wars between countries and our ongoing war with the environment; it also gives us the power to end the war in our hearts. Waging peace not only gives us the power to heal societal wounds such as racism, sexism, and other forms of injustice; it also gives us the power to heal psychological wounds such as betrayal, abuse, and other forms of trauma.

If I truly wanted to defeat the war system, I realized I would have to recruit my trauma as an ally in this struggle. I would have to turn my nemesis into a friend. By exploring, understanding, and learning to make peace with my trauma, I have increased my empathy, awareness, and love of humanity. This has made me more effective as a soldier of peace. My trauma is the cause of much of my pain, but it is also the source of much of my strength.

Although trauma has become my ally, for me it remains unpredictable. I am thirty-two years old as I write this, and I still struggle with my deep psychological wounds. On dark days, my ally sometimes turns against me, but I am working hard to win its trust, heal its wounds, and strengthen my alliance with the wounded part of myself. I hope to continue making progress for the rest of my life. Perhaps someday, my Ahab will be at peace with the white whale within me, and I will be at peace with myself.

It is not easy to escape the labyrinth of trauma. We must embark on a journey of personal growth and understanding to free ourselves from the mazelike tunnels of rage, meaninglessness, addiction, mistrust, and shame. Since trauma affects people in different ways, those who suffer from trauma can experience these five self-destructive behaviors in varying amounts. Some spend much of their time lost in the dark tunnels of rage. Others rarely feel rage, but are lost in the confusing corridors of meaninglessness. Some are lost in the maze of addiction, while others wander aimlessly through the winding tunnels of mistrust. Some spend most of their lives struggling to free themselves from the shadows of shame. Although people who suffer from trauma experience these five self-destructive behaviors in varying amounts, most of them experience all five to at least some extent.

Our existence is filled with adversity, and most human beings who live a long and full life will probably experience some form of rage, meaning-lessness, addiction, mistrust, and shame. People who suffer from trauma tend to experience these five self-destructive behaviors in large amounts, but nearly all human beings experience these behaviors in some amount. Haven't most people felt anger: the little brother of rage? Haven't most people struggled to find purpose in their lives: the cure for meaninglessness? Haven't most people had difficulty controlling their impulses and desires: the temptations that lead to addiction? Haven't most people been betrayed: the cause of mistrust? Haven't most people felt inferior, inadequate, or been humiliated: the causes of shame?

What is the difference between suffering and trauma? A knife can wound us by cutting open our flesh, or it can penetrate deeper and split open our bone. We can compare our conscious mind to flesh, and our unconscious mind to the bone structure that lies underneath. Metaphorically speaking, suffering is the kind of wounding that cuts the flesh of our conscious mind, while trauma is a deeper kind of wounding that splits open the bone of our unconscious mind. Suffering and trauma both hurt, but trauma can drastically change our personality, just as an injury that shatters our bone can have severe and long-lasting consequences.

Trauma can certainly happen to adults, but it is far more likely to happen to children. Psychologist Bruce Perry, whom I quoted in the first chapter, said:

> Unfortunately, the prevailing view of children and trauma at the time—one that persists to a large degree to this day—is that "children are resilient." . . . If anything, children are more vulnerable to trauma than adults . . . The developing brain is most malleable and most sensitive to experience—both good and bad—early in life. (This is why we so easily and rapidly learn language, social nuance, motor skills and dozens of other things in childhood, and why we speak of "formative" experiences.) . . . Consequently, we are also rapidly and easily transformed by trauma when we are young. Though its effects may not always be visible to the untrained eye, when you know what trauma can do to children, sadly, you begin to see its aftermath everywhere.[3]

There is a fine line between suffering and trauma. Self-reflection has helped me understand where this line is drawn within myself, and the art of waging peace has helped me heal and grow as a human being. Waging peace empowers us to heal the pain within us, and it also enlarges our empathy for the pain of others. No matter how much suffering and trauma we have experienced, we can all make progress on the path of inner healing, and we can help each other walk this path.

Our World Needs Warriors Trained to Wage Peace

My existence is proof that peace is possible. During a television interview on the PBS station in San Diego, I was asked if peace can develop between groups that have had long and deadly conflicts. I replied:

> I think [peace] is possible. I think a good example would be Europe. Europe was the bloodiest place on earth for around five hundred years, constant warfare—a lot of that was religious conflict—culminating in two world wars. But now it's very hard to imagine a war in Western Europe. It's very hard to imagine France and Germany going to war with each other. And Europe was the bloodiest place on earth for centuries, and if a place as bloody as Europe—as divided by religious conflict as Europe—could become peaceful, it gives a lot of potential for other places to possibly become peaceful. I think another very protracted conflict is African Americans in the United States. I'm half Korean, a quarter white, and a quarter black. My father was half white and half black, and African Americans lived under over three hundred years of slavery and segregation and lynching. If you look at Birmingham, between 1957 and 1963, in Birmingham alone, eighteen black homes and churches were bombed.* And today African Americans aren't trying to take revenge because there was a peaceful resolution through the civil rights movement that was able to give them equality and kind of create the conditions for forgiveness. So I think that if you look at the centuries of conflict between African Americans being brutalized, if you look at how violent [Western] Europe was, it does offer the potential for other places on earth to also become peaceful.

* Earlier I quoted King saying that seventeen black churches and homes of civil rights leaders were bombed in Birmingham between 1957 and January 1963, but here I am saying eighteen because I include the bombing of Sixteenth Street Baptist Church on September 15, 1963, which killed four young girls.

Despite centuries of brutal oppression, many African Americans have shown the power of love, peace, and forgiveness. Frederick Douglass said that one hour of slavery was worse than all the decades of British oppression inflicted on the white Founding Fathers.[4] As a testament to the power of their humanity, it is remarkable that Frederick Douglass, Martin Luther King Jr., and many other African Americans became some of the most patriotic Americans our country has ever created. Tavis Smiley said, "Our contribution to the nation is that we didn't create a black Al Qaeda. Look at all that black people have endured and gone through, and then look at the patriots that we have become. That's the beauty of the black experience."[5]

As humanity confronts our current global problems, an uprising of peace warriors from the African American community and all racial demographics is foretold by a Hopi Native American prophecy, which I see as an important metaphor for the twenty-first century. Sherri Mitchell, executive director of the Land Peace Foundation and member of the Penobscot tribe, tells us:

> The prophecy that I was told by Hopi elder, Thomas Banyaca, before he died was this: There will come a time when a group of people from all corners of the earth will rise up during a time of great conflict and environmental destruction. These individuals will bring the people on this planet together to heal the earth and overcome oppression. When these warriors rise up from all corners of the earth, the road that we follow will become a rainbow path, honoring the colors represented by the sacred directions and the colors of all the races of people. The warriors that rise up out of this time will lead the way toward peace and unity for the planet.[6]

Male and female peace warriors from all nations must now rise and unite in the struggle to end war, stop oppression, and protect the health of our planet. The prologue of this global movement has already been written by the lives of people such as Wangari Maathai, who in 2004 became the first African woman to receive the Nobel Peace Prize. She and the other Kenyan women of the Green Belt Movement simultaneously advocated three controversial issues: women's rights, the struggle for democracy, and the need to protect the environment. As a brilliant strategic thinker, Wangari Maathai waged peace by attacking the underlying causes of these problems rather than just their symptoms. She said, "The more I looked into the problems that people were complaining about . . . the more I understood that what we were complaining about were the symptoms, and that we needed to understand the causes of those symptoms."[7]

Wangari Maathai and all those who waged peace before us were underdogs, and the journey of waging peace is in fact a tough and often dangerous underdog journey. On the long and challenging road to peace, the warrior code offers a lot of useful guidance for underdogs, because true warriors embrace the challenge of being an underdog. When others give up before taking the first step, true warriors train themselves to win against all odds. When others are selfish and greedy, true warriors serve the well-being of their community. In *The Art of War*, Sun Tzu said, "The general who advances without coveting fame and retreats without fearing disgrace, whose only thought is to protect his country and do good service for his sovereign, is the jewel of the kingdom."[8]

Ancient warrior codes, such as the *Code of the Samurai*, taught warriors to protect their homeland by serving a sovereign feudal lord. But today, our world has become so interconnected that the fate of our country is tied to the fate of every other country. As warriors in the twenty-first century, we can best serve our country by serving the ideals of justice, liberty, peace, and truth. In an interconnected world, our homeland has truly become the planet Earth, and we must defend and spread these ideals in order to protect our homeland.

The warrior code is a philosophy of life that includes ideals such as selflessness, perseverance, and discipline. Martin Luther King Jr. used many warrior metaphors to inject these and other warrior ideals into the civil rights movement. In the following excerpt from King's book *Why We Can't Wait*, I have italicized his use of warrior metaphors and military references:

> Fortunately, history does not pose problems without eventually producing solutions. The disenchanted, the

disadvantaged and the disinherited seem, at times of deep crisis, to summon up some sort of genius that enables them to perceive and capture the appropriate weapons to carve out their destiny. Such was the *peaceable weapon* of nonviolent direct action . . . Acting in concert with fellow Negroes to assert himself as a citizen, he would embark on a *militant program* to demand the rights which were his: in the streets, on the buses, in the stores, the parks and other public facilities . . .

In the *nonviolent army*, there is room for everyone who wants to join up . . . *Nonviolent soldiers* are called upon to examine and burnish their *greatest weapons*—their heart, their conscience, their courage and their sense of justice . . . *We did not hesitate to call our movement an army . . . It was an army that would move but not maul. . . It was an army to storm bastions of hatred, to lay siege to the fortresses of segregation, to surround symbols of discrimination . . . The battle hymn of our movement [was] "We Shall Overcome."*[9]

In his "I Have a Dream" speech, King expressed the importance of discipline (one of the most important warrior ideals) and what he called *marvelous new militancy*:

But there is something that I must say to my people, who stand on the warm threshold which leads into the palace of justice: In the process of gaining our rightful place, we must not be guilty of wrongful deeds. Let us not seek to satisfy our thirst for freedom by drinking from the cup of bitterness and hatred. We must forever conduct our struggle on the high plane of dignity and *discipline* [emphasis added]. We must not allow our creative protest to degenerate into physical violence. Again and again, we must rise to the majestic heights of meeting physical force with soul force. The *marvelous new militancy* [emphasis added] which has engulfed the Negro community must not lead us to a distrust of all white people, for many of our white brothers, as evidenced by their presence here today, have come to realize that their destiny is tied up with our destiny. And they have come to realize that their freedom is inextricably bound to our freedom.[10]

By arming us with leadership skills and strategic thinking, the warrior code empowers us to improve our lives and the world around us. In order to empower us, the warrior code puts a priority not only on being idealistic, but also on being highly skilled. It is important for military commanders to lead by example and treat their soldiers with empathy, but good intentions are not enough. Effective military commanders must also be highly skilled. To effectively wage peace, we must be as well trained and proficient in the art of waging peace as military commanders are in the art of waging war.

This book offers the basic building blocks of waging peace, and there is much more to explore. Just as we must learn the basic building blocks of math in order to learn engineering, we must learn the basic building blocks of waging peace in order to learn how to engineer a more humane and peaceful world. This book can serve as a road map on your personal journey to understand peace, what it means to be human, and how to live well.

Waging peace skills are also life skills, because the same skills that help us create peace in our society and throughout the world also help us create peace in our family, among our coworkers, and within ourselves. When we learn to wage peace well, we also learn to live well. When we learn to wage peace well, we also become warriors in the struggle for a brighter future. During a lecture I gave at the MK Gandhi Institute in Rochester, New York, a member of the audience asked me why I use military metaphors to describe waging peace. I said:

> I reached a point in my life where I was very bitter, and I rejected all military metaphors. I rejected all that kind of language. But then I saw Gandhi use it effectively. Gandhi said [he is] "a soldier of peace."[11] Martin Luther King Jr. said, "Nonviolence is a powerful and just weapon.

It is a sword that heals . . ." That language is not only effective, it's also accurate. Because if you think about what
waging peace really is . . . You are trying to use truth to
defeat ignorance. You're not trying to befriend ignorance.
You're trying to overcome it with truth or with an idea . . .
You are trying to defeat hatred, and the only way to defeat
hatred is with love or compassion or understanding. If you
try to defeat hatred with hatred, it magnifies and amplifies
hatred.

So if you actually think about what we're doing [when
we wage peace], when a doctor fights illness he's trying to
destroy a virus . . . We are trying to destroy ignorance. And
when you make that distinction, you realize your opponent is not that person in particular. Every person is a
potential ally. Every person is a potential friend. Their
minds have been held by these things. And you also have
this understanding that we're all journeying, trying to learn
truth. If you look at Gandhi and King, they were so willing not just to teach but also to learn . . .

In my case, when I didn't use that kind of metaphor,
I had a hard time communicating these concepts. It's really
hard to communicate these concepts, because people
think, "Oh peace, that's being on the beach, that's sitting
in a room and just singing "Kumbaya." People have that
misconception [that] peace is easy, it's just doing nothing,
lying around, wearing a peace t-shirt, doing nothing. But
when you use that kind of metaphor, you get people prepared for what waging peace really is, and it's a struggle.

Bernard Lafayette, a civil rights activist who helped desegregate
Nashville, Tennessee, also described how waging peace is a struggle: "Unfortunately, the concept of nonviolence for many people is that you get hit
on one cheek, you turn the other cheek, and you don't do anything. But
nonviolence means fighting back, but you are fighting back with another
purpose, and other weapons. Number one, your fight is to win that person

over, and that is a fight, that is a struggle. That is much more challenging than fisticuffs . . . We were warriors in that sense."[12]

History shows us that oppression and injustice can be defeated by warriors who strategically wield the sword of truth. As I explained in chapter 9, when people said racial segregation in America must end, those who supported segregation controlled the society, government, military, corporations, many universities, and most of the money. What did the advocates of desegregation have on their side? The truth. Contrary to widely believed myths, it was not true that African Americans were inferior to whites. It was not true that racial harmony was impossible.

When people said women should have equal rights with men, those who opposed women's rights controlled the society, government, military, corporations, many universities, and most of the money. What did the advocates of gender equality have on their side? The truth. Contrary to widely believed myths, it was not true that women were intellectually inferior to men. It was not true that women were less than human. Injustice is built on lies, and every lie has a fatal flaw—it isn't true.

Today ending war is necessary for the survival of humanity, yet those who perpetuate war control the society, government, military, corporations, many universities, and most of the money. What do we have on our side? The truth. Contrary to widely believed myths, it is not true that human beings are naturally violent. It is not true that war is inevitable. It is not true that war protects our way of life and makes us safe.

Truth is eternal, but the lies that sustain oppression and injustice have a lifespan. Since the birth of humanity it has always been true that women are not less than human and no race was designed for slavery, but lies suppress these truths. Unlike truth, which can be concealed but never destroyed, a lie can eventually grow old and die. However, unlike the struggles for civil and women's rights—primarily moral issues—ending war is a matter of survival. The great question of our era is, What will die first, the myths that support war or the human species? Unlike the movements that furthered racial and gender equality around the world, the struggle to end war is a race against time in which our survival is at stake.

During the twentieth century, the Cold War between the Soviet Union and United States held the world hostage. Today, if we fail to take action we could face far more dangerous situations: a nuclear arms race might escalate not between two superpowers but among many countries, or terrorist organizations could obtain nuclear weapons.

The war system threatens our survival in another way. In the past, human beings fought many wars over greed, profit, fear, and ideology. But in the middle and latter part of the twenty-first century, climate change will put humanity under an unprecedented amount of pressure. Climate change will cause rising ocean levels and population migrations, while increasing the amount of droughts, famines, and natural disasters at a time when there will be more people on the planet than at any other time in history. Never will our planet have had so many people on it with such a high demand for food and other natural resources, while climate change, overfishing of the oceans, and other problems threaten food production.

When the political leaders of one country are greedy and able to manipulate their population, it can plunge many countries into war. Although wars in the past have often been fought over greed, profit, fear, and ideology, as climate change escalates during the middle and latter part of the twenty-first century, over 2 billion people could face starvation, and humanity will have something far more serious to fight over. Countries will no longer be threatened by illusionary dangers conjured by manipulative politicians, but receding shorelines, displaced populations looking for a place to live, and increased competition over vital resources such as food, oil, and access to clean water.

During the Cold War of the twentieth century, the United States and Soviet Union had a dispute over ideology, and this conflict nearly escalated into nuclear war during the Cuban Missile Crisis. Imagine how much likelier nuclear war would have been if the United States and Soviet Union had instead fought over basic resources like food and access to clean water. Imagine if political leaders willing to wage war over greed are given serious problems to fight over such as diminished global food supplies. This is why the greatest threat to human survival is not climate change by itself, but the combination of climate change, nuclear armed nations, and political leaders who serve the war system. When these three dangers exist in the world at the same time, they create a "perfect storm" that threatens human survival in the twenty-first century.

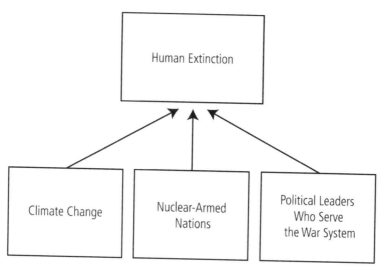

Figure 12.2 The Three Dangers That Create a Perfect Storm for Human Extinction in the Twenty-first Century

Considering that so many wars have been fought over illusions conjured by manipulative politicians, do you trust the political leaders of all the nuclear-armed nations to keep us safe when climate change will give them very serious problems to fight over? If we can transform enough attitudes about war during the coming years and replace the obsolete war system with a more effective *peace system*, we will not destroy each other as climate change gives us more serious reasons to fight. If we can replace the paradigm of waging war, the master of deception, with a more effective paradigm of waging peace, the master of truth, humanity will even work together as a global family and help those in need during the upcoming climate crisis.

Most of the debate today is not about whether climate change is happening, but whether climate change is a natural process or a product of human activity. For those who believe that climate change is a natural process and not manmade, then the upcoming climate crisis is inevitable and cannot be avoided. Isn't that more reason for us to end war, abolish nuclear weapons, and create a peace system before that crisis escalates? And if climate change is in fact a product of human activity, many of the climate scientists are now saying it is too late to avoid a major catastrophe in the twenty-first century because we have already passed the tipping point. According to them, even if we dramatically reduce all carbon emissions tomorrow, we will still face a major climate crisis, especially toward the middle and latter part of this century. Isn't that also a good reason for us to end war, abolish nuclear weapons, and create a peace system?

The war system is a powerful opponent. All systems of oppression are goliaths, but the war system is a goliath among goliaths. For thousands of years it has ruled countries and empires. When we confront such a powerful opponent, one of two things will happen. We will either become hopeless and cynical, or we will become stronger. The only way to defeat a goliath as mighty as the war system is to unlock our full potential as human beings. When trauma tried to defeat me, I had to become stronger and grow as a human being in order to survive. In a similar way, we must strengthen our humanity if we want to effectively confront the war system. By waging peace as warrior underdogs and committing ourselves to a noble and challenging struggle, the war system can bring out the best in us. During my struggle to defeat the war system, I have experienced spiritual change that has made me more hopeful, empathetic, appreciative, conscientious, rational, disciplined, and in awe of the world.

Many who wage peace have also experienced spiritual change. Gandhi lived under British colonialism. He was beaten for challenging injustice, arrested numerous times, imprisoned for seven years, and eventually assassinated. Martin Luther King Jr. lived under segregation. He was arrested multiple times, his house was bombed, and from the age of twenty-six until his assassination at thirty-nine his life was constantly threatened. Nelson Mandela lived under apartheid, and he spent twenty-seven years in prison. But instead of becoming hopeless and cynical, these peace warriors used their struggle to increase their hope, empathy, courage, and determination. Just as the friction of a whetstone sharpens a knife, the friction of struggle made them sharper, stronger, and wiser during their journey to defeat the systems that oppressed them. If they could grow as human beings despite the horrible circumstances that surrounded them, why can't we? This is our challenge.

Because those who wage peace must undertake the underdog journey, perseverance is vital. All systems of oppression, including the war system, defeat activists by making them hopeless and cynical. When people become hopeless and cynical, they are more likely to resort to violence and other acts of desperation. They are also more likely to give up. Promoting truth in a society filled with deception is a challenging path. Frederick Douglass reminds us, "The simplest truths often meet the sternest resistance, and are slowest in getting general acceptance. There are none so blind as those who will not see, is an old proverb . . . Our friends of the woman's suffrage movement should bear this fact in mind, and share the patience of truth while they advocate the truth. It is painful to encounter stupidity as well as malice; but such is the fate of all who attempt to reform an abuse, to urge on humanity to nobler heights, and illumine the world with a new truth."[13]

If we want to persevere, we must also strengthen the seven muscles of our humanity. In *Peaceful Revolution* I describe these seven muscles. They are hope, empathy, appreciation, conscience, reason, discipline, and curiosity. If we do not strengthen the muscles of our humanity, we will not be strong enough to lift the infinite shield and the sword that heals, let alone wield them effectively. But when we strengthen these muscles, we can wield the infinite shield and the sword that heals with great power.

Why is perseverance so important? Imagine being a women's rights activist during the 1840s and dedicating your life to this important cause. For thirty years you work and struggle for women's right to vote, but then in 1875 the Supreme Court rules in the case *Minor v. Happersett* that it is legal to forbid women from voting. This was one of the worst Supreme Court decisions in American history. Can you imagine how this terrible decision could have crushed your spirit? After this setback to their life's work, however, many women's rights activists did not despair, but instead found a way to maintain a strong foundation of realistic hope. At a women's rights convention in the late 1870s, nearly forty years before women had a constitutional amendment granting them the right to vote, Frederick Douglass said:

> In judging of the possible success of this cause [women's rights], we shall do well, not to measure its progress by the great distance at which it seems now to stand from its ultimate aim and object, or by the stupendous obstacles it has yet to overcome, but rather from the

point way back in the past, from which it started, and by the tremendous obstacles it has already surmounted.

Woman has already secured a vast vantage ground. Her voice and pen are both free. Archimedes only wanted a place for the fulcrum of his lever in order to move the world. Woman has found the place in her ability to speak, write, publish, organize and agitate. She has in this a weapon superior to swords, guns, or dynamite. No man even now, running for Congress or the presidency or any other office, wants to have the voice of the women against him.

See how wisely she has conducted this movement, how guarded have been all her approaches to the vast citadel she has determined to storm and capture. Her first demand was not for suffrage, but for the right of speech. Her next was for higher education, and her next was for an enlargement of her opportunities for making an honest living. She has measurably compelled compliance with all of these demands. She has found her way into colleges and universities, and greatly enlarged the boundaries of her industrial avocations. Forty years ago there were not thirty occupations open to women. Now there are more than three hundred. Forty years ago there were no colleges open, now there are none where she cannot enter.[14]

When we broaden our perspective, we can appreciate how far humanity has come. In 400 BC in ancient Athens, around 30 percent of the people were slaves. In Roman Italy during the first century BC, around 35 percent of the people were slaves. In 1850 in Brazil, around 30 percent of the people were slaves. In 1861 in Cuba, around 30 percent of the people were slaves. In Alabama and other southern states during 1860, around 33 percent of the people were slaves.[15] Although state-sanctioned slavery has been abolished, there are still an estimated 27 million illegal slaves in the world today. But in a population of over 7 billion people, that means less than 1 percent of the world's population are slaves. That is still an unacceptable number, but if we have reduced slavery per capita so dramatically, why can't we continue to make progress?

An article in the *Christian Science Monitor* summarized the views of Dr. Kevin Bales, president of the nonprofit organization Free the Slaves: "Yet despite this new largely unacknowledged slavery epidemic, Dr. Bales is optimistic . . . Today, he adds, we don't have to win the legal battle; there's a law against it in every country. We don't have to win the economic argument; no economy is dependent on slavery (unlike in the 19th century, when whole industries could have collapsed). And we don't have to win the moral argument; no one is trying to justify it any more. The fact that it's still thriving, he explains, comes down principally to ignorance about the institution and lack of resources directed at eradicating it."[16]

As soldiers of peace, we must hunt injustice relentlessly. We must not allow it to have any safe refuge. We must end illegal slavery and other forms of injustice no matter where they are, no matter whom they affect. People are still being harmed by oppressive systems other than state-sanctioned slavery and illegal slavery. For example, Frederick Douglass and Martin Luther King Jr. both said that many poor white Americans have lived in impoverished economic conditions not too different from slavery. Douglass explained:

> The slaveholders, with a craftiness peculiar to themselves, by encouraging the enmity of the poor laboring white man against the blacks, succeeded in making the said white man almost as much a slave as the black slave himself . . . Both [white and black men] were plundered, and by the same plunderers. The slave was robbed by his master of all his earnings . . . and the white laboring man was robbed by the slave system of the just results of his labor, because he was flung into competition with a class of laborers who worked without wages. The slaveholders blinded [poor white men] to this competition by keeping alive their prejudice against the slaves as *men* . . . The impression was cunningly made [by slaveholders] that slavery was the only power that could prevent the laboring white man from falling to the level of the slave's poverty

and degradation. To make this enmity deep and broad between the slave and the poor white man, the latter was allowed to abuse and whip the former without hindrance.[17]

The propaganda that causes poor people to blame each other for their problems and see each other as enemies, which Frederick Douglass described during the nineteenth century, still echoes in our society today. Many Americans blame poor immigrants for stealing from American taxpayers, while not realizing that the war system is secretly conducting one of the largest robberies in world history. As soldiers of peace we must defeat this propaganda and the many unjust systems that still exist. If someone like me—who grew up in Alabama, a descendant of slaves—can write these words today, why can't we continue making progress on the road to peace? Why can't we continue to win victories against injustice?

I see so much in our world that is beautiful and worthy of celebration, yet we still have much to do in the struggle for peace. When I witness war, oppression, and environmental destruction on a large scale, I do not perceive our world as ugly. Instead, I see our world as an unfinished masterpiece where peace can be painted. The painter does not hate a canvas while caressing it with a brush dipped in vivid color. The sculptor does not despise a stone while chiseling away its rough edges. Nor should we hate our world as we strive to magnify its beauty. Our world, no matter how unjust and cruel it may seem, is simply an incomplete work of art. As artists who paint with the brush of nonviolent action, we can add the beautiful colors of waging peace to the blank canvas of ignorance. As warrior underdogs armed with the infinite shield and the sword that heals, we can transform our world into a masterpiece. It will not be easy, but it is up to us.

Notes

Preface

1. Voting rights for white men increased dramatically around the 1820s, especially during the era of "Jacksonian Democracy," and universal voting rights for African Americans and women came much later (although I have read about a couple of rare places where free black men could vote in the early nineteenth century).

2. There were some places, such as ancient Sparta, where women had more rights than was common for that era, but the rights usually associated with women's rights today did not exist in much of the world for most of recorded history.

3. Frederick Douglass, *Narrative of the Life of Frederick Douglass* (New York: Dover Publications, 1995), 1–4.

4. Frederick Douglass, *The Life and Times of Frederick Douglass* (New York: Dover, 2003), 16, 17, 32, 33, 44, 68.

5. Ibid., xi–xiii.

6. Yale Law School, Fugitive Slave Act of 1850, sections 5 and 7, http://avalon.law.yale.edu/19th_century/fugitive.asp.

7. *The Words of Martin Luther King Jr.*, selected by Coretta Scott King (New York: Newmarket Press, 1987), 90.

8. *A Force More Powerful,* A Force More Powerful Films, 2002, DVD.

9. Gandhi's Farewell Talk in Europe, http://www.youtube.com/watch?v=RlJ00KvsHuQ.

10. Martin Luther King Jr., *Why We Can't Wait* (New York: New American Library, 2000), 65–66, 81.

11. Ibid., 16.

12. Henry David Thoreau, *Walden* (New York: Dover Publications, Inc., 1995), 49.

13. The Roman Catholic Church actually threatened to torture Galileo on the rack. But being tortured in this way would have likely killed him, since he was in his early seventies and in poor health. Also, if Galileo somehow survived the rack and still refused to recant, the church would have executed him rather than allow him to continue expressing his ideas. Nevertheless, the church preferred that Galileo recant rather than face torture and execution, because publically rejecting his own ideas would do a lot more to strengthen the church's position on the issue.

14. Martin Luther King Jr., "Why I Am Opposed to the War in Vietnam" speech, http://www.lib.berkeley.edu/MRC/pacificaviet/riversidetranscript.html.

15. *A Force More Powerful*, DVD.

16. I heard James Lawson discuss this in a workshop I attended in 2011.

Chapter 1

1. Jonathan Shay, *Achilles in Vietnam* (New York: Scribner, 2003), xiv–xv.

2. Malcolm Day, *100 Characters from Classical Mythology* (Hauppauge, NY: Barron's Educational Series, 2007), 98, 102, 104. There are different interpretations of the labyrinth story, but I based my interpretation on the descriptions in this book. I paraphrased a few sentences from this book.

3. Bruce Perry and Maia Szalavitz, *The Boy Who Was Raised As a Dog* (New York: Basic Books, 2008), 38–39.

Chapter 2

1. Douglass, *Narrative of the Life of Frederick Douglass*, 11.

2. I had a genealogist research this in 2012. I used the information from the 1870 census, the earliest data the genealogist could find.

3. Douglass, *Narrative of the Life of Frederick Douglass*, 25.

4. Carly Lucille Baldwin, "Slavery Is Not Dead, Just Less Recognizable," http://www.csmonitor.com/2004/0901/p16s01-wogi.html/(page)/3.

5. Interview on Chicago TV with Jim Hurlbut, http://www.youtube.com/watch?v=izy6BiCV3Nw.

6. "Malcolm X Killer Heads Mosque," BBC News, http://news.bbc.co.uk/2/hi/americas/71838.stm.

7. Alex Haley, *The Autobiography of Malcom X* (New York: Ballantine Books, 1999), 31–32.

8. Ibid., 401.

9. The Pierre Berton Interview, http://www.malcolm-x.org/docs/int_pbert.htm.

10. Interview with Gordon Parks, http://www.malcolm-x.org/docs/int_parks.htm.

11. Day, *100 Characters from Classical Mythology*, 56.

12. Sun Tzu, *Sun Tzu on the Art of War: The Oldest Military Treatise in the World*, trans. Lionel Giles (El Paso: El Paso Norte Press, 2005), 170.

13. Shay, *Achilles in Vietnam*, 79.

14. Ibid., 86–87.

15. Ibid., 78–79.

16. Ibid., 75, 83–84.

17. *Tyson*, Sony Picture Classics, 2009, DVD.

18. Ibid.

19. Ibid.

20. Thomas Cleary, ed. and trans., *Training the Samurai Mind* (Boston: Shambhala, 2008), 194–95.

21. Shay, *Achilles in Vietnam*, 97.

22. *The Bulletproof Mind*, Dave Grossman and Gavin de Becker, 2008, DVD.

23. Shay, *Achilles in Vietnam*, 97.

24. Ibid., 94–95.

25. Douglass, *Narrative of the Life of Frederick Douglass*, 56–57.

26. Ibid., 57.

27. Frederick Douglass, *The Life and Times of Frederick Douglass* (New York: Dover, 2003), 94–95.

28. Ibid., 96, 98.

29. *Tyson*, DVD.

30. Victor Frankl, *Man's Search for Meaning* (Boston: Beacon Press, 2006), 149.

Chapter 3

1. MLK: A Call to Conscience, http://www.pbs.org/wnet/tavissmiley/interviews/mlk-a-call-to-conscience-part-2/?show=8623.

2. Andrew Meldrum, "The Guard Who Really Was Mandela's Friend," http://www.guardian.co.uk/world/2007/may/20/nelsonmandela.

3. Ibid.

4. Ibid.

5. West Point Bugle Notes, http://www.west-point.org/academy/malo-wa/inspirations/buglenotes.html.

6. Arun Gandhi, *Legacy of Love* (El Sobrante, CA: North Bay Books, 2003), 83–84. There is another version of this story that replaces "fifteen days" with "three days." I first heard the "three days" version from peace studies professor Michael Nagler before reading this, and I used the "three days" version in my earlier interviews.

7. Matthew 7:3–5, New International Version.

8. Martin Luther King Jr., *The Autobiography of Martin Luther King Jr.* (New York: Warner Books, 1998), 197–98.

Chapter 4

1. Dave Grossman with Loren W. Christensen, *On Combat* (Milstadt, IL: Warrior Science, 2008), 347.

2. King, *Why We Can't Wait*, 16.

3. Martin Luther King Jr., *A Testament of Hope*, ed. James M. Washington (New York: HarperOne, 2007) 12–13.

4. Grossman, *On Combat*, 135–36.

5. Ibid., 44.

6. King, *The Autobiography of Martin Luther King Jr.*, 70.

7. Perry and Szalavitz, *The Boy Who Was Raised As a Dog*, 245.

8. Erich Fromm, *The Art of Loving* (New York: Perennial Classics, 1956), 27.

9. Philip S. Foner, ed., *Frederick Douglass on Women's Rights* (Cambridge, MA: Da Capo Press, 1992), 57.

10. Grossman, *On Combat*, 337.

Chapter 5

1. George W. Bush, *Decision Points* (New York: Crown, 2011), 325.

2. Robert Miles and Malcolm Brown, *Racism* (New York: Routledge, 2003), 58.

3. Ernest Cashmore, ed., *Encyclopedia of Race and Ethnic Studies* (New York: Routledge, 2003), 213, 214.

4. David Margolick, "Elizabeth Eckford and Hazel Bryan: The Story Behind the Photograph That Shamed America," http://www.telegraph.co.uk/news/worldnews/northamerica/8813134/Eliz...zel-Bryan-the-story-behind-the-photograph-that-shamed-America.html.

5. Alex Chadwick, "Little Rock Remembers Troops' Arrival," http://www.npr.org/templates/story/story.php?storyId=14654126.

6. "Central High School Integrated," http://www.history.com/this-day-in-history/central-high-school-integrated.

7. Interview conducted by Martin Agronsky on *Look Here*, October 27, 1957.

8. King, *The Words of Martin Luther King Jr.*, 18.

9. Sun Tzu, *Sun Tzu on the Art of War*, Giles, trans., 5.

10. Homer, *The Iliad*, trans. Robert Fagles (New York: Penguin, 1990), 193.

11. M. K. Gandhi, *Mahatma Gandhi: Selected Political Writings*, ed. Dennis Dalton (Indianapolis: Hackett, 1996), 78–79.

12. Kirsten Grieshaber, "Museum Created for Germans Who Hid Jews." http://www.washingtonpost.com/wp-dyn/content/article/2007/05/08/AR2007050800197.html.

13. Klaus P. Fischer, *Nazi Germany: A New History* (New York: Continuum, 2006), 502.

14. *Code of the Samurai: A Modern Translation of the Bushido Shoshinshu*, trans. Thomas Cleary (Boston: Tuttle, 1999), 50.

Chapter 6

1. Thomas Merton, ed., *Gandhi on Non-violence* (New York: New Directions, 2007), 52.

2. Seneca, *Moral Essays; Volume I*, trans. John W. Basore (Cambridge; MA: Harvard University Press, 1928), 59.

3. Grossman, *On Combat*, 322.

4. Louis Fischer, ed., *The Essential Gandhi* (New York: Random House, 2002), 137.

5. Merton, *Gandhi on Non-violence*, 51.

6. Peter Brock, "Gandhi's Nonviolence and His War Service," *Peace and Change: A Journal of Peace Research*, March 5, 2009, 80.

7. Merton, *Gandhi on Non-violence*, 49.

8. Ibid., 50.

9. Interview conducted by Martin Agronsky for *Look Here*, October 27, 1957.

10. Yamauchi Tomosaburo, "Kaibara Ekken: The Founder of Japanese Neo-Confucianism," *Memoirs of Osaka Kyoiku University*, ser. II, vol. 59, no. 2, February 2011, 97–110.

11. Cleary, *Training the Samurai Mind*, 72, 74–76.

12. Although many Eastern thinkers look at violence from a practical perspective, some also have a version of just war theory that tries to reconcile warfare with Lao Tzu's anti-war views.

13. I received permission from Rick Wayman to use his story.

14. Sun Tzu, *The Art of War*, trans. Ralph D. Sawyer (New York: Barnes & Noble, 1994), 177.

15. Carl von Clausewitz, *On War*, trans. J. J. Graham (New York: Penguin, 1982), 116.

16. Tony Dokoupil, A New Theory of PTSD and Veterans: Moral Injury. http://www.thedailybeast.com/newsweek/2012/12/02/a-new-theory-of-ptsd-and-veterans-moral-injury.html.

17. Abraham Maslow, *The Psychology of Science* (Chicago: Gateway, 1966), 15–16.

18. Mark Benjamin, "Is the Army Lying about Friendly Fire Deaths?" http://www.salon.com/2009/01/15/friendly_fire_6/.

19. Ibid.

20. Cleary, *Code of the Samurai*, 35.

21. Ibid., 13.

22. Interview conducted by Martin Agronsky on *Look Here*, October 27, 1957.

Chapter 7

1. Jennings L. Wagoner Jr., *Jefferson and Education*, (Charlottesville: University of Virginia Press, 2004), 61–63.

2. Michael Adkins, "Liberal Arts Education Is Undervalued," http://www.marshall-parthenon.com/opinion/liberal-arts-education-is-undervalued-1.2458922#.T8Z mvI6rU20.

3. Christopher D. Kolenda, ed., *Leadership: The Warrior's Art*, (Carlisle, PA: Army War College Foundation Press, 2001), 254.

4. D. Clayton James, *The Years of MacArthur: Volume I* (Boston: Houghton Mifflin, 1970), 275.

5. Ibid., 270–71, 273.

6. When I was at West Point every cadet was required to take an "engineering track," which my professors told me was roughly equivalent to a minor.

7. Cleary, *Code of the Samurai*, 11.

8. Cleary, *Training the Samurai Mind*, 34–35, 40. I added "ethical" in front of "psychology" because he is referring to Confucian psychology, which is focused on ethics rather than psychoanalysis.

9. The American Experience: MacArthur, http://www.pbs.org/wgbh/amex/macarthur /filmmore/description.html.

10. Thomas J. Fleming, *West Point* (New York: William Morrow, 1969), 308.

11. Sun Tzu, *Sun Tzu on the Art of War*, Giles, trans., 49.

12. Zhuge Liang and Liu Ji, *Mastering the Art of War*, ed. and trans. Thomas Cleary (Boston: Shambhala, 1989), 81.

13. Ibid., 82.

14. Ibid., 47, 52, 60.

15. Diodorus Siculus, *Library of History: Books 16.66–17*, trans. C. Bradford Welles (Cambridge, MA: Loeb Classical Library, 1963), 299.

16. Plutarch, *Themistocles and Aristides*, trans. Bernadotte Perrin (New York: Charles Scribner's Sons, 1901), 131.

17. Plutarch, *Plutarch's Lives*, trans. Bernadotte Perrin (Cambridge: Loeb Classical Library, 1917), 351.

18. Diodorus, *The Fragments of Diodorus*, trans. G. Booth (London: W. McDowall, 1814), 68.

19. Kolenda, *Leadership: The Warrior's Art*, 104.

20. Ibid., 105.

21. J. F. C. Fuller, *The Generalship of Alexander the Great* (New Brunswick: Da Capo Press, 1960), 263.

22. Kolenda, *Leadership: The Warrior's Art*, 105–7.

23. Ibid., 102, 111–14, 119–20, 398. The information about Hermolaus's stoning is from Colonel Kolenda's footnote on page 398 of *Leadership*.

24. Rajmohan Gandhi, *Gandhi: The Man, His People, and the Empire* (Berkeley: University of California Press, 2008), 86, 108–110.

25. Matthew Trundle, *Greek Mercenaries* (New York: Routledge, 2004), 71.

26. Ibid., 43, 62.

27. I moved the first two sentences to the front to put the narrative in chronological order.

28. Livy, *Hannibal's Wars*, trans. J. C. Yardley (Oxford: Oxford University Press, 2009), 4–5.

29. David C. Sears, *Xenophon's Anabasis Lessons in Leadership*, thesis for Naval Postgraduate School, 2007, 19, 30, 37–38; http://calhoun.nps.edu/public/handle/10945/3524.

30. Shay, *Achilles in Vietnam*, 39, 49.

31. After the Show: How the Gift of Fear Can Save Your Life, video clip, http://www.oprah.com/spirit/After-the-Show-How-the-Gift-of-Fear-Can-Save-Your-Life.

32. Merton, *Gandhi on Non-violence*, 52.

33. Fleming, *West Point*, 308.

34. Shay, *Achilles in Vietnam*, 125–27.

35. Smedley D. Butler, *War Is a Racket* (Feral House, 2003), 23.

36. Brock, "Gandhi's Nonviolence and His War Service," 72, 76.

37. Merton, *Gandhi on Non-violence*, 53.

38. King, *The Words of Martin Luther King Jr.*, 23.

39. Nicholas D. Kristof, "Our Lefty Military," http://www.nytimes.com/2011/06/16 /opinion/16kristof.html?_r=2&fb_source=message.

40. James, *The Years of MacArthur: Volume III*, 681–82.

41. Eric F. Goldman, *The Tragedy of Lyndon Johnson* (New York: Alfred A. Knopf, 1969), 399–400.

42. Edward T. Imparato, ed., *General MacArthur: Speeches and Reports: 1908–1964* (Paducah, KY: Turner Publishing, 2000), 247.

43. Imparato, *General MacArthur*, 216. MacArthur called blockades "the most effective weapon known to military science," 148.

44. Letter to Professor Shermer, March 22, 1961. Letter courtesy of MacArthur Archives.

45. Imparato, *General MacArthur*, 241.

46. Letter to Oscar Hammerstein, March 23, 1955, courtesy of MacArthur Archives.

Chapter 8

1. John McCain, "War Is Hell: There Is No Substitute for Victory," http://www.mccain. senate.gov/public/index.cfm?FuseAction=PressOffice.OpEds&ContentRecord_id=21e7f 3d7-d14a-48fc-a44d-5f800a3fe0a0&Region_id=&Issue_id=73379446-ed00-4a32-8ef1-9f1e12737746.

2. Homer, *The Iliad*, trans. Richmond Lattimore (Chicago: University of Chicago Press, 2011), 141–42.

3. Day, *100 Characters from Classical Mythology*, 17, 32.

4. Paul Cartledge, *Sparta* (New York: Overlook Press, 2003), 56.

5. Athena Promachos, http://www.britannica.com/EBchecked/topic/40735/Athena-Promachos.

6. William Smith, ed., *Dictionary of Greek and Roman Biography and Mythology* (Boston: Little, Brown, and Company, 1867), 398.

7. Barry Ladendorf, the president of the San Diego Veterans for Peace chapter, told me about the Strategic Air Command's motto. He also pointed out that many other weapons have been referred to as bringers of peace, such as the Colt 45 Peacemaker.

8. Day, *100 Characters from Classical Mythology*, 35.

9. Imparato, *General MacArthur*, 215.

10. G. M. Gilbert, *Nuremberg Diary* (Cambridge: Da Capo Press, 1995), 278.

11. War and Peace in Afghanistan, *World Have Your Say*, BBC News, May 2, 2012.

12. Mars, the God of War, http://www.forumancientcoins.com/moonmoth/reverse_mars.html.

13. Virgil, *The Aeneid*, trans. Robert Fables (New York: Viking Press, 2006), 244.

14. Ibid., 245.

15. Mars, the God of War, http://www.forumancientcoins.com/moonmoth/reverse_branches.html.

16. The Official Truth: Propaganda in the Roman Empire, http://www.bbc.co.uk/history/ancient/romans/romanpropaganda_article_01.shtml.

17. Ata-Malik Juvaini, *The History of the World-Conqueror*, trans. John Andrew Boyle (Cambridge: Harvard University Press, 1958), 77.

18. Adolf Hitler, *The New Germany Desires Work and Peace* (Berlin: Liebheit and Thiesen, 1933). From the introduction; no page number listed.

19. Ibid., 13, 53, 62.

20. Mars, the God of War, http://www.forumancientcoins.com/moonmoth/reverse_mars.html.

21. Chomsky Explains Cold War in 5 Min, http://www.youtube.com/watch?v=j9Z05xyGB0c.

22. James G. Blight and Janet M. Lang, *The Fog of War*, (Lanham, MD: Rowman and Littlefield, 2005) 100–101.

23. King, *The Autobiography of Martin Luther King Jr.*, 335.

24. Fuller, *The Generalship of Alexander the Great*, 277–78.

25. Kolenda, *Leadership: The Warrior's Art*, 114–16, 119–20.

26. Day, *100 Characters from Classical Mythology*, 35.

27. Cleary, *Training the Samurai Mind*, 79.

28. Ibid., 81–82, 84.

29 Interview with David Pakman, https://www.youtube.com/watch?v=zYOqrcpTzC8.

30. Liang, *Mastering the Art of War*, 20–21.

31. King, *The Autobiography of Martin Luther King Jr.*, 197.

Chapter 9

1. There were some places, such as ancient Sparta, where women had more rights than was common for that era, but the rights usually associated with women's rights today did not exist in much of the world for most of recorded history.

2. James L. Crouthamel, *Bennett's New York Herald and the Rise of the Popular Press* (Syracuse, NY: Syracuse University Press, 1989), 4.

3. Foner, *Frederick Douglass on Women's Rights*, 12. Eric Foner does not include the year this article was published, but it seems to have been published sometime during the 1840s.

4. Ibid., 49.

5. Diane F. Halpern et al., "Sex, Math and Scientific Achievement" (*Scientific American Mind*, December 2007/January 2008), 48. I moved this sentence up from a later part in the article because it elaborates on the issue of standardized test scores.

6. Ibid., 47.

7. Tamar Lewin, "Perfect's New Profile, Warts and All," http://www.nytimes.com/2006/09/03/weekinreview/03lewin.html. The article explains that a student can miss a couple of questions and still get a "perfect score"; the number of students who scored "perfect perfect" on the test is unknown.

8. Sue Davis, *The Political Thought of Elizabeth Cady Stanton* (New York: New York University Press, 2010), 103.

9. Charles Darwin, *Descent of Man and Selection in Relation to Sex, Volume II* (London: John Murray, Albemarle Street, 1871), 327.

10. Foner, *Frederick Douglass on Women's Rights*, 106.

11. Ibid., 114–15.

12. Ibid., 113.

13. Ibid., ix.

14. King, *Why We Can't Wait*, 171.

15. Douglass, *The Life and Times of Frederick Douglass*, 125, 145.

16. Douglass, *Narrative of the Life of Frederick Douglass*, 20, 23–25.

17. Howard Zinn on *Bill Moyers Journal*, PBS, December 11, 2009.

18. King, *Why We Can't Wait*, 16.

19. Foner, *Frederick Douglass on Women's Rights*, 95.

20. Merton, *Gandhi on Non-violence*, 47.

21. Michael R. Hall, *Historical Dictionary of Haiti* (Toronto: Scarecrow Press, 2012), 210.

22. Ibid.

23. Interview conducted by Martin Agronsky on *Look Here*, October 27, 1957.

24. King, *Why We Can't Wait*, 27, 100, 146, 147, 148. (I rearranged the order of some of these paragraphs to illustrate his points.)

25. Thomas F. X. Noble, *Western Civilization: Beyond Boundaries*, 5th ed. (New York: Houghton Mifflin, 2008), 66.

26. Keith Hopkins, *Conquerors and Slaves* (Cambridge: Cambridge University Press, 1978), 101.

27. David Sacks, *Encyclopedia of the Ancient Greek World* (New York: Facts on File, 2005), 326.

28. Michael Whitby, ed., *Sparta* (New York: Routledge, 2002), 229.

29. Paul Cartledge, *The Spartans*, (Woodstock, NY: Overlook Press, 2003), 72, 29, 229.

30. Keith Bradley and Paul Cartledge, eds., *The Cambridge World History of Slavery: Volume 1* (Cambridge: Cambridge University Press, 2011), 84.

31. Paul Cartledge, *Sparta and Laconia* (New York: Routledge, 2002), 305.

32. Cartledge, *The Spartans*, 227.

33. Whitby, *Sparta*, 229.

34. Robert B. Strassler, ed., *The Landmark Thucydides*, (New York: Free Press, 1996), 596.

35. Gandhi, *Gandhi: The Man, His People, and the Empire*, 109–10.

36. Brock, "Gandhi's Nonviolence and His War Service," 79–80.

37. Merton, *Gandhi on Non-violence*, 71.

38. Ibid., 42.

39. Ibid., 40–42.

40. Ibid., 54.

41. Fischer, *The Essential Gandhi*, 311.

42. Study finds nonviolence more effective than violence, http://www.mettacenter.org/nonviolence-in-the-news/study-finds-nonviolence-more-effective-than-violence.

43. Erica Chenoweth, "Give Peaceful Resistance a Chance," http://www.nytimes.com/2011/03/10/opinion/10chenoweth.html.

44. Foner, *Frederick Douglass on Women's Rights*, 115.

45. According to Persian mythology, the hero Arsalan used the magic sword to kill Fulad-Zereh, but before that Arsalan used deception to trick Fulad-Zereh into giving him the sword. In a similar way, Frederick Douglass had to mislead people in order to learn how to read and escape from slavery. This raises an interesting question: Although deception should not be used when waging peace, can we justifiably use deception if there is no other way for us to gain information and escape from ignorance?

Chapter 10

1. Erich Fromm, *The Anatomy of Human Destructiveness* (New York: Henry Holt, 1992), 223.

2. Basil H. Liddell Hart, *Strategy* (New York: Henry Holt, 1954), xx–xxi.

3. Clayborne Carson and Kris Shepard, eds., *A Call to Conscience: The Landmark Speeches of Dr. Martin Luther King Jr.*, (New York: Grand Central Publishing, 2002), 81–82, 85–86.

4. I got this idea from something Noam Chomsky said in an interview: "Either we stop talking or we try to use the words in a sensible way." Noam Chomsky Answers Questions from Six Personalities, http://www.youtube.com/watch?v=eTMfel0CCK0.

5. Mark Twain, *Collected Tales, Sketches, Speeches, and Essays: 1891–1910*, sel. Louis J. Budd, "The Czar's Soliloquy," 645.

6. Stewart Burns, *To the Mountaintop* (New York: HarperOne, 2003), 404.

7. Foner, *Frederick Douglass on Women's Rights*, 85.

8. Dwight D. Eisenhower, address at the Columbia University National Bicentennial Dinner, New York City, May 31, 1954, http://www.presidency.ucsb.edu/ws/index. php?pid=9906.

9. Cleary, *Code of the Samurai*, 50.

10. Carson and Shepard, *A Call to Conscience*, 153.

11. *King: Man of Peace in a Time of War,* Passport Video, 2007, DVD.

12. Foner, *Frederick Douglass on Women's Rights*, 82.

13. The Declaration of Sentiments, http://www.fordham.edu/halsall/mod/senecafalls.asp.

14. Foner, *Frederick Douglass on Women's Rights*, 67.

15. Ibid., 137.

16. Ibid., 129.

17. Imparato, *General MacArthur*, 192. In this quote he also says "whose sacred duty it became, once the guns were silenced, to carry to the land of our vanquished foe the solace and hope and faith of Christian morals." I replaced this with an ellipsis because that comment is misleading and can make him seem like a crusader, if one does not understand his overall views toward religion. As the MacArthur quote mentioned later clarifies, MacArthur supported religious freedom and when he said "Christian morals" he was referring to the ideals of the Sermon on the Mount. If people embraced those ideals "it would mean little whether a Japanese were a Buddhist, a Shintoist, or a Christian."

18. Albert Einstein, *The Expanded Quotable Einstein*, ed. Alice Calaprice (Princeton: Princeton University Press, 2000), 167.

19. Merton, *Gandhi on Non-violence*, 55.

20. Sermon on the Mount, http://www.biblegateway.com/passage/?search=Matthew+5-7&version=NIV.

21. David J. Dionisi, *American Hiroshima* (Victoria, BC: Trafford Publishing, 2006), 1.

22. Imparato, *General MacArthur*, 222.

23. Interview conducted by Gordon Parks, http://www.malcolm-x.org/docs/int_parks.htm.

24. Merton, *Gandhi on Non-violence*, 37, 59.

25. Ibid., 57.

26. *Roads to Memphis*, PBS, American Experience, 2010, DVD.

27. Janine di Giovanni, "The Quiet American," http://www.nytimes.com/2012/09/09/t-magazine/gene-sharp-theorist-of-power.html?_r=1&pagewanted=all&_moc.semityn.www.

28. Martin Luther King Jr., *The Trumpet of Conscience* (Boston: Beacon Press, 2010) 56, 57, 62, 63.

29. Martin Luther King Jr., *Where Do We Go from Here?* (Boston: Beacon Press, 2010), 59.

30. Martin Luther King Jr., "The Crisis in America's Cities," http://www.thekingcenter.org/archive/document/crisis-americas-cities.

31. Clayborne and Shepard, *A Call to Conscience*, 158–59.

32. Louis Fischer, *Gandhi: His Life and Message for the World* (New York, Mentor, 1982), 39.

33. Blase Bonpane said this when he interviewed me on his radio show in 2010.

34. Seth Rosenfeld, "Activist Richard Aoki Named as Informant," http://www.sfgate.com/crime/article/Activist-Richard-Aoki-named-as-informant-3800133.php.

35. Seth Rosenfeld, *Subversives* (New York: Farrar, Straus, and Giroux, 2012), 418–19.

36. *A Force More Powerful*, DVD.

37. King, *Why We Can't Wait*, 153.

38. Grossman, *On Killing*, 119, 128.

39. *A Force More Powerful*, DVD.

40. Ibid.

41. Cleary, *Training the Samurai Mind*, 88–90.

42. King, *Why We Can't Wait*, 50.

43. Clayborne and Shepard, *A Call to Conscience*, 162–64.

Chapter 11

1. Imparato, *General MacArthur: Speeches and Reports*, 215.

2. David A. Nichols, "Ike Liked Civil Rights," http://www.nytimes.com/2007/09/

12/opinion/12nichols.html.

3. Sun Tzu, *The Art of War*, Giles, trans., 7.

4. Thom Hastings, "Finding Common Ground in a Battlefield," http://hastingsnonviolence.blogspot.com/2011/01/finding-common-ground-in-battlefield.html.

5. Sun Tzu, *Sun Tzu on the Art of War*, Giles, trans., 37.

6. Sun Tzu, *The Art of War*, Cleary, trans., 163.

7. Tony Jones, "Bin Laden wanted US to invade Iraq," http://www.abc.net.au/news/2007-08-24/bin-laden-wanted-us-to-invade-iraq-author-says/648888.

8. Niels Annen, "Echoes of the Soviet Surge," http://www.foreignpolicy.com/articles/2011/03/02/echoes_of_the_soviet_surge.

9. "Transcript: Translation of Bin Laden's Videotaped Message," http://www.washingtonpost.com/wp-dyn/articles/A16990-2004Nov1.html.

10. "One 9/11 Tally: $3.3 Trillion," http://www.nytimes.com/interactive/2011/09/08/us/sept-11-reckoning/cost-graphic.html.

11. Jonathan Fahey, "Golden Decade Is Ending for Defense Industry, and Stocks," http://www.usatoday.com/money/economy/2011-08-20-defense-stocks_n.htm.

12. Robert Schlesinger, *White House Ghosts* (New York: Simon and Schuster, 2008), 74–75.

13. Imparato, *General MacArthur*, 182.

14. Ibid., 237.

15. Fact Sheet: The Discretionary Budget: Military v. Non-Military, The National Priorities Project, www.nationalpriorities.org.

16. Sun Tzu, *The Art of War*, Cleary, trans., 25–27.

17. Sermon on the Mount. http://www.biblegateway.com/passage/?search=Matthew+5-7&version=NIV.

18. Noam Chomsky, *World Orders Old and New* (New York: Columbia University Press, 1994), 79.

19. CBS News Online: 60 Minutes, http://www.youtube.com/watch?v=LxJK6SxGCAw.

20. Interview with Andrew Bacevich on *Bill Moyers & Company*, http://billmoyers.com/segment/andrew-bacevich-on-changing-our-military-mindset/.

21. Stephen Kinzer, *All the Shah's Men* (Hoboken, NJ: Wiley, 2003), 2, 3, 4, 68, 95, 127, 128, 140, 164, 195.

22. Carson and Shepard, *A Call to Conscience*, 146–48.

23. Ibid., 157–58.

24. Failed States, http://www.c-spanvideo.org/program/FailedSt.

25. Noam Chomsky, *Rogue States* (Cambridge, MA: Rogue States, 2000), 33.

26. Imparato, *General MacArthur: Speeches and Reports*, 214.

27. Bill Moyers Journal: Brian Fishman and Fawaz A. Gerges on Al Qaeda and Iraq. http://www.pbs.org/moyers/journal/07272007/watch2.html.

28. Ibid.

29. Andrew Bacevich, "Osama bin Laden Is Gone, but US War in the Middle East Is Here to Stay," http://www.csmonitor.com/Commentary/Opinion/2011/0502/Osama-bin-Laden-is-gone-but-US-war-in-the-Middle-East-is-here-to-stay.

30. Post on General Dempsey's Facebook page, August 17, 2012.

31. Natalie Pompilio, "The Real Reason the Military Is Going Green," http://www.yesmagazine.org/issues/making-it-home/the-real-reason-the-military-is-going-green.

32. U.S. Army Sustainability Report 2009, http://www.aepi.army.mil/docs/whatsnew/FINALArmySustainabilityReport2010.pdf.

33. 60 Minutes: Golf Company, http://www.cbsnews.com/video/watch/?id=6690267n.

34. Imparato, *General MacArthur*, 247.

35. "War and Sacrifice in the Post-9/11 Era," http://www.pewsocialtrends.org/2011/10/05/war-and-sacrifice-in-the-post-911-era/.

36. Paul Harris, "Drone Attacks Create Terrorist Safe Havens, Warns Former CIA Official," http://www.guardian.co.uk/world/2012/jun/05/al-qaida-drone-attacks-too-broad.

37. Interview with Andrew Bacevich on *Bill Moyers & Company*, http://billmoyers.com/segment/andrew-bacevich-on-changing-our-military-mindset/.

38. Foner, *Frederick Douglass on Women's Rights*, 117.

39. Ibid., 96.

40. The U.S. Employment Effects of Military and Domestic Spending Priorities:

An Updated Analysis by Robert Pollin and Heidi Garrett-Peltier, http://www.peri.umass.edu/fileadmin/pdf/published_study/spending_priorities_PERI.pdf.

Chapter 12

1. Herman Melville, *Moby-Dick* (Lawrence, KS: Digireads.com Publishing, 2011) Kindle book, 107.

2. In the novel it is unclear whether Moby Dick actually dies at the end.

3. Perry and Szalavitz, *The Boy Who Was Raised As a Dog*, 38–39.

4. Frederick Douglass, *The Life and Times of Frederick Douglass* (New York: Dover 2003), Kindle Edition, Location 7680.

5. "Tavis Smiley on Quentin Tarantino's Django Unchained," The Daily Beast, http://www.thedailybeast.com/newsweek/2013/01/04/tavis-smiley-on-quentin-taran-tino-s-django-unchained.html?utm_medium=email&utm_source=newsletter&utm_campaign=cheatsheet_morning&cid=newsletter%3Bemail%3Bcheatsheet_morning&utm_term=Cheat%20Sheet.

6. She sent this quote to me in an e-mail.

7. *Taking Root*, Mongrel Media, 2008, DVD.

8. Sun Tzu, *The Art of War*, Giles, trans., 49.

9. King, *Why We Can't Wait*, 30, 33–34, 65–66, 81.

10. Carson and Shepard, *A Call to Conscience*, 83,

11. Gandhi's exact words were "I regard myself as a soldier, though a soldier of peace."

12. *A Force More Powerful*, DVD.

13. Foner, *Frederick Douglass on Women's Rights*, 92–93.

14. Ibid., 133, 134.

15. Hopkins, *Conquerors and Slaves*, 101.

16. Susan Llewelyn Leach, "Slavery Is Not Dead, Just Less Recognizable," http://www.csmonitor.com/2004/0901/p16s01-wogi.html.

17. Douglass, *The Life and Times of Frederick Douglass*, 125.

INDEX